The Artist and the Garden

The Artist & the Garden

ROY STRONG

published for
the Paul Mellon Centre for Studies in British Art
by Yale University Press, New Haven & London

Designed by Sally Salvesen
Set in Sabon and printed in Singapore

Library of Congress Cataloging-in-Publication Data
Strong, Roy C.
The artist and the garden / Roy Strong
p. cm.
Includes bibliographical references and index.
ISBN 0-300-08520-6 (cloth: alk. Paper)
Gardens in art. 2. Painting, English. 3. Painting, Modern–England. I. Title.
ND1460.G37S77 2000
758'.9635–dc21   00-035922

Half-titlepage: detail from plate 313
Richard Wilson, *Wilton House: view from the south-east, c.* 1758–9
Collection of the Earl of Pembroke and the Trustees of the Wilton House Trust

Frontispiece: detail from plate 90
Alexander Nasmyth, *The Family of Neil, 3rd Earl of Rosebery, c.* 1787
By permission of the Earl of Rosebery

Endpapers
Jacques Rigaud, *Stowe. The View from the Head of the Lake*
Metropolitan Museum, New York (Harris Brisbane Dick Fund)

For

JULES PROWN

*American friend
whose tree grows in
our garden*

CONTENTS

1. Detail from Paul Sandby, *The Flower garden at Nuneham Courtney*, 1777. Private collection

PREFACE

In 1979 John Harris published his enormous corpus of pictures of country houses, *The Artist and the Country House*. Twenty years have passed, during which garden history has taken off as an academic discipline, signalling that the time is ripe for a renewed examination of this pictorial evidence. More, it now needs to be placed in its European context, and also considered alongside the appearance of gardens in emblems and in portraits.

Several years ago I began to collect photographs and references to garden pictures with the idea that one day I might attempt such a book, but it remained on the mental back burner until I was asked to deliver the Andrew Carnduff Ritchie Lectures at the Yale Center for British Art in New Haven. Andrew Ritchie and his wife Jane I remember with great affection from the 1960s when they were generous to a young man still making his way in the world of museums and British art history. The opportunity to renew my acquaintance with the Yale Center, which had been part of my life since its inception, and with old friends provided an added incentive. Many have helped me on my journey, with John Harris at the head of the list. Only he could cheerfully allow me to cart away from his files such a mound of photographs without asking for a checklist. Others who have spurred me on or answered particular queries include Mavis Batey (Garden History Society), Professor J. B. Trapp (Warburg Institute), Dr Christopher Lloyd (Royal Collection), Dr Alastair Laing and Warren Davies (National Trust), Edward Morris (Walker Art Gallery, Liverpool), Peter Boyd (Shrewsbury), Samuel Whitbread, Professor H. J. Höltgen, Kate Harris (Longleat House), Joseph Leduc (Rhode Island School of Design) and Dr Jan Woudstra, who kindly read one of the chapters, making helpful suggestions. I have also greatly benefited from the careful reading of Julia MacRae. Nor should I forget the staff of the archives of the National Portrait Gallery, still a happy hunting ground after nearly half a century, the staff of the Lindley Library and its librarian, Dr Brent Elliott. To these must be added the enthusiasm of those at the Press headed by John Nicoll. In particular, this book owes much to its editor and designer, Sally Salvesen, who among other things, ironed out what had always been a difficult chapter.

Finally, I think that I can say that this book would not have been written without the encouragement of Dr Brian Allen of the Paul Mellon Centre in London, who read each chapter as I wrote it and urged me on in what otherwise would have been an all too solitary quest.

Roy Strong
The Laskett, Herefordshire

2. Jonathan Myles-Lea, *The Laskett Garden,*
1995. Collection the author

INTRODUCTION

When I was sixty I happened to be writing a regular column in that quintessentially English periodical *Country Life*. Its subject indeed was precisely that, in my case how two people lived and gardened in the remote and rural county of Herefordshire on the borders of Wales. In one issue I described our garden which, after twenty-five years of hard toil and plant growth, had reached a point when it seemed worthy of the brush of one of those seventeenth-century view painters.[1] The enchanting bird's-eye panoramas of Jan Siberechts and Leonard Knyff had crossed my mind as I wrote, artists ideal for delineating a formal garden stretching over some four acres and made up of compartments, avenues and vistas. Not long after that particular column was published a letter arrived from a twenty-seven-year-old man called Jonathan Myles-Lea. I am destined, he wrote or rather announced, to paint your garden, and enclosed photographs of some of his recent canvases. And, taking a leap of faith in the young, we commissioned him to paint it for my sixtieth birthday (2).

This anecdote may seem a curious point of departure for a book about pictures of English gardens. But it was this painting that caused me to ask some of the questions which this book sets out to answer: who was the first person to paint an English garden accurately, and is seeing always believing, for it certainly should not be in the case of Myles-Lea's representation of the Laskett garden. In what we called the Silver Jubilee Garden, planted to commemorate that royal milestone in 1977, for example, features like the double circle of flowerbeds are in fact inaccurate. Indeed the whole picture is a monument to tidying up and formalising into pattern a garden of which the experience on foot is very different. In short this is not an ultra-realistic record of our garden but rather a realisation of its spirit. An aerial photograph would be far more accurate, and photographs taken at ground level would certainly provide a more vivid impression of what it is like to move through the reality. Although, I might add, I am equally aware that garden photographs too are works of art, monuments to interpretation and manipulation by the wielder of the camera's lens.

Those were only a few of the problems that the picture threw up in my mind. Another was the whole question of viewpoint. Here, on the whole, the approach was cartographic, as though the whole triangle of land had been up-ended for us to look straight at, but yet, on examination, this is not quite true, for areas, like the pleached lime avenue, are seen from an angle and there are cast shadows. Then there is the choice of season, in this case certainly early summer before the garden becomes ruffled and blowsy, the hedges calling for trimming and the leaves on the trees starting to yellow. There are other more stridently anti-naturalistic elements like the cartouches, four of them, like jewels with masks of our cats at the top. They frame individual garden prospects, a parterre, a temple, a fountain and a monument, each one caught in a different mood, from the golden effulgent light of autumn to winter snow beneath a star-spangled night sky. Nor should the role of the patrons be forgotten for there we stand flanking an even larger cartouche, and we certainly had a hand in how this garden picture should look and what it should record.

I begin with this picture not only because it demonstrates that picturing the English garden still goes on, but because it was my point of departure. The act of commissioning it prompted me to collect reproductions of pictures of English gardens and to ask a whole series of questions about them. When did they start being painted and why? What was chosen to be painted and why? And what was the significance and meaning of these views within each particular period? Was it just pride of possession or could such a picture express deeper motives, like the desire to be at harmony with Nature and to reflect on the marvel of God's creation? Then there is the extreme unevenness of the material. In early pictures we catch only glimpses of gardens through an aperture or an arch as though the artist was hesitant to reveal more. But by the eighteenth century the sitter has walked through that arch and called for the painter to depict him and his family actually in the garden. Why, one asks, did this happen? What ideological and social change did this reflect? And nagging at the back of my mind was the eternal question of idea and reality, was seeing believing? Did all these gardens recorded in paintings, drawings, maps, book illustrations and single prints actually exist or were some of them merely wishful-thinking if not downright fantasy?

Ever since garden history took off in the 1980s, galleries, museums, country houses and archives have been ransacked for garden images. Pictures which until then had barely seen the light of day, had, within two decades, become clichés of garden history publishing, as garden historians sought to illustrate their texts with images of what had gone. But little if any consideration was given to the images themselves, occupying as a genre a place midway between the landscape painting and the country house view. By now a large corpus of such images has come to be known and exhibitions have assembled them for public display. Obviously the most important are those that record gardens before the advent of the landscape style, when the garden was banished in favour of the park.

Such a topic could be treated either chronologically or thematically. Both options have their advantages, although I have opted for the latter, aware that such an approach can from time to time involve arbitrary separation of material that has relevance for more than one topic. On the other hand it makes for clarity by emphasising what were the driving forces which precipitated these images and determined the forms which they took.

Garden images are by no means an insular phenomenon – they are part of a wider European trend.[2] From the late sixteenth century onwards they could already act as a topographical document, an illustration, a design or a map. They could delineate a real garden as much as one that existed only in the imagination. All these images sustained in perpetuity a memory of the ephemeral art of garden design. They evoked things material – earth, water, plants and artefacts – as well as things immaterial, such as the response of the senses and the intellect, as well as reflecting a concern for political and social prestige. Whether on paper, panel or canvas the garden picture bestows an immortality comparable to the portrait, enabling the viewer to walk through an existing, lost or imagined garden. The artist's role was essentially to capture this transient and fragile art, one which was subject to the mutation of the seasons and the vicissitudes of time in a way unknown, for example, to a building.

The opening chapter explores unfamiliar territory, the appearance of gardens in portraits. These reflect the rise of the garden as a secular status symbol, which began during the late medieval period and was to continue on a steady ascent, reaching a climax in Louis XIV's Versailles. So little visual evidence survives of early English gardens that any glimpse of one lurking in the background of a portrait is to be pondered upon. In them, as I shall demonstrate, we can uniquely trace the history of the knot garden, a development otherwise wrapped in total obscurity. As the garden gains hold as a major attribute we have crucial records of seminal creations. Thomas Howard, Earl of Arundel's garden at Arundel House was the first to be filled with a collection of classical statuary, and that of the Capel family at Much Hadham must have been designed by the Frenchman Isaac de Caus with sculpture by Nicholas Stone.

The appearance of actual, as against imaginary, gardens in portraits tell us much about the dialogue between garden and owner during a period when that relationship was dramatically shifting. Pride and display motivate their appearance in early portraiture. There is an element too of superior detachment between sitter and garden, the latter presented as an attribute much like a jewel or an order of chivalry. Although gardens continued to be an aristocratic symbol strangely they vanish from portraiture in the 1640s, not to surface again until a century later and then something quite spectacular happens. Pride and display continue to be motives but a great shift occurs, sitters are seen singly or in groups actually standing or sitting in the garden. These pictures are a reflection of a profound change in the human psyche, the fruit of new philosophical concepts introduced by John Locke. This involved the discovery of a self-created world as a direct expression of that newly discovered psyche. In this scheme of things the garden was to hold a highly complex place as an index of a range of sensibilities from a response to the effects of light and shade to being a vehicle for stimulating the imagination. These new thought currents account for the renaissance of the garden in portrait painting in a flood of canvases by painters including Arthur Devis and Johann Zoffany. Far from being just a convenient setting for a sitter, the choice of the garden (often of the painter's invention) is a reflection of some of the deepest resonances of the age.

In parallel with this the second chapter explores the status of the garden as emblem. Before the middle of the seventeenth century most garden images were emblematic. The gamut of their allusions ranged from the kingdom as a garden to the *jardin d'amour*; from Eden to the *hortus conclusus* of the Virgin Mary; from the classical golden age of eternal springtime to the seductive haven of forbidden delights. The fact that such gardens occupied a primarily symbolic role does not mean that they did not record a horticultural reality. In these images we can trace the development of the garden in England as it moved from its late medieval into its renaissance phase through the sixteenth and into the seventeenth centuries. The twin influences that formulated the Tudor garden were the Netherlands and France. In these garden pictures we can trace the reordering of the elements of the medieval garden, the raised beds, the shaped trees, the turf seats, tunnel arbours and fountains, in response to the new renaissance ideals of symmetry. In this process the compartment was the key component. A garden was made up of a series of compartments, each one hedged or fenced or surrounded by an arbour and each one having within it a pattern of turf beds, a maze or knot. Carpentry work was to multiply and by the close of the century the fantasies typical of Antwerp mannerism began to take hold. This type of garden was to have a life stretching into the 1630s, though by then upper-class taste had moved on.

The new garden style became fashionable in the reign of James I under the aegis of his queen, Anne of Denmark, and their son, Prince Henry, and even more forcefully during the reign of Charles I and Henrietta Maria. But it was still used as a vehicle for allegory and for symbol. The richest quarry of garden images for the early seventeenth century comes from the designs by Inigo Jones for the scenery of the court masques, those glittering entertainments that apotheosised the crown. In them Jones propagated a garden style which looked far more directly to Italy and also to new currents in French garden making under the aegis of the Mollet dynasty. Classical statuary and architecture appear along with the parterre of clipped box, soaring Italianate cypresses, elegant fountains and cavernous grottoes. These were visual propaganda for Jones's audience at court to change its garden style; but they were also emblems of the kingdom and of the realm of courtly love in the same way as the gardens in the old manner. The continuing force of that emblematic tradition should not be forgotten for the garden in a sense was able to give Protestantism images which were not graven ones through which to meditate on the divine. Gardens as compendiums of God's miraculous creation and hence as settings for spiritual meditation were to retain their hold into the Georgian age and beyond.

The emergence of the separate garden picture is the subject of the third chapter. The meagre topographical tradition in England in the Tudor and early Stuart periods was revolutionised by a flood of new artists from abroad. Among those who arrived were men like Leonard Knyff, Jan Siberechts and Jan Kip. During the last forty years of the seventeenth century they painted and engraved views of the great country houses. As a result between 1670 and 1730 there is a multiplication of accurate information about gardens. Illustrated county histories were produced and owners of great houses called for them to be immortalised in paint. These images are crucial, providing sometimes our only information about an era of English gardening that was to vanish in the next century. In particular these pictures offer us material on two obscure subjects, the development through the seventeenth century of the flower garden and of town gardens.

There is a plethora of visual information on the English garden during its French-dominated phase, when the model was Versailles and the master was André Le Nôtre. In England his equivalent was the team of George London and Henry Wise, who laid out most of the great gardens of the age from William III's Hampton Court to the Duke of Devonshire's Chatsworth. One publication may be said to encapsulate this achievement, Kip's *Britannia Illustrata*, which includes virtually every major garden created during the era.

Chapter four takes the story on to the gradual disintegration and eventually the collapse of the formal tradition, first at the hand of Charles Bridgeman early in the eighteenth century and then at that of William Kent in the 1720s and 30s.

This was without doubt the most innovative phase in the whole history of gardening in England. And a reflection of that fact can be found in the chapter's theme, the garden panorama – sets of pictures or engravings devoted to delineating a single garden. Chiswick House, Wrest Park, Stowe, Hartwell House, Westcombe House and Claremont: each was the subject of a set of images. Their very existence presupposes that their makers knew that they were different and these sets have no parallel in Europe at the time. In the light of the fact that the premise of the new gardening was to make a series of pictures it is hardly surprising that it was in just such a way that their owners chose to have them immortalised. That they and their successors were often engraved meant that *le jardin anglais* was to wing its way around the civilised world from St Petersburg to Washington.

Once the line between the garden and the landscape had been eroded and the park, under the aegis of 'Capability' Brown and his imitators, took over in the 1750s, garden painting gave way to landscape painting. Chapter five forms an epilogue in which the triumph of the landscape park and the emergence of a major school of landscape painting led by Richard Wilson coincide. The English garden all but vanishes from aesthetic record not to resurface again until the Victorian era. In the work of watercolourists like George Elgood and Beatrice Parsons there was to be a glorious revival of garden painting in the half century before the First World War. But that is another story and one that has already been told.[3]

For me garden pictures always exert an extraordinary visual hold. Lurking behind every garden view, however seemingly particularised, is always that greater image of the earthly paradise, that blissful state of nature lost at the Fall. That could only be recaptured by man through an exercise of the imagination in poetry and in art and in the taming of nature into a garden. Actual gardens never quite shed their relationship to a rich literary inheritance. Such concepts would have been part of the furniture of the mind of any educated viewer of both actual and imaginary gardens. It would equally have affected the pictorial interpretation of gardens, for what we see must inevitably be selective, an image that to some degree works from a premise of what the onlooker will expect to see. The increasing demand for garden pictures indicates the significant and progressive hold of the garden on the public's imagination. Record, reverie, instruction and vision have all continued to meet across the centuries in the image of the garden.

I

PRIDE OF POSSESSION

GARDENS IN PORTRAITS

The earliest exact topographical record of an English garden appears in a portrait group depicting Henry VIII and his family (4).[1] The king sits enthroned beneath a canopy of state, flanked by his third wife, Jane Seymour, and his son, the future Edward VI. Distanced from this regal trinity by columns decorated with grotesque work in gold are his two daughters, Mary and Elizabeth. Silhouetted in the flanking arches looking into the garden are two figures, generally believed to be a serving wench and a court fool with a monkey capering on his shoulders. The canvas dates from about 1545, two or three years after the death of Holbein and about eight from that of the queen who appears here in her capacity as mother of the heir apparent. Apart from her all the sitters are observed from life, as indeed is the Great Garden of Whitehall Palace.

This picture is an essential document, not only on account of the portraits, but also for the information it provides about the vanished palace of Whitehall.[2] That location is firmly established by the glimpses through, on the left, to the Princess Mary's lodging with its grotesques in grisaille and, to the right, towards one of the turrets of the great close-tennis court. The tableau is

4. Unknown artist, *The Family of Henry VIII*, *c.*1545. The Royal Collection © HM Queen Elizabeth II

3. View of the major garden at Hadham Hall, Hertfordshire, laid out for Arthur, Lord Capel of Hadham in the 1630s. Detail from plate 61

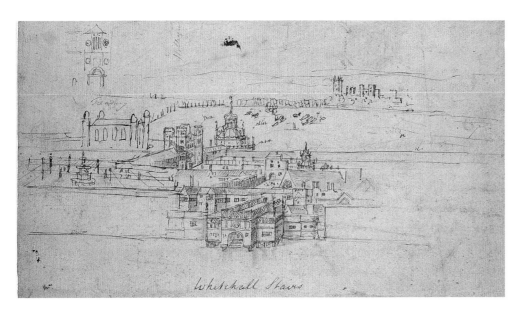

Whitehall Stairs

arranged on the ground floor of the king's lodgings and, even if the interior has been rearranged, it certainly delineates what we know to have been major features of the internal decoration.

But what of the garden? Compared with the Privy Garden at Hampton Court (164) information about the Great Garden is meagre.[3] Whitehall had been Cardinal Wolsey's London residence under its previous name of York Place. It passed into the hands of the king in 1529 and work continued on it throughout the thirties and into the forties. Huge tracts of land were purchased, so that the palace finally sprawled over twenty-three acres, almost four times the area covered by Hampton Court. By the time that the family group was painted the original privy garden had been transformed into the Sermon Court and the Great Garden elevated to the rank of privy garden, an extremely large one, some 120 metres long by 75 metres wide. Its lay-out is known from two other visual sources, both inadequate. One is an aerial view, *c.*1557–62, by Anthonis van den Wyngaerde (7) and the other a map of London attributed to Ralph Agas based on a survey made about 1558 (8). From these we can establish details not visible

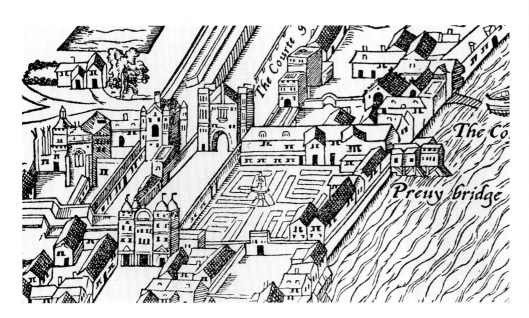

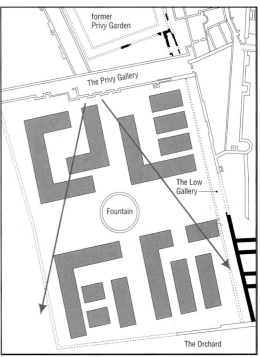

in the painting: the garden was quartered and at the centre intersection stood a major fountain, which, written sources tell us, also incorporated an elaborate sundial by the humanist and Greek scholar, John Ponet. The fountain was of the descending bowl type, close to one in the famous garden of the Cardinal d'Amboise at Gaillon that he had imported from Italy. Both the fountain and the ordering of the garden into quarters suggests an Italian input in its design, which can be ascribed to Nicholas Bellin of Modena whom we know to have been busy in 1541 working on another of the garden's major features, the banqueting house.

None of this is seen in the picture which records the garden's most retrogressive feature, the raised rectangular beds made up of courses of red brick encompassed by wooden rails painted white and green, the Tudor colours. From the Agas view we know that these beds were arranged pell mell into each of the four quarters. Elsewhere in Europe the compartment system, in which any space could be divided into a series of generally square compartments of equal size, each surrounded by a lattice fence or hedge and each having its own particular geometric patterns for flowers, was already well established. It originated in Italy, before spreading to France in gardens such as Gaillon and Blois; by 1600 it had become universal.[4] However, the picture does record what without doubt was the Whitehall garden's most splendid feature – the celebration of the dynasty by the introduction throughout the garden of stanchions topped by carved heraldic beasts. Through the archways can be discerned Edward III's griffin, the Beaufort yale, the Richmond white greyhound and possibly a white hind. Since the picture celebrates the royal family, the inclusion of these references to their ancestry and hence their legitimacy as rulers might well have provided the motivation to include the two unprecedented garden views.

In compositional terms the picture refers directly back to Holbein's celebrated wall painting of the Tudor family in the privy chamber. The division of space by means of columns certainly draws on Raphael's *Healing of the Lame Man* from his tapestry series, *The Acts of the Apostles*, a set of which belonged to Henry VIII. But there is another source. The painter would have been familiar with images of the Virgin and Child flanked by saints. He has applied a sacred formula to a secular subject which, in a post-Reformation context, was in its own way also sacred, for the king was now head of the Church. So the Virgin and her attendants within her *hortus conclusus*, a familiar subject in late-medieval religious art, has been replaced by the Supreme Head of the Church of England set within a new kind of *hortus conclusus*, that of the Tudor state.

The Family of Henry VIII raises the topic I wish to pursue in this chapter: gardens in portraits and why they were seen as appropriate attributes not just for the ruling family but, as time went on, for the aristocratic and gentry classes too. The contribution of portraits to garden history has been largely overlooked as a source and as a consequence some of the most evocative images of gardens have either been ignored or lain unappreciated for the richness of vision and accuracy of horticultural information that they provide. Before the middle of the seventeenth century no other source is better able to flesh out the reality.

The Garden as Status Symbol

René, titular king of Naples, Duke of Anjou and Count of Provence was the most famous horticulturalist of his age.[5] Between 1447 and his death in 1480 he was to create a series of spectacular gardens at his many castles and estates scattered across France. These opened with one at Aix-en-Provence which

10. *René d'Anjou at work in his gardens.* From the *Book of Hours of Isabella of Portugal*, *c.* 1480. Brussels, Royal Library of Belgium; MS 10308f.1

included a great circular mount bordered with wickerwork, a garden at Saumur based directly on the advice found in Piero de'Crescenzi's *Liber ruralium commodorum*, one on an island at Pont-de-Cé in the Loire and, finally, another at his castle at Angers which had an aviary and a two-storied pavilion from which to view the fish ponds.

The miniature at the opening of his treatise on the 'Mortification of Pleasure' shows him seated at a lectern beneath a canopy in what must be a garden pavilion (10). The compositional formula is the one for an evangelist or for St Jerome in his study, but the view to the left is something quite new – a bird's-eye panorama of one of the king's gardens. It is on an island, approached by a drawbridge opening onto a walk flanked by walls leading to a wicket gate which, in its turn, leads on to a door in a wall giving access to a garden of the kind already seen in *The Family of Henry VIII*. Four raised beds are filled with turf and flowers, one of which has a topiary bush, the paths between the beds being checkered. Off this main enclosure is a square bay turfed with grass with a fountain at its centre and with turf benches against the walls. The figure of René is certainly a portrait and the implication is that the garden scene also records a reality. René of Anjou's territorial authority was fragile and his concern with the pageantry of chivalry and his deliberate cultivation of a glamorous court were intended to keep his nobility loyal to the crown. The delights afforded by the garden represent one aspect of the late-medieval escalation of the trappings of rulership whereby that was achieved.

One of René's estates was, as we have seen, laid out according to the dictates of Piero de'Crescenzi whose *Liber ruralium commodorum* (*c.* 1304–9) was the most copied and published text on gardening at the close of the Middle Ages.[6] Charles V of France had commissioned a French translation in 1373 and fifteen manuscript copies survive, not to mention the fifteen printed editions between 1486 and 1540. Copies moreover are recorded in all the most important royal and aristocratic households in the fifteenth century.

Book VIII of the *Liber ruralium* deals with the pleasure garden and although he derived much of this from Albertus Magnus, he went on to add two sections of his own, one on gardens of a medium size and, more significantly, one on gardens appropriate to royalty.[7] Crescenzi introduces 'kings and other illustrious and rich lords' to the notion that gardens are an index of social hierarchy. He opens this section with the lordly statement: 'Because such persons, by reason of their riches and state are quite able to order things in such gardens so as to satisfy their desires, therefore they for the most part only need labour...' Crescenzi then describes a pleasure ground extending to twelve and a half acres with walls, summer houses, singing birds, fish ponds, leafy walks and bowers, vine-covered arbours, game, fruit trees and many other delights.

Thus the garden became an attribute of that central virtue for great personages during the Renaissance and Baroque periods – magnificence.[8] Aristotle had classified it as a virtue in the *Nichomachean Ethics*: 'great expenditure is becoming to those who have suitable means to start with, acquired by their own efforts or from ancestors or connexions, and to people of high birth or reputation, and so on; for all those things bring with them greatness and prestige.'

No court responded to this princely virtue with more alacrity than that of the Dukes of Burgundy. The gardens were highly developed as a setting both for occasions of frivolity and solemnity.[9] Charles the Bold's wife, Isabella of Portugal, took as her device the *hortus conclusus* thereby enmeshing into the dynasty's iconography the whole gamut of garden images from chastity to the state and to love. Guilbert de Lannoy, ducal adviser and diplomat, is depicted presenting Charles the Bold with his *L'Instruction d'un jeune prince* in 1470 in what must be a record of one of the ducal gardens (11). Behind the courtly group we see a walled garden with a summerhouse in which two lovers linger. There are the usual raised beds, a table for outdoor games and a maiolica container with a topiary plant.

One final illumination can be added to this line of descent to *The Family of Henry VIII*. In it Henri d'Albret, titular king of Navarre, plucks a daisy in honour of his approaching marriage to the sister of François I, Marguerite d'Angoulême, in 1526 (12). The setting is the garden of his castle of Alençon; it is more up-to-date than the Great Garden of Whitehall, for Henri stands on the edge of a compartment walled in by a lattice-work fence and laid out in a symmetrical geometric pattern. Already by the 1520s French gardens had responded to the Italian system of compartments and at Alençon there are further Italianate touches like the temple sheltering a fountain in the classical style.

Although all these images are an index of the rise of the garden as a royal and aristocratic status symbol, they are all characterised by being inward-looking, a walled world of delights to which only those bidden entered. That sense of admittance granted only to a chosen elite as opposed to flamboyant display for wider consumption is a key motif in these early garden images. They reflect accurately how such pleasure grounds were deployed to impress, for example, visiting dignitaries. In 1464 Georges Chastelain, Philip the Good's chronicler, recounts how the duke overwhelmed an English embassy by staging a complex

progress for them through his legendary park of Hesdin, near Montreuil. This comprised a huge area given over to ducal delight including lodges, fishponds, fountains, orchards, gardens, stables, even whole hamlets scattered over a landscape that embraced both hills and woodland.[10] Passing across a river flowing with fountains the visitors were intoxicated to find themselves given a banquet off silver-gilt in a specially constructed gallery. Eventually they made their way through the wood to the castle where they were received by the duke in his private apartments and then led to be presented to the king of France who happened to be staying there.

Such an experience can be exactly paralleled in Henry VII's reception of the great embassy which brought Katherine of Aragon to England in 1501. Her marriage to the heir apparent, Prince Arthur, was the summit of early Tudor foreign policy. Richmond Palace had been virtually rebuilt with that event in mind, modelled directly on the splendid residences and garden complexes of the Burgundian court. Here too the garden was inward looking:

In the aftirnon, the kinges hignes yede with a right pleasant company of gen-

11. *Guillbert de Lannoy presenting his book 'L'Instruction d'un jeune prince' to Charles the Bold in a garden*. Bibliothèque de L'Arsenal, Paris, MS 5104 f14

12. *Henri d'Albret in the garden of the castle at Alençon*, 1526. Bibliothèque de l'Arsenal, Paris, MS 509.f.1

13 Flemish Artist working in England, *Tudor Court Scene in a walled enclosure, probably a garden*, 1500. Illumination from *Poems of Charles d'Orléans*. British Library, MS Royal 16 F 11

tils and estates through his goodly gardeyns, lately rehersid, unto his galery uppon the walles apreparyd pleasantly for his highnes.[11]

There the guests found tables for chess, dice and cards, bowling alleys, the butts for archery 'and othir goodly and pleasant disportes, for every person as they wolde chose and desire.' One of the earliest productions of the recently established royal manuscript atelier at Richmond Palace, a copy of the poems of Charles d'Orléans dated 1500, shows a courtly scene of precisely this kind (13). Elaborately attired aristocrats parade in the vicinity of what is virtually certainly a garden fountain (its surroundings are obscured by the throng), the craggy mountains beyond firmly shut out by a high crenellated wall.

The Family of Henry VIII merely magnifies to picture size a format established earlier in illuminations. These, however, are potent reminders of the twin influences that framed early Tudor gardens, France and Burgundy. In another role *The Family of Henry VIII* is the precursor of two other pictures. The first, a reworking of the same formula attributed to Lucas de Heere, is discussed in Chapter 2 (115) where the garden may or may not reflect a reality and is primarily symbolic, but the second seems without doubt to be the result of observation. That picture is the small full length of Elizabeth I painted by Marcus Gheeraerts I during the opening years of the 1580s (14).[12] It is not devoid of allegory, for the sword at her feet and the sprig of olive in her right hand betoken her regal role as bringer of peace and justice. The most puzzling feature is the garden view which opens out to the right and in which a Yeoman of the

14. Marcus Gheeraerts the Elder, *Queen Elizabeth I with a view to a walled garden*, c. 1580–85. Private collection

Guard bows while he swings wide a door admitting a lady (the Queen again?) whose train is borne up by a lady-in-waiting. Three courtiers are engaged in conversation in the foreground. Like the view of the Great Garden of Whitehall all the indications are that this picture is site specific. It is a view of a royal privy garden within a courtyard which has an arcaded loggia running around part of its sides. The architecture of that arcade, seen from another angle, reappears in another portrait of Elizabeth, the famous picture of her at Siena.[13] The garden is a small one but it is stylistically advanced, for the enclosed area is treated as a single compartment; the beds within are arranged in a geometric symmetrical pattern, each one outlined with some low growing plant, probably a herb like germander or rosemary. The setting, however, bears no relation to any known royal palace garden.

This portrait establishes that even in Britain, on the fringes of the cultural currents emanating from Italy, gardens were understood as appurtenances of splendour and magnificence, their increasing grandeur through the sixteenth century mirroring exactly the rise of absolutism and the reassertion of aristocratic hierarchy. Under the impact of the Renaissance, however, both portrait and garden were to respond to one of the fundamental principles of the new art – the application of new laws by which the ideal coherence of space could be represented. Space and the figures it held were reordered with reference to man as the beholder and this was achieved by the new science of mathematical perspective as it was evolved in fifteenth-century Italy. In England that new disposition of space was slow to be adopted both in the portrait and in the garden. Indeed the fact that it was so slow meant that the Elizabethan optical aesthetic lingered on allowing artists to incorporate into a picture's surface inset views of gardens which ceased once the new optics fully gained sway.

PICTURES WITHIN A PICTURE

All over Europe by the second half of the sixteenth century gardens assume a greater presence in depictions of royal and aristocratic personages. One of the series of drawings made by the French court artist Antoine Caron (15), used as a basis for the cartoons for the celebrated tapestries depicting Valois fêtes staged under the aegis of Catherine de'Medici, demonstrates their changing status.[14] In his drawing of the entertainment given by the queen at the Tuileries for the Polish ambassadors in 1573 Caron has deliberately discarded the temporary building in which it was staged to reveal the garden beyond. That had been planted only seven years before and included beds which depicted the arms of the reigning dynasty. The prime objective of this series of designs was to represent everything that reflected the magnificence of the French crown. The fact that the Tuileries gardens are included is index enough of their new-found significance. French royal gardens had begun to assume the upward curve of importance which led to Versailles.

From this time on gardens also appear in aristocratic portraiture. In 1642 when the Genoese nobleman Gio Vincenzo Imperiale wanted his family immortalised the background was filled with a panorama of the great garden at his villa at Sampierdarena (16).[15] That villa had been built by his father in the 1560s but work continued on the gardens, which stretched up a hillside in terraces, into the 1580s. Gio Vincenzo was both a politician and a man of letters, so that his choice of the garden as backdrop symbolised not only patrician power but also its role as a magical domain inspired by the pastoral poetry of Tasso and, under his aegis, as a Parnassus of the arts. Few portraits give a gar-

16. Gio Bernardo Carbone, *Gio Vincenzo Imperiale and his Family before the gardens of Villa di Sampierdarena*, 1642. Villa Cattaneo-Imperiale, Genoa

den such undiluted presence. In most we catch only a detail, like that in Van Dyck's portrait of a Genoese noblewoman, painted in the 1620s (Musée du Louvre, Paris),[16] where we glimpse a garden through a small forest of triumphal columns, but the garden is a very grand one with balustrading and a seated figure of Jove. It leaves us in no doubt, however, as to the lady's rank.

In the main during the sixteenth century in England the garden in portraits retains its symbolic role. It is only after 1590 that the pace quickens and a steady succession of portraits give us what must have been the reality of Tudor and early Stuart gardening. Whole gardens are tucked away in the backgrounds. No other visual source gives us such a unique insight into the evolution of garden style as these pictures which deserve to occupy a position centre stage in any account of the history of gardening between about 1590 and 1640. The rarest are those which give any impression of English gardens before the death of Elizabeth I in 1603.

TUDOR GARDENS

The first important view of a garden in a non-royal portrait presents a problem. It appears in the background of a miniature by Rowland Lockey of *The Family of Sir Thomas More* (19).[17] It is one of three versions after Holbein's famous family group, all of which were commissioned by his son Thomas More II in the early 1590s. Two of the versions change the original composition to add the younger More, his wife and his two sons, John and Cresacre. As a result we are able to date the miniature quite closely, for the last named son is clean faced in the large oil version dated 1593 whereas in the miniature he has a slight moustache and beard.

George Vertue, the eighteenth-century antiquary, saw this miniature in 1742 when it was in the possession of James Sotheby whose father 'bought this limning many years ago of a Gentlewoman who was under some necessity. – and was as I heard before (sold to him by a) daughter of one of the More family...'[18] Vertue was hypnotised by the object, especially by the garden view, for he made a little sketch of it in his manuscript and wrote: '– a prospect of his [Sir Thomas

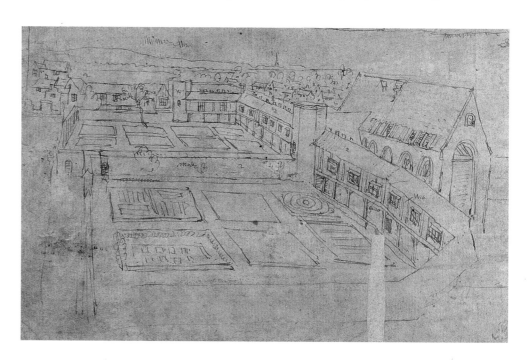

17. Anthonis van den Wyngaerde, *View of the Privy Garden at Richmond Palace*, with compartments filled with beds pell-mell *c.* 1550. Ashmolean Museum, Oxford

18. Sir Thomas More's garden at Chelsea. Detail of plate 19

19. Rowland Lockey, after Holbein, *Thomas More and Family*, 1593–4. Victoria & Albert Museum, London

More's] Garden at Chelsea appears part of his Gallery & chappel at the distance. London spire very small...' This indeed is what we see, a gallery stretching out along the left from the house towards the Thames, which terminates with what must have been his chapel and a distant view of London as seen from Chelsea beyond. The garden, in which a couple are seen to stroll, consists of one large compartment (18).

The reference to the fact that this depicts More's garden would lead us to conclude that it must record the garden of the manor house, which was forfeit on More's attainder in 1535, being granted to William Paulet, later 1st Earl of Winchester and later, in 1595, to Gregory Fiennes, Lord Dacre of the South, whose widow left it in 1595 to Lord Burghley.[19] The latter had a plan made of both house and garden which is irreconcilable with the miniature. But in fact there was a second part of the estate which was not lost at the attainder because it had been given to William Roper on his marriage to More's daughter, Margaret, in 1521. It was here that as Roper records in his life of his father-in-law, 'a good distance from his mansion-house builded he a place called the new building wherein there was a chapel, a library, and a gallery...' This remained in the possession of the Ropers and in 1618 was referred to in a letter as the 'Moorhouse'. It was sold in 1622–3 to Sir John Danvers, and this is the garden that we see in the miniature.

The garden is still medieval, in that it is enclosed. It blocks out the river panorama with a wall and a gate. Within the hedged square there are further geometric enclosures, all defined by more clipped hedges, four squares to the left, from one of which arises a tree, there is another that is not geometrically positioned, and, to the right, a long L-shaped bed within which there is a larger square bed with double hedges and a tree. This is a very early example of the compartment system in England.[20]

The number and contents of compartments could vary. The grander the garden, the more compartments. Lord Burghley's Theobalds, the apogee of Elizabethan aristocratic garden style, had nine, but in the case of More's house in Chelsea it is early days and there is just one. Their size could also vary between thirty-five and seventy feet square and, although such compartments could be railed (see plate 182), more often than not they were, as here, surrounded by a clipped hedge of whitethorn or privet. Frequently, though not in this case, the corners were marked by fruit trees. Within the compartment there is a knot, but not of the kind normally associated with the name.

Knots in the form of complex interlacing patterns did not appear before the 1580s. Before and even after that time any arrangement within a compartment of beds was also referred to as a knot. This type of garden can already be seen in Anthonis van Wyngaerde's view of the privy garden of Richmond Palace laid out about 1500 (17), which shows compartments containing beds arranged in various patterns, including ones in a basket weave design. From the drawing it is impossible to tell whether these beds were raised as in *The Family of Henry VIII* or hedged. The extraordinary L-shaped bed in the More compartment is duplicated in the pell-mell arrangement of the quarters of the Great Garden of Whitehall (8). By the middle of the 1590s garden fashion had moved on. The fact that More bought the land for his Chelsea house in 1520 and that he was executed in 1535 exactly dates the garden. The importance of this tiny view of an early Tudor manor house garden can hardly be overestimated.

Thirteen years later Lettice Newdigate was painted at the tender age of two, with a view of a complete garden stretching behind her through an archway (20). The picture is dated 1606 and has always remained at Arbury Hall, Warwickshire, from when it was painted just three years into the reign of James I. The garden, judging from its growth alone, must be late Elizabethan. Lettice was the daughter of John Newdigate and granddaughter of another John Newdigate.[21] In 1591 Lettice's father inherited Arbury, marking an upturn in fortunes for he had married well. The house was on the site of an Augustinian priory which in 1577 Sir Edmund Anderson had demolished 'and built out of their ruins a very fair structure in a quadrangular form.'

Nothing of the gardens visible in a view drawn in 1708 survives today but these must have been on the site of what we see in Lettice's portrait where the compartment system of the More garden is multiplied by three – two hedged squares in alignment with each other and a third strangely slightly set to one side, although this could be the fault of the painter. The latter compartment is punctuated by two entrances giving access to a square central fountain into which the water flows from a circular bowl whose source is a pissing figure. Beyond that there is a circular arbour with a seat in it and trees beyond. To the right the garden appears to be held in by a line of turf and then a hedge.

20. Unknown artist, *Lettice Newdigate aged two*, 1606. Arbury Hall, Warwickshire

Thomas Hyll's *The Gardeners Labyrinth* (1577) is an invaluable guide to the late Elizabethan garden and tells us all we need to know about the Arbury garden. The circular arbour is a herber:

> The herber in a garden may be framed with Juniper poles, or the willow, either to stretch, or to be bound togither with Osiers, after a square forme, or in arch maner winded, that the branches of the Vine, Melone, or Cucumber, running and spreading all ouer might so shadow and keepe both the heat & sun from the walkers and sitters there vnder.[22]

For an arched herber of the Arbury kind he recommends juniper poles, which will last for a decade, or willow which will call for repair every third year. The planting should be of fragrant roses, jasmine or privet 'to shoote vp and spread ouer this Herber, which in time growing not onely defendeth the heate of the Sunne, but yeeldeth a delectable smell, much refreshing the sitters vnder it.'[23] Hyll goes onto describe what we see – walks two or three feet broad of sand 'that the owner may diligently view the prosperitie of his hearbes and flowers.'

Opposite the herber is a fountain of a type whose origin is a woodcut in Francesco Colonna's *Hypnerotamachia Poliphili* (1499) which was translated into English in 1592 as *Hypnerotamachia. The Strife of Loue in a Dreame* (22). This book, a fundamental source for so many Renaissance garden motifs, includes in the English version the fountain of the pissing child which Poliphilus encounters. It consisted of two nymphs who 'held vp the Boyes shirt, aboue his nauil. The infant holding his little Instrument in both his hands, and continued pissing into the hotte water, fresh coole water…'[24] Subsequently Poliphilus was bidden to fetch some of this water: 'I had no sooner set my foote vpon the steppe, to receiue the water, as it fell, but the pissing Boye lift vp his pricke, and cast sodeinly so colde water vppon my face, that I had lyke at that instant to haue fallen backward.' Subsequent to this publication fountains of this kind, but without the mechanical marvels, were certainly introduced into gardens. Two designs for them are among the drawings of John Smythson (23).

The most striking feature, however, is the two knots for this is the only view we have of an Elizabethan knot garden. The earliest designs for interlocking knots appear in the *Hypnerotamachia Poliphili* but they find no echo in what we know of sixteenth-century Italian gardening. Nor is there any evidence of them in Androuet du Cerceau's engravings of French château gardens, although they do exist in one unexecuted design by him.[25] Their first appearance in England is in the form of what could only be an embroidery pattern in Thomas Hyll's *Proffitable Art of gardening* (1568). He refers to it as a 'propre knot' to

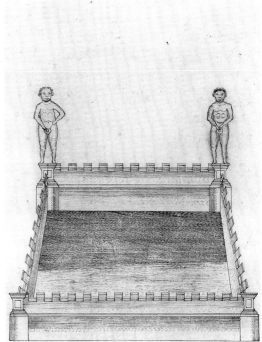

22. Pissing fountain from the 1592 translation into English of the *Hypnerotamachia Poliphili*.

23. John Smythson, *Design for a Fountain*. RIBA, London.

21. A unique view of an Elizabethan knot garden with a herber. Detail from plate 20

24. Two Elizabethan knots, one derived from plate 27, opposite. Detail from Hovenden's map of All Souls. *c.* 1586–1605. Codrington Library, All Souls College, Oxford

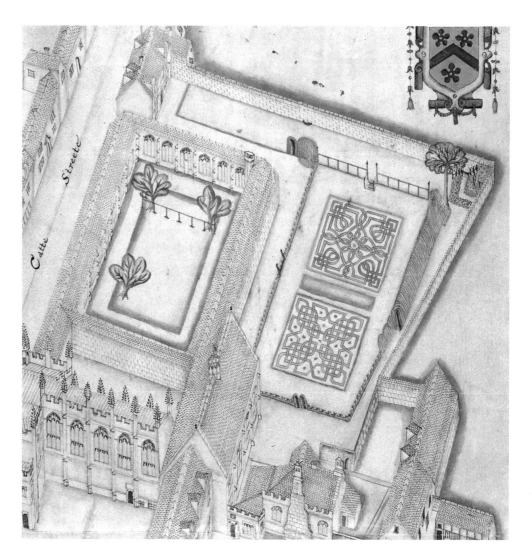

distinguish it from that seen in the More garden. But in the 1594 edition of *The Gardeners Labyrinth* he includes designs for twelve knots and the likelihood is that his source was French. The earliest evidence that we have that such knots were actually being planted is a map of All Souls College, Oxford (24), one of a series commissioned by Warden Hovenden between 1586 and 1605.[26] It shows two gardens, the warden's and the fellows', each with two knots, two of which are based on those in Hyll. The map belongs to the 1590s so these gardens were probably laid out in the eighties. The knots in the Arbury portrait are also variants of the designs provided by Hyll (25–7). They are planted in precisely the manner described slightly later by Gervase Markham in *The English Husbandman* (1613): 'you shall then set it either with Germander, Isoppe, Time, or Pinke-gillyflowers, but if of all hearbes Germander is the most principall best for this purpose...'[27]

One other portrait extends our knowledge of knots and that is the one of Jane Shirley, Baroness Holles of Ifield (29, 124). Although the portrait is allegorical (see p. 104) it includes a garden view that has all the indications of having been observed from life. By about 1630, the date of the picture, knots were extremely old-fashioned and the garden must have been planted at least ten years earlier. Jane Shirley, co-heiress of Sir John Shirley of Ifield, Sussex, was born 1596/7 and did not marry Denzil Holles until 1642. The garden we see

25, 26, 27. Knot designs from Thomas Hyll, *The Gardeners Labyrinth*, 1594

28 (bottom centre). Knot design from William Lawson, *The Country Housewifes Garden*, 1617

29. Knot in the manner of plate 28. Detail from plate 124

should be that of her second husband, Sir Walter Covert of Slaugham, Sussex, whom she married sometime after the death of his wife in 1610.[28] This again is a garden of compartments, two framed by paths and with a hedge and trees beyond. In the corners of the main knot there are junipers, an Italianate touch, and the format has changed somewhat since the portrait of Lettice Newdigate. The knot which can be seen in detail closely resembles those of William Lawson in his *The Country Housewifes Garden* (1617) (28). This records the sparse planting of flowers within it, emphasising how costly such things were.

JACOBEAN GARDENS

The previous portraits were Jacobean and Caroline but the garden style they record is firmly late Elizabethan. They herald a series of inset scenes in portraits which record either entire gardens or substantial parts of them. Collectively they accurately chart an upsurge in garden-making parallel to the building boom in country houses that is such a marked feature of the opening decades of the new century. This was to last until the disruption of civil war in 1642. The sudden burst was due not only to social stability and economic confidence, but also to the reassertion by the crown of a leading role in framing taste and fashion.[29] Under Elizabeth garden-making at court had stood still for the Queen lived within her father's *mise-en-scène*. Then suddenly after 1603 all that

30. Marcus Gheeraerts the Younger, *Anne of Denmark*, probably with a view of the garden of Somerset House. By kind permission of the Marquess of Tavistock and the Trustees of the Bedford Estate

31 (facing page, top left). *Design for a grotto and orangery.* Engraving from Salomon de Caus, *Les Raisons des forces mouvants*, 1624

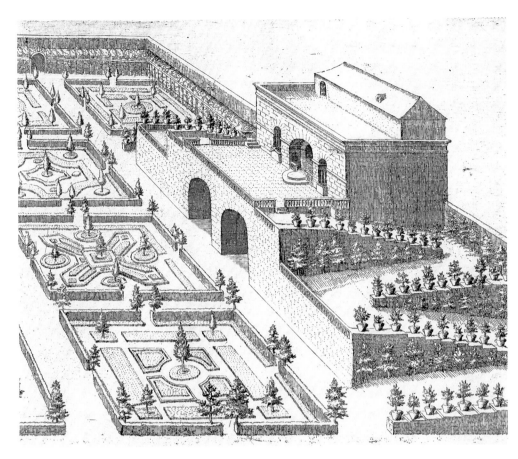

changed, with the new Queen, Anne of Denmark, and her son, Henry, Prince of Wales being in the vanguard. Both of them embarked on ambitious projects under the auspices of the French Huguenot garden designer and hydraulic engineer, Salomon de Caus, Anne at both Somerset House and Greenwich Palace and Henry at Richmond. The latter, in addition, made use of a Florentine artist, Constantino de'Servi. All of these royal projects involved elaborate water effects incorporating statuary, grottoes, aviaries, fountains, automata and the construction of whole islands. Although the long-term fount of these innovations was to be found in mannerist Italy in the late sixteenth century, in particular the gardens created by the Medici grand dukes, the style that reached England had first been interpreted in France and also the Netherlands. None of the major royal projects figures recognisably in portraits, which is a loss, but what is chosen nonetheless is of a deeply innovatory nature.

In Marcus Gheeraerts's portrait of Anne (*c*.1611–14) (30), an archway frames a garden encircled by a classical arcade and composed of hedged compartments, each of which is laid out with beds of green turf cut into symmetrical geometric patterns.[30] The arrangement is seen in engravings of similar garden compartments in de Caus's *Les Raisons des forces mouvantes* (1624) (31) which incorporates designs he made while he was in England before 1613. In Anne's portrait, therefore, the treatment of the compartment is quite unlike either that in the More group or those in the portrait of Lettice Newdigate. There are no interlacing knots recalling Markham's remark in 1613 that such things were now only popular with the 'vulgar' whereas 'great persons' were wholly 'given ouer to nouelties.'

Four other portraits offer corroborative evidence of the change. In the por-

32. Artist unknown, *Elizabeth Brydges, Lady Kennedy*, c. 1615. Woburn Abbey, by kind permission of the Marquess of Tavistock and the Trustees of the Bedford Estate

33. Garden compartment with a turf pattern similar to plate 31. Detail from plate 32

34. Artist unknown, *Sir Thomas Lucy III and his Family*. Board of Trustees of the National Monuments and Galleries on Merseyside (Walker Art Gallery)

35. Garden of turf compartments enclosed by a crenellated hedge. Detail from plate 34

trait of an unknown lady of 1611 discussed in chapter 2 (122) there is a similar view through an archway to a garden of cut-turf compartments. Another of the same type appears in the background of a portrait of Elizabeth Brydges, Lady Kennedy, at Woburn Abbey (32).[31] The incident depicted must have some meaning for a man is bowing low to a lady in proximity to a compartment of the same cut-turf variety; the whole garden is held in by a hedge which has been cut into curved crenellations (33). A third appears in a group portrait of Sir Thomas Lucy III of Charlecote Park, Warwickshire, and his wife, Alice, together with their seven children (34, 35).[32] The picture exists in two versions, both said to be early copies of one lost in a fire. The costume dates the picture to about 1620 and the family is arranged in some kind of carpeted garden pavilion. Access can be gained by a flight of steps up which Sir Thomas's heir, Spencer, bears a bowl of apples. The scene is peppered with objects reflecting the preoccupations of the family: a falcon on a perch, dogs, a bow and books, not to mention the garden. The role of the garden is emphasised by Lady Lucy who extends her fingers to a bowl of cherries held by her eldest daughter. The Lucys were rich through marriage and landowning; Sir Thomas was a scholar and a friend of the philosopher Lord Herbert of Cherbury and the poet John Donne. Although the garden view is somewhat crepuscular it clearly follows the latest court fashion.

A final portrait of an unknown young man, wrongly identified as Henry, Prince of Wales, also of about 1620, shows him standing in front of a garden. It is railed in with an arbour of carpenter's work in the corner of which two people sit gossiping to a third who stands. A couple strolls along one of the

36. Artist unknown, *Called Henry, Prince of Wales*, *c.* 1620. The Viscount Cowdray's collection

37. Robert Peake *Henry, Prince of Wales*, *c.* 1610–12. National Portrait Gallery, London

paths which surround a geometric pattern of raised or hedged beds. Indistinct though this image is, it is a rare record of the reality of the social use of gardens at the close of the reign of James I (36, 38).

Perhaps de Caus was responsible for introducing this new kind of compartment. Collectively they represent the English preoccupation with grass. This was to become a feature which was to set English seventeenth-century gardens apart from those of mainland Europe where the emphasis instead was always on elaborate parterres. In this country the preference was for what became known as grass *plats* which in the end earned their own designation of *parterre à l'Angloise*, although it has recently been argued that these could be 'enamel'd with flowers'.[33] The great French gardener, André Mollet, who worked for Charles I and Henrietta Maria in the 1630s, wrote of this predilection for scythed grass in his seminal *Le Jardin de plaisir* (1651) in discussing 'compartiments de gazon'.[34] The beauty of English turf, he wrote, was achieved by frequent cutting during the summer months and by the use of both wooden and stone rollers to beat the grass down, compact the ground and eliminate worm casts.

Two portraits of royal children offer tantalising garden evidence of another kind. One is a full length attributed to Robert Peake of James's eldest son, Prince Henry (37), who was to die tragically young at eighteen in 1612, and includes an enigmatic view through a window. The panorama is of a winding

38. View of a geometric garden compartment with a herber of the kind seen in plate 183. Detail from plate 36

39. Panorama of part of Prince Henry's Richmond Palace garden. Detail from plate 37

40. Robert Peake, *Elizabeth, Queen of Bohemia*, 1603, National Maritime Museum

41. The tree arbour. Detail of plate 40

stream or river with banks planted with trees and shrubs. In the foreground a flight of wooden steps leads to a landing stage. Whoever ascended from the water up the steps then took a path to the right to a puzzling and strange creation. It is set against a brick wall and consists of a projecting canopy in an ornate mannerist style with what would seem to be two benches beneath it. Undoubtedly we are looking at some aspect of the prince's Richmond Palace project where de Caus created island grottoes in the Thames. In addition a design for the project by Constantino de'Servi has recently come to light in the Medici archives.[35] Indeed we can see what must be an island for there is a promontory surrounded on three sides by water.

The second portrait is of Henry's sister, Elizabeth, later Electress Palatine and Queen of Bohemia, and is also by Robert Peake but earlier, being dated 1603 (40).[36] Once again we are faced with a view of an artificial landscape deploying water. To the right there is an arched bridge over a stream leading to a wooden gate or stile in a palisade dividing the pleasure grounds from the park beyond where the hunt is in progress. Far more interesting is what can be seen to the left, another stream, this time bridged by a single plank of wood that leads to a winding path to a summit on which sits an extraordinary arbour. This

is the only representation that we have of tree pleaching on this scale in an English garden (41). The nearest parallel occurs in one of the series of lunettes painted by Utens depicting the Medici gardens in 1599 (42). There a central tree has been trained into a dome with finials rising from it and a circle of trees has been clipped to form what resembles a colonnaded circular temple. Similar features are recorded in pictures of Netherlandish gardens, usually trained to form some kind of alfresco banqueting house (43) and mingling trained living plants with carpentry work, as in the picture of Elizabeth. In the portrait two ladies are seated on a turf bank whose sides are held in by wattle fencing, an arrangement typical of a medieval garden feature, the *estrade* tree, whereby one was trained into a shape, for example in tiers like a cake-stand. The central tree has been trained upwards to form the dome and a circle of trees has likewise been trained to form walls, an arched entrance and windows. The whole tableau is surrounded by a further circle of trees. We know that such training happened in English gardens for John Parkinson gives a description of an astonishing two-story banqueting house constructed by plashing a single tree in the garden at Cobham Hall.[37] But where was the garden in Peake's portrait? As the picture was almost certainly commissioned by Elizabeth's guardian, Lord Harington of Exton, to whose care the princess was entrusted in October 1603, it is likely that the view is of the grounds of his seat in Warwickshire, Combe Abbey.

During this period and down into the 1620s water gardens of this kind were made on a stupendous scale. In 1611–12 Robert Cecil was busy creating the Dell at Hatfield – a complex of canals with an island banqueting house at its centre. There was Francis Bacon's amazing complex nearby at Gorhambury, also in Hertfordshire, to which we can add a list of similar water gardens constructed at Bindon Abbey, Devon, for Lord Howard who died in 1608 and which still exist; at Raglan Castle for the 5th Earl of Worcester, described as 'divers artificial islands and walks'; and at Campden House, Chipping Campden for Sir Baptist Hickes. The earthworks for these, revealed in our cen-

42. A tree arbour at the Medici Villa of Pratolino. Detail from Utens's lunette, 1599, Museo Topografico, Florence

43. Garden with two trees, one trained with an ariel room, the other with a lower and upper chamber, both with a tree growing through the centre. Detail from Hans Bol, *Spring*. Uffizi, Florence

tury thanks to drought and the use of aerial photography, were on a very large scale embracing the deployment of water to form canals and islands.[38] These pictures are evidence of the latest fashions in garden style at court.

Markham's allusion to the fancies of 'great ones' can be put into context if we turn to the other portrait evidence. One is the likeness of a lady of the Kentish Byng family, later of Southill Park, Bedfordshire, painted about 1620 (45).[39] The garden here consists of two identical compartments with a striking concern for mirror-image symmetry of the kind propagated by Inigo Jones's masque designs after his visit to Italy (plate 134). It is caught again in the Netherlandish mannerist entrance gate with its scrolls and obelisks being placed in alignment to the central vista to the fountain instead, for example, to one side as in the More garden. The railings around the compartment are painted red and the whole garden is contained within a hugely extravagant wooden arcaded loggia that replaces the usual wall or a hedge or indeed a tunnel arbour as the enclosing boundary. External loggias to houses had evolved by 1600, favoured particularly for the garden façade of a house but this record of one surrounding a garden is unique. There are plenty of precedents for the garden it encloses in the engravings in Vredeman de Vries's *Hortorum Formae*.

A modest fountain is the focal point of the Byng garden, but by the 1620s fountains were proliferating in gentry gardens. An unlocated portrait of Anne, daughter of Sir Richard Houghton and widow of Sir John Cotton of Landwade, Cambridgeshire, shows her seated in a garden with her son and heir by her side (46, 47).[40] She is attired as a widow, her husband having died in March 1620 or 1621. The portrait, judging from the costume, was painted soon after. It is difficult to determine whether this garden is fact or fantasy, for the spire in the foreground with ivy entwined around it must be symbolic. It is almost certainly taken from an emblem in Geoffrey Whitney's *A Choice of Emblemes* (1586), where it is used to symbolise the interdependence of the Queen – the spire – and the Church – the ivy (48). Interdependence of another kind is the theme of the portrait, perhaps of widow and son. But stretching behind the spire is a garden

Te ſtante, virebo.

44. View of a complete garden in the manner of de Vries's *Hortorum Formae*, with a typically sparse planting of flowers. Detail of plate 45

45. Artist unknown, *Lady of the Byng Family*, c.1620. Private collection

46. Artist unknown, *Lady Cotton and her son*, c. 1620. Location unknown

47. Garden with a fountain of Diana. Detail from plate 46

48. *Spire entwined with Ivy*. Device in Geoffrey Whitney, *A Choice of Emblemes*, 1586

49. Artist unknown, possibly Abraham
Blyenberch, *Portrait called Sir Francis
Walsingham*, *c.* 1625. Reproduced by per-
mission of the Marquess of Bath, Longleat
House, Wiltshire

50. A unique depiction of a Jacobean house
and garden conceived as an interlocking
unit. Although the garden style is Flemish
mannerist, the geometry and perspective are
Italianate. Detail of plate 49

with flowers and a large bowl fountain with the huntress Diana at its summit attended by two dogs. In type it is not so far from the Venus fountain at Bolsover Castle, which was in place by July 1634 when it formed part of the décor for the Earl of Newcastle's reception of Charles I and his queen.

By far the most spectacular record of a Jacobean garden appears in the background of a portrait wrongly called Sir Francis Walsingham (50). The costume belongs to the mid-1620s and the view is to the garden façade of a house virtually identical in style but not scale to Blickling Hall, Norfolk (1619–27). A flight of steps leads down from the central doorway to a garden which is the exact width of the house. The garden is clearly designed to be aligned to it on a central axis that runs through its component parts and out beyond through a topiary arch in a hedge at the boundary. The main part of the garden consists of a large compartment delineated by a tunnel arbour with pavilions at its corners as in the portrait of Sir George Delves (103). In the two pavilions nearest the house a central tree goes up through the dome in the same way as in the garden emblem in Peacham's *Minerva Britanna* (99). The tunnel arbour has arched entrances and numerous windows from which to gain access to and look out upon a flower garden of the kind seen in the print in De Passe's *Hortus Floridus* (118). The positioning of the garden would mean that the pattern of the beds would have been visible from the upper windows of the house. Beyond the tunnel arbour there is firstly an expanse of grass planted with shrubs and two cypresses flanking the central arch, then a sanded or gravelled path and finally a stretch of grass filled with what were probably fruit trees. On one side the whole composition is held in by a wall while, on the other, it continues with what is likely to be an orchard.

Both garden and house must be relatively new. The scale is modest, the owner belonging to the gentry or office-holding classes. It is difficult not to associate the house with Robert Lyming, the 'architect and builder' of Blickling, who had earlier worked at Hatfield. All three houses are in an ornate Flemish style of classicism typical of Jacobean prodigy houses, the final flourish of a style which by the 1620s was being superseded in court circles by the stricter classicism of Inigo Jones. The garden too belongs to the tail end of a tradition, the type we have encountered since the 1590s, deriving from the *Hortorum Formae*; and the inset scene can be paralleled in Flemish paintings and prints of spring or courtly life. Gardens like this continued to be made even in the 1630s as the portrait of William Style testifies (111), but by then the court had moved on. Already by 1620 the virtuoso Thomas Howard, Earl of Arundel, was creating a revolutionary kind of garden at his Thames-side mansion, one that was the direct result of first-hand experience of the Renaissance villas of Italy. He was in the vanguard of a new phase in the history of garden-making in Britain.

Caroline Gardens

In the background of a full length portrait of Thomas Howard, 2nd Earl of Arundel, proud aristocrat, connoisseur, collector and promoter of all things Italian (51),[41] a view of a garden has been inserted, in exactly the same way as in the Walsingham portrait (49). It represents the revolutionary garden that he laid out on his return from his tour of Italy with Inigo Jones from 1613 to 1614 (52). Today the portrait hangs skied in the underground ballroom of Welbeck Abbey, by no means easily accessible to study. Nevertheless this inset scene of

51. Ascribed to Daniel Mytens, *Thomas Howard, Earl of Arundel, c.* 1627. Private collection

52. The East Garden of Arundel House with the antique sculpture collection and a gateway by Inigo Jones. Detail of plate 51

the first Italianate garden filled with classical statuary ever to be laid out in this country is one of the crucial images in the history of gardening in Britain.[42]

The portrait is ascribed to Daniel Mytens and it certainly belongs to the style introduced by the new wave of painters who started to arrive in England around 1620 signalling a marked change of fashion at court. Paul van Somer, Abraham Blyenberch (the likely painter of plate 49), Cornelius Johnson and the young Van Dyck were other new arrivals. This view is an early instance of the use of perspective in a portrait with the bold central path providing the strong converging lines emphasising recession in precisely the way Inigo Jones was doing in his masque sets in the years immediately after 1615. Suddenly the garden is no longer one of compartments, but is conceived of as a whole, where space is orchestrated in terms of vista. It is an arrangement which directly reflects the earl's and presumably Inigo Jones's personal knowledge of the gardens of the Italian renaissance. The main vista, which terminates with a piece of sculpture, is towards a classical arcade with rambling medieval and Tudor buildings seen arising beyond it. The approach to the path is by way of a flight of steps flanked by two life-size classical statues. Either side of this walk there is grass and more statuary sited on what is clearly the top of the retaining wall of an upper garden, revealing that this part of the Arundel House garden was an essay in terracing in the renaissance manner. The second garden filled with trees and a classical arch can be seen below. This is Arundel's response to the papal Villa Belvedere and to the great villa gardens of the cardinals of the church in Rome which were used as museums in which to display collections of antiquities.

The origins of the museum garden goes back to the fifteenth century, but Bramante's Villa Belvedere, in which antique statuary and modern architecture were integrated in a deliberate re-creation of an imperial villa, was seminal.

That garden also inspired the taste for re-landscaping the terrain into terraces. By the 1530s what had begun as haphazard collections of excavated fragments had been orchestrated in the great Roman gardens as focal points at the end of a vista or used to line a path.[43] While in Rome Arundel had purchased the so-called *Homerus* and commissioned Egidio Moretti to carve him four statues *à l'antique*. A year after the earl's return to England William Cecil, Lord Roos, gave him 'all the Statues he brought out of Italie at one clap'. Sir Dudley Carleton presented him with a head of Jupiter which he placed 'in his utmost garden, so opposite the Gallery dores, as being open so soon as you enter into the front Garden you have the head in your eie all the way.'[44]

In 1627, at precisely the period when this view was painted, the German biographer, Joachim von Sandrart, visited the garden and wrote a description:

> Foremost amongst the objects worthy to be seen stood the beautiful garden of that most famous lover of art, the Earl of Arundel, resplendent with the finest ancient statues in marble, of Greek and Roman workmanship. Here were to be seen firstly the portrait of a Roman Consul, in long and graceful drapery, through which the form and proportion of that body could be readily perceived. Then there was a statue of Paris, and many others, some full-length, some busts only; with an almost innumerable quantity of heads and reliefs all in marble and very rare.[45]

Sandrart describes the garden in the aftermath of the arrival of the massive consignment of antiquities from Greece and Asia Minor which were to be published in 1628 as *Marmora Arundeliana*. In all the house and garden contained thirty-two statues, one hundred and twenty-eight busts and two hundred and fifty inscriptions, sarcophagi and other fragments.

But is the picture an accurate record of the reality of that garden? Initially we have to approach it with some caution in the light of what we now know about the other two views of parts of Arundel House in Daniel Mytens's two full lengths of about 1618 of the Earl and Countess.[46] That date is provided by a letter from the artist in the August of that year refering to them. The Earl is shown seated with his sculpture gallery stretching behind him, a vista which closes with a classical arch framing a view across the Thames. The view is a fiction, for the sculpture gallery was in fact on the ground floor and the gallery ended not in an arch but a pair of windows. The picture gallery in the countess's portrait is no more accurate for it certainly did not terminate in a vista into the garden with a tunnel arbour and fountain. Both are inventions , though founded on a degree of reality, for Arundel certainly did revamp an old Tudor gallery leading to a landing stage to house his collections. The explanation may be that the portraits depict intentions, rather than actuality still in the making.

Arundel House was in fact a somewhat ramshackle collection of old buildings whose appearance is graphically caught in Hollar's engraving of 1646 (53). These are the buildings glimpsed on the skyline in the Welbeck portrait, in particular the steep roofed great hall with its belfry. It is easy to forget that the apparent grandeur was cosmetic. The Earl's grandfather, Thomas Howard, 4th Duke of Norfolk, had been executed for treason and his father, Philip Howard, Earl of Arundel, had died in the Tower, having converted to Catholicism. The family fortunes were low both politically and financially. Although that began to be reversed under the Stuarts Arundel never fully enjoyed royal favour or

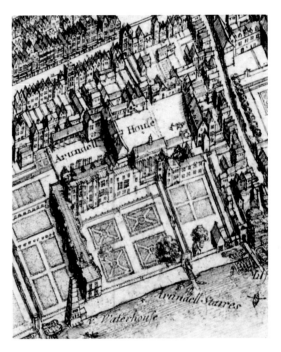

53. Bird's-eye view of Arundel House from Wenceslaus Hollar's map of London, 1646, showing the East and West Gardens and the gallery leading to the river. British Museum, London

54. Daniel Mytens, *Alathea Talbot, Countess of Arundel, sitting before the picture gallery at Arundel House*, 1618. National Portrait Gallery, London

55. An entirely fictitious view of the garden at Arundel House. Detail of plate 54

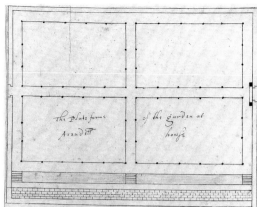

lucrative office and much must have depended on the fortune brought him through his heiress wife, Alathea, daughter of Gilbert Talbot, 7th Earl of Shrewsbury (54).

On their return from Italy Inigo Jones was commissioned to apply a cosmetic overlay to an existing building, in the main remodelling windows, fireplaces and doorways as essays in the new Renaissance classical style. Central to the plan were the alterations to the old long gallery to house the collections and the creation of a new garden to the west. The fact that there were two gardens at Arundel House accounts for much of the confusion about the surviving evidence. To understand this we need to start with Ralph Agas's map of c.1558 which shows the eastern garden, which was quartered and walled along the waterside (56). Just beyond it was a public landing leading into Milford Lane. That garden can be seen again laid out in four compartments in geometric shapes, of the kind seen in Gheeraerts's portrait of Anne of Denmark (30), in Hollar's map of London of c. 1660–6 (53). It is the groundplan of that garden which is given by John Smythson in 1619 in his drawing labelled 'The platforme of the garden at Arundell house' (57) on a sheet which contains also drawings of the two new Italian gates by Inigo Jones, one which bears the date 1618 (58).[47] The 'platforme' shows the area still quartered, with dots along the edges of each quarter, presumably marking trees. Along the river wall there must have been a raised walk for three flights of steps are indicated leading up to it. The Welbeck portrait records that the simple rusticated gate was located in the new western garden. But the whereabouts of the more important one, derived by Jones from Genoese and Roman sources is less obvious. Smythson's groundplan indicates a gate from the walled pathway above the new landing stage into the courtyard of Arundel House leading into the eastern garden and that surely was it.

The sources for the new western garden again can confuse. It lay between the gallery and a public right-of-way from the river up to the Strand. Jones had partially refaced and re-fenestrated the old north–south wing in order to make the

56. Arundel House, c. 1558, from Ralph Agas's map showing the East Garden and the future site of the West Garden. Museum of London

57. John Smythson, *Plan of the East Garden of Arundel House,* 1619. RIBA, London

58. Inigo Jones, *Design for the Italian Gate for Arundel House,* c. 1618. RIBA, London

59. Cornelis Bol, *View of Arundel House and the West Garden, c. 1640* (detail). Private collection

60. Wenceslaus Hollar, *Panorama of Arundel House from the south bank of the Thames*, from left to right: the terraced West Garden, the sculpture and picture gallery, the wall of the East Garden. The Royal Collection © HM Queen Elizabeth II

galleries for sculpture and pictures, adding a colonnade to the western garden side at ground level for the display of antiquities. This can be seen in a picture by Cornelis Bol painted about 1640 (59) which records also the wall along the riverside and that the lower garden within consisted of four grass plats. There is no sign of any classical statuary. The plats in the Bol picture fully accord with the ground plan of the western garden seen in Hollar's map of *c.* 1660–61 which goes on to give us the plan of two further gardens. These are caught from a different angle in another Hollar view, this time from the south bank of the Thames looking across towards Arundel House (60). From this it is clear that the western garden had changes of level which the Welbeck portrait with its terrace corroborates. The Hollar engraving also shows that some of this area was planted with trees.

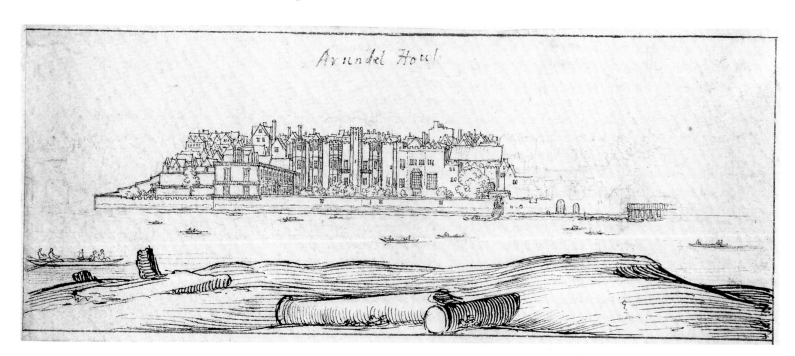

Arundel Hous

61. Cornelius Johnson, *Arthur, 1st Baron Capel and his family*, c. 1641. National Portrait Gallery, London

The conflicting evidence leads one to question the accuracy of the view in the Welbeck portrait. Our viewpoint must be looking across the upper part of the garden from the west towards the remodelled gallery, above which the roof and belfry of the great hall rise in the distance. At ground level the gallery has not a colonnade as on the lower terrace seen in the Bol picture, but an arcade. The rusticated Serlian gateway glimpsed through the trees of the lower garden is seemingly sited directly by the gallery when logic would place it at the opposite western end of a walk like the one we see. Furthermore the garden view in the Mytens portrait of the Countess with its tunnel arbour and fountain accords with none of the other sources. The conclusion must be that this is largely if not entirely imaginary. Overall the evidence favours the reliability of the panorama in the Welbeck picture as a genuine monument to pride of possession.

Arundel's museum garden was only to be emulated by the king at St James's Palace in order to house the classical antiquities acquired from the ducal collections at Mantua. Both, however, signalled a more direct interest and contact with Italy after 1620. John Aubrey recorded that it was his relative Sir John Danvers 'who first taught us the way of Italian gardens'.[48] The first three, he wrote, were at Danvers's house at Chelsea, Danvers's country house at Lavington in Wiltshire and, lastly, the famous garden laid out by Isaac de Caus during the 1630s at Wilton for the Earl and Countess of Pembroke (see chapters three and four). But Aubrey makes no reference to what, next to the royal gardens and to Wilton, must have been the most extravagant garden of the age, that created by Arthur Capel, Lord Capel of Hadham.

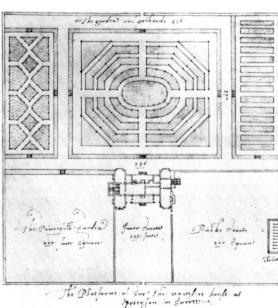

62. Artist unknown, *View to the east front of Hadham Hall, Hertfordshire, across the garden wall*, late seventeenth century. Hadham Hall

63. Robert Smythson, *Plan of the garden at Ham House, Petersham, Surrey, c. 1609.* RIBA, London

64. Artist unknown, *Aerial view of the garden and east front of Hadham Hall*, nineteenth-century copy after a drawing of 1649. Hertfordshire County Council

This garden is graphically recorded in Cornelius Johnson's masterpiece, the group depicting Lord Capel and his family (61).[49] This spectacular set piece with its breathtaking garden is the nearest equivalent we have to the picture of the Genoese Imperiale family painted only a few years later (16). The composition draws on Van Dyck's group of Charles I and Henrietta Maria, bestowing by its reference almost regal attributes on a mere Hertfordshire knight and his wife, enthroned beneath pillars and swirling baroque draperies. The portrait is a monument to dynastic pride with the garden as its ultimate symbol.

Hadham Hall in Hertfordshire was inherited by Arthur Capel in 1632 on the death of his grandfather.[50] The house was an Elizabethan brick one built by his great grandfather, Henry Capel, between 1572 and 1578. Arthur was elected a knight of the shire in the Short Parliament of 1640 and again to the Long Parliament in 1641 where he spoke in protest against the imposition on the county's freeholders of Ship Money. Shortly after that he was so shocked by the violence of the attack on the crown that he adopted an unswerving loyalty to it, being rewarded on 6 August 1641 with a peerage as Lord Capel of Hadham. Unusually he was not knighted until his appointment as a privy counsellor in January 1645. His steadfast loyalty to the crown was to cost him his life, for he was executed two months after the king in March 1649.

The garden was created in the late 1630s and in view of its grandeur the portrait must surely commemorate Capel's elevation to the peerage in 1641, making it in its way a last glimpse of a world about to be shattered. This is a hugely expensive garden. In November 1627 Capel had married Elizabeth Morrison who was the sole heiress of Sir Charles Morrison. The latter owed his vast fortune to another great heiress, one of the two daughters of Sir Baptist Hickes, Viscount Campden. She was said to have brought him £100,000. By his marriage to Elizabeth Morrison Capel came into the estate of Cassiobury and became one of the richest commoners in England, and by 1636 his elevation to the peerage was under consideration. Although the garden is usually considered in the light of Arthur Capel it may well far more reflect the interests of his wife. She came from a gardening family, her grandfather Baptist Hickes had laid out a major complex at Chipping Campden in the reign of James I.[51] Also she had a connexion with the sculptor Nicholas Stone who was responsible for the magnificent and costly tombs of the Morrisons in Watford Church.[52] And Stone at this period was busy on another major garden project, Wilton.

The Morrison tombs are listed by the sculptor in his Note-book and Account Book, but there is no mention of any work for Capel. However the lists are not exhaustive, for his nephew admits 'Hee did many more workes of Eminency in many places…'[53] The garden at Hadham Hall must have been one of them. Besides Johnson's picture there are two other sources for its appearance, one a primitive painting looking from beyond the garden back to the retaining wall and to the garden front of the house (62) and the other a crude drawing of 1649 now only known from a nineteenth-century copy (64). Both show that on that side the old Elizabethan house had been updated with new fenestration and roundels above with classical busts inset.

From that façade the visitor walked out onto a balustraded terrace, across a broad walk through a second entrance in a wooden fence, with newel posts topped by urns of flowers, leading to a second terrace looking down onto the parterre below reached by a second flight of steps. The containers are stone vases in the classical style, not placed haphazardly as in a medieval garden but to enhance the geometry of the composition. On each side the garden was contained by a stone wall with espaliered fruit trees and in the middle of each wall there was a handsome classical garden gate in the style of Jones. Down the centre ran a broad path cutting through a *compartiment de gazon* of the familiar English kind with four symmetrically placed statues and fountains. Only two of the statues are visible in the painting but they have attributes which suggest an identity, one a cornucopia – Ceres perhaps – the other an eagle indicating Jupiter. The central path ends in either a flight of steps leading down into a grotto house and out through a door into the country beyond or upwards via two other flights to a terrace running the width of the garden with banqueting houses at either end.

This garden closely resembles a garden scene by Inigo Jones in *The Shepherd's Paradise* (136) which in turn is based on Callot's *Le Grand Parterre de Nancy* (discussed in Chapter two). The overall arrangement of the garden recalls one of the terraces at Henri IV's palace of Saint Germain-en-Laye and there are also echoes of Sir Thomas Vavasour's orchard at Ham House (63) in

65. Detail of the bird's-eye view of the garden at Wilton, from Isaac de Caus, *Wilton Garden*, c. 1645–6. See plate 228.

the general disposition of the space and parterre. But none of these sources quite eclipses the relationship to the last section of the garden at Wilton. It is virtually identical. The connexion of Elizabeth Capel with Nicholas Stone, who carried out the sculpture commissions there, makes it difficult not to associate this garden with the designer of Wilton, Isaac de Caus. Indeed if we look at de Caus's design for a reduced version of the south front of Wilton made about 1636 (65) there is a double staircase of the Hadham kind descending from a Serlian doorway with a roundel also of the Hadham kind above it.[54] Everything would suggest that the Capel garden is by de Caus.

There is one final point about these appearances of gardens in portraits before 1640 and that is their connexion with women. A garden is far more likely to appear as an attribute for a woman than a man. Over the medieval garden presided the Virgin Mary, over the Renaissance one the reborn classical deities, Venus, Ceres and Flora, goddesses of love, fertility and abundance. On a more mundane level gardens were the province of the good housewife, a source of produce for the kitchen and the storeroom. In a long stream of English female portraits the generative role is alluded to by garlands and flowers. Some women like Lucy Harington, Countess of Bedford, were also important garden-makers, although no portrait of her in that context survives. In the case of royal patronage it was the two queens, Anne of Denmark and Henrietta Maria, who had a commitment to garden projects. The garden as the domain of the lady of the house is amply demonstrated in the title of William Lawson's book *The Country Housewifes Garden* (1617):

> The skill and paines of Weeding the Garden with weeding kniues or fingers, I refer to her selfe, and her maides, willing them to take the opportunity after a showre of raine: with all I aduise the Mistresse, eyther to be present her selfe, or to teach her maides to know hearbes from weedes.[55]

The female role in the garden is alluded to in Sir Thomas Hanmer's reference to 'ye old common way of Cuttings and Slips set in the Spring or Autumne in moist, shaded places, as women usually doe Gilliflowers...'[56] Such advice re-introduces the realms of practicality to the aura of symbolism and pretentious grandeur of these gardens.

THE END OF PICTURES WITHIN A PICTURE

In aesthetic terms Cornelius Johnson's group of the Capel family was old-fashioned. Although the artist attempted to incorporate the garden as a logical part of the picture's internal space the result is only slightly removed from the inset emblems typical of Elizabethan and Jacobean portraiture. When placed beside portraits by Van Dyck, in which sitter and setting are as one, the group is revealed as a throw back to an earlier age. After 1640 gardens in portraits disappear for virtually a century, until suddenly, from about 1740 onwards, there is an extraordinary resurgence when sitters clearly demanded to be presented in the garden. During the intervening hundred years portraits that record the reality of a garden are rare. And, as in the earlier instances, their appearance can be put down not to the whim of the artist but the dictates of the sitter.

John Michael Wright, ironically a painter who was trained in Italy and who was the only British member of the Roman Accademia di San Luca, is an artist whose work uniquely fuses continental baroque allegory with a lingering senti-

ment for Elizabethan emblematics. The iconic tradition lives on in his at times awkward if hieratic portraits in which his sitters are bedizened in archaic symbolic splendour. In 1673 Wright painted his group masterpiece, the family of Sir Robert Vyner (66), in a canvas which recalls the Capel family group.[57] The subjects are Sir Robert and his wife, Mary Whitchurch, the heiress widow of Sir Thomas Hyde; her daughter by that marriage, Bridget, future Duchess of Leeds; and her son by the present marriage, Charles. They are arranged as a frieze with columns and swirling drapery to one side and a garden backdrop let down behind them.

Sir Robert Vyner, forty-two in the year that this picture was painted, was at the apogee of his career as both goldsmith and banker. In the aftermath of the Restoration he had made the crown jewels for the coronation and became as a consequence King's Goldsmith. In 1665 he was knighted and the year after made a baronet. Pepys recorded in the former year that 'now he lives no man in England in greater plenty'.[58] The year after the portrait was painted Vyner became Lord Mayor. Thereafter troubles followed, first the death of his wife in 1674, then endless legal squabbles over his stepdaughter's marriage and finally,

66. John Michael Wright, *The Family of Sir Robert Vyner seated before the garden at Swakeleys, Middlesex*, 1673. National Portrait Gallery, London

in 1688, the tragic death of his only son, Charles, aged twenty-two. Vyner, heart-broken, died a few months later.

None of that could have been foreseen in 1673 when Vyner chose to present himself and his family in the context of the splendid garden which must recently have been laid out at his country mansion of Swakeleys in Middlesex.[59] He had purchased the estate in 1665, the year in which Pepys visited it, being shown round both the house and grounds by Vyner himself: 'He took us up and down with great respect and showed us all his house and grounds; and is a place not very moderne in the gardens nor house…' Swakeleys was built in the 1630s in the artisan craftsman style; by the 1660s it was desperately in need of updating, and that is precisely what the plutocratic Vyner did. The scheme included the decoration of the stair-well in the full-blown baroque manner with the story of Dido and Aeneas painted by an artist now designated as an anonymous follower of Laguerre or Verrio.[60] The garden chosen for inclusion in the portrait must have been another part of the project.

The garden is not so different from the one in the Capel group. Access to it through a wooden gate painted blue can be seen between the couple. Balustrading to the right would indicate that we view the garden from a terrace next to the house. It is a walled enclosure divided down the middle by a path that leads to a large wooden gate set between handsome gate piers. A little door in the gate opens into the landscape beyond. On either side of the path there are fountains with dolphins and putti, with, to the right, a classical statue on a plinth depicting Hercules and the Nemean lion. At ground level there are indications of that familiar English predilection, plats of verdant turf. The ingredients and disposition are virtually the same as at Hadham but the stylistic idiom has shifted to the baroque. It contains one feature, however, not found at Hadham for beyond the outside gate there is a cut through the distant trees indicating that there was a vista from this garden through the entire length of the estate. This reflects the influence of France and André Mollet, who had worked in England both before and after the Civil War, and whose book *Le Jardin de Plaisir* (1651) advocated the extended axis.[61]

The garden at Swakeleys was laid out between 1665 and 1673. As in the case of Hadham it is a hugely expensive one dependent for its effect on lavish built structures and an abundance of statuary. The year before, 1672, Vyner had been responsible for erecting an equestrian statue of Charles II in the London Stock Market. The horse he had purchased in Rome but the figure of the king was the work of Jasper Latham who was later to work on St Paul's under Wren,[62] raising the possibility that Latham was the author of the Swakeleys garden ornaments.

The Vyner family group is a late instance of the presentation of a new garden as an accoutrement of a *nouveau riche* family. Other portraits by Wright include garden details but none conveys any sense that they record a reality.[63] That applies to numerous portraits by other artists through these decades that often hint at a garden with trees or include a fountain or an orange tree in an urn without a specific allusion. One instance of this kind is the group portrait by an unknown artist of Elihu Yale with the second Duke of Devonshire, Lord James Cavendish and a lawyer, Mr Tunstal, gathered at the signing of the contract on the occasion of the marriage, in 1708, of Yale's daughter to Lord James (67). In the background five children (a later addition) play before a massive

67. Artist unknown, *Elihu Yale, the 2nd
Duke of Devonshire, Lord James Cavendish,
Mr Tunstal and a Page*, c. 1708, the view
may represent the garden at Chatsworth,
Derbyshire. Yale Center for British Art, New
Haven. Gift of the 11th Duke of Devonshire

68. Jonathan Richardson, *Richard Boyle,
3rd Earl of Burlington, with the bagnio at
Chiswick House, Middlesex, c.* 1717.
National Portrait Gallery, London

69. *A View of the bagnio at Chiswick,
c.* 1729–30. Detail of plate 256

vista of clipped yews and a fountain which may or may not
represent Chatsworth.[64]

One other portrait bridges the gap into the eighteenth century. Attributed to Jonathan Richardson, it represents the
young Richard Boyle, third Earl of Burlington, standing non-
chalantly holding a pair of compasses. The garden vista is at
his house at Chiswick and culminates in his first architectural
essay, the celebrated bagnio (68).[65] Constructed after his
return from his Grand Tour, the bagnio was completed by
1717 and the portrait was clearly designed to commemorate
that event (69).[66] It was one of the three buildings erected to
terminate the great *allées* which dominated the garden at
Chiswick structurally in an old-fashioned manner, that
looked back to André Mollet's radial planting at Hampton
Court shortly after the Restoration. At this stage the garden
was far from revolutionary but the building, which was
designed under the tight supervision of Colen Campbell,
most decidedly was. This was a manifesto for the palladian
revolution to come. And with it came a radical change in the
style in which gardens were portrayed in portraiture as they
moved centre stage in a new and final statement celebrating
pride of possession.

INTO THE GARDEN

After about 1740 gardens suddenly figure quite prominently
in portraiture for about two decades. This was the result of
a converging series of circumstances that made them not
only, as in the past, indexes of power and possession, but also the expression of
the new sensibilities cultivated by Georgian polite society. This evolved in the
era of Steele and Addison and is epitomised in the key phrase, 'the pleasures of
the imagination'. Its roots go back to Locke and a fundamental philosophical
shift in the perception of the human psyche.[67] The 1694 edition of Locke's
Essay Concerning Human Understanding contained a new chapter entitled 'Of
identity and diversity', which argued that personal identity was only derived
from awareness of the ongoing activities of one's consciousness. The assertion
was revolutionary; decades of philosophical controversy followed, which had,
by the 1740s, been settled firmly in Locke's favour. The notion that we each create a personality as a necessary fiction opened the door to the first representations of the private self.

This concept was to have profound repercussions in many spheres – portraiture and gardening among them. In the case of portraiture the focus was
redirected to record the sitter's world as an extension of his new-found consciousness, including the cultivation of sensibilities like taste. This was an
attribute keenly sought in polite society, for it allowed man to exercise his
higher perceptions and thus to reveal his true judgement, above all in the newly
defined domain of the fine arts. Gardening and gardens provided an arena in
which both the old public and the new private ideals could be expressed by
means of associative elements – buildings, inscriptions, columns and obelisks –
introduced as part of the landscape revolution.[68] In eighteenth-century portraiture the garden, actual or invented, became a vehicle for a complex of mean-

ings far beyond those of status and emblem in the pre-landscape era. Sitters chose to be represented in gardens, indicating a dramatic ideological change. Landscape assumed the role of a stimulant to the imagination and a vehicle for the gratification of the senses. The old spiritual and meditative tradition was to continue, as did the emblematic, but this was increasingly overlaid by a concern for an aesthetic response which was the direct consequence of Locke's epistemology. This led to associationist theories and emphasis on individual subjective responses, including the effects of colour and light as expounded in Newtonian optics. The new garden style was also seen as a mirror of English liberties. These portraits, therefore, contain complex resonances far beyond those of mere possession. They are celebrations of man's ability to re-shape his terrain in a way radically different from the previous century, meeting new objectives that included a worship of variety, novelty and a sense of motion along with an apotheosis of the prospect.

The portraits situated in gardens fall almost without exception after 1740 and record the closing phases of the dissolution of the old formal style which began after 1720.[69] The move started as one towards simplification, banishing elaborate parterres and topiary, gradually doing away with rigid enclosures and, above all, enlarging the wilderness area until that could be extended almost to incorporate an entire estate. This form was advocated by Stephen Switzer in *Ichnographia Rustica* (1718). The style was typified by the work of Charles Bridgeman and can be categorised as late geometric, for it never quite dissolved the boundaries, which finally disappeared after 1760 with 'Capability' Brown. The new style enjoyed widespread popularity because it was relatively inexpensive to maintain and accommodated working agricultural land within its orbit. Already in the 1730s, however, it began to change with a movement towards excluding any signs of physical labour even if it meant moving whole villages and roads. The architect and garden designer William Kent was especially influential, championing the serpentine line with a set route to guide the visitor to contemplate a series of 'pictures', often expressing the new-found preoccupation with personal relationships and experiences.

One other development is crucial. The old garden style had been about pattern; it was meant to be looked down upon to appreciate the swirling pattern, for example, in a baroque parterre, hence its placing beneath the windows of the *piano nobile* and the role of the terrace within the garden. Plants could be ranged in the *plate-bande* like illustrations in a botanical book. The border was to be strolled along and each plant viewed individually. The new gardens were radically different. More and more they demanded other attributes of the visitor whose role now was to move through a garden contemplating a series of pictures. These were gardens designed to be seen at ground level. It was but a short step from a person looking at one of these new garden pictures to wishing actually to be depicted standing in one.

Simultaneously and in response to these developments new forms of portraiture came into being, the conversation piece and the small full length.[70] The former represented people at home either within an interior or outside before their houses or in the park. Coming into favour during the 1720s, by the 1730s the new styles had established a distinctive tradition of their own. For the first time sitters stepped out and stood or sat in their gardens, either actual or composed in a manner suitable to their status and aspirations.

Three pictures anticipate this development. The first, dating from as early as

the 1670s, must be recorded as an unexplained aberration. This is the picture depicting the presentation of a pineapple to Charles II who stands in a formal garden (70).[71] There are no less than four versions of this painting, two of which are certainly later copies. The most important belonged to Horace Walpole and came from the grandson of George London, the partner of Henry Wise. Together they ran the famous Brompton Nurseries responsible for laying out the great formal gardens of the 1680s and 1690s. In a letter to the Rev. William Cole on 6 March 1780 Walpole wrote: 'It is Rose, The Royal Gardener, presenting the first pineapple in England to Charles II.' It is likely that the suppliant is correctly identified for London worked under John Rose who, in 1666, billed himself as 'Gardener to His Majesty at his Privy Garden in St James's'; he

70. Artist unknown, *John Rose, the royal gardener, presenting a pineapple to Charles II before a fictitious garden*, 1670s. Private collection

died in 1677. But it cannot be the first pineapple grown in this country for that event did not occur until after 1690. The house used to be identified as Dorney Court near Windsor. The garden is in the familiar format of grass plats with fountains and containers planted with exotics like agaves. Despite the mystery of its subject matter, no survey of garden pictures can omit this one which anticipates the potential of portraiture in the garden, although it is significant that the king is depicted here in a private capacity and not in ceremonial robes. In both stylistic and iconographic terms this picture fits far more easily into the work being produced in the Low Countries than into painting of the post-Restoration period in England.

The second picture dates from about 1733 and is a direct precursor of the garden pieces of the 1740s. It is by Peter Tillemans, teacher of Arthur Devis who was to become the chief exponent of the new formula. Tillemans trained as a painter in Antwerp and came to England in 1708. He specialised in country house views and by 1715 had obtained a permanent patron in George II's chaplain, the Rev. Dr Cox Macro, an antiquarian and collector who lived at Little Hough Hall, Suffolk, where the artist was to die in 1734. But not before he had painted the portraits of the owner's two children, Edward and Mary, in the garden (71).[72] Dressed like miniature adults they actually stand amid the vegetation, albeit probably invented. In contrast to earlier portraits foreground and background are as one. Behind them to one side the artist has included one of Dr Macro's improvements to his Suffolk estate, a vista to a classical temple. This is part of a garden that must have been laid out in the late geometric manner with buildings terminating perspectives formed by hedges holding in woodland. It is but a short step to Devis's portraits only eight years later.

William Hogarth's painting never reached a final form, for it was one of two proposals for a group portrait of George II and his family.[73] One sketch sets the figures in a garden against a circular temple with trees behind (72, 74), the second moves the group indoors. Scholars concur that this solution followed the first and that the likeness in it of Frederick, Prince of Wales, was the result of a sitting but that was not true of the others. Hogarth never gained the commission to paint that picture on account of William Kent. In 1733 the painter's hopes of royal favour ran high and in particular he sought the commission to paint the forthcoming marriage of the Princess Royal, with all its potential for a money-making print after the event. In anticipation of gaining that commission he secured access via Queen Caroline to make preliminary studies of the chapel where the marriage was to take place. However, William Kent, then rising high in royal favour, saw Hogarth and ordered him out of the building. The projected royal family conversation piece came to an abrupt end.

All of this has a sharp relevance if we turn to Hogarth's initial proposal of a garden setting, for the royal family are surprisingly arranged before one of Kent's recent buildings for the Queen in the gardens of Richmond Lodge (73). George II and his consort sit in splendid throne chairs with William, Duke of Cumberland, to the left. In the foreground Princesses Mary and Louise play with a spaniel, while, from the right, the Prince of Wales advances towards a table near to which are ranged his other sisters, the Princesses Anne, Amelia and Caroline. Perhaps the garden idea has some connexion with Philippe Mercier's group of Frederick, Prince of Wales, and his sisters making music in the grounds of Kew House, a signed version of which is dated 1733 but which must have been underway simultaneously with Hogarth's proposal.[74]

71. Peter Tillemans, *Master Edward and Miss Mary Macro*, c. 1733, with a view of the garden at Little Hough Hall, Suffolk. Norfolk Museums Service, Norwich Castle Museum

72. William Hogarth, *The Family of George II*. The Royal Collection © HM Queen Elizabeth II

73. William Kent's Temple on the Mount in Richmond Gardens. From *A Description of the Royal gardens at Richmond*

74. Detail of plate 72

The sketch must be prior to 1733, when the scheme foundered, and post 1730, when Cumberland was accorded the Order of the Garter, which he wears. Richmond Lodge had been given to Queen Caroline by the King on his accession in 1727 and she immediately set about changing the vast gardens (their circumference extended to some six miles).[75] She employed Charles Bridgeman, who, in the late geometric tradition, loosened up a formal domain, turning it into one with winding walks and vistas out to the Thames. More unusually he introduced cultivated fields thus bringing in, as part of the scheme, the working farmland. William Kent was commissioned to provide the fashionable associative buildings dotted through the gardens as focal points and terminations of vistas. The most notorious, Merlin's Cave, came later, but, by 1732, when Hogarth was putting forward his royal group proposal, the Dairy, the Hermitage and the Temple were already completed. The latter stood on a steep mount overlooking the river and the approach to it from Richmond Lodge was via a meandering serpentine walk through woods. Hogarth has transported it to a flat terrain in his composition.

It is extraordinary that he chose to incorporate the temple at all. There was no love lost between the painter and Kent. Even before the final rift of 1733 Hogarth had begun to swipe at Kent and his great advocate, Lord Burlington. In his earliest satire, *Masquerades and Operas (The Bad Taste of the Town)* (1724), he lambasted the leaders of what he regarded as 'foreign' taste, represented by Burlington and

THE TEMPLE.

75. Arthur Devis, *Unknown Man in a landscape garden*, 1740–41, the garden is probably fictitious. Private collection

Kent. In the background over the new portico of Burlington House labelled the 'Academy of Art' Kent stands flanked by Michelangelo and Raphael.[76] Kent in fact embodied everything Hogarth detested, not only in personal terms – for the architect unlike the painter was easy going and confident – but also in aesthetic ones – for he stood for the new Italianate palladian style. To make matters worse Kent could turn his hand to everything and anything and Hogarth loathed him for it. In this light the only possible explanation for Hogarth making Kent's Temple the main feature of his royal family group was that he knew that it would please the queen and she, after all, would have had influence over the king.

Hogarth's group anticipates by a few years what was to become a portrait formula in which specific gardens are depicted. The painter who more than any other responded to this demand or who made it fashionable was Arthur Devis.[77] Side by side with his long stream of interior conversation pictures there runs a parallel alfresco series covering the decades 1740 to 1760 portraying sitters either singly or in groups in gardens. The interiors in these pictures are virtually all fictitious compiled from engraved and other sources to provide settings appropriate to the rank of his sitters. Exceptionally his portrait of Sir Roger Newdigate show him in his new Gothick library at Arbury. In the case of the gardens the issue is, I believe, far more complex for it is arguable that virtually all of them record a reality and are the result of on-the-spot observation.

Devis was the son of a Preston carpenter who was trained under Peter Tillemans from whom he gained the skill to paint bird's-eye views of houses and gardens. His career as a portrait painter began in 1737 and five years later he settled in London where he continued to work until his death in 1787. By then he was a survivor from another era, one whose work must have seemed desperately archaic by 1760 when the new wave led by Reynolds and Gainsborough took over. This eclipse should not obscure the fact that for two decades Devis attracted the patronage of important members of the aristocracy, gentry and landowning classes. The bulk of his early sitters were conservative, High Tory and, early on, known for their Jacobite sympathies. His was a style formed by Dutch genre painting of the previous century, by current French rococo elegance, but also by the native iconic tradition filtering down from the Elizabethan age via painters like Wright. As a result his images of sitters in their gardens are quite extraordinary for they deploy a naive insular aesthetic to record a revolution in taste – one which was to have European repercussions. They are important reminders that the creators of these gardens may have viewed Devis as representative of a style that was apt for an English phenomenon.

His alfresco portraits fall into two groups. One series has little relevance as garden evidence. These are the pictures in which he arranges sitters in the foreground against a winding river and beyond that distant landscape. All these record is the dominance of the fashionable serpentine line and the pleasures of irregularity. There are, however, some twenty canvases in which single figures or groups are placed in specific garden settings.[78] They begin about 1740 and record the final phases of the gradual dissolution of the formal style. The ele-

76. Arthur Devis, probably *Dorothy Savile, Countess of Burlington, seated in the Orange Tree Garden at Chiswick*, c. 1741–2. Private collection

77. Arthur Devis, *Mrs Edward Travers in a landscape garden*, 1751. Private collection

ments within these canvases are the new found proliferation of associative buildings and ornaments, urns, obelisks, temples and classical eye-catchers, as well as formal pools of water and plantings of young trees. Some admittedly could be fictional as in the case of an early portrait of an unknown gentleman (75).[79] It would be difficult not to conclude that the obelisk in the distance behind him was inserted as anything other than a *momento mori* but it is possible, although unlikely, that he indeed erected it.

Early on Devis attracted important sitters. One of them was a middle-aged lady who is depicted seated in the Orange Tree Garden of Lord Burlington's villa at Chiswick with its Temple behind her and a part of the obelisk in the middle of the round pond to the left (76).[80] The picture dates from about 1741/2 by which time all these features were in place and they are recorded on Rocque's engraved survey of 1736 (252). Although no identification has ever been suggested surely the lady could be no one else but Dorothy Savile, Countess of Burlington. At that date she would have been in her early forties and she was certainly no beauty as Kent's sketches capture.[81] From the evidence of his other garden compositions Devis would never have placed anyone other than a member of the owner's family in such a setting. Moreover the Burlingtons, in the light of recent scholarship on the Jacobite affiliations of the

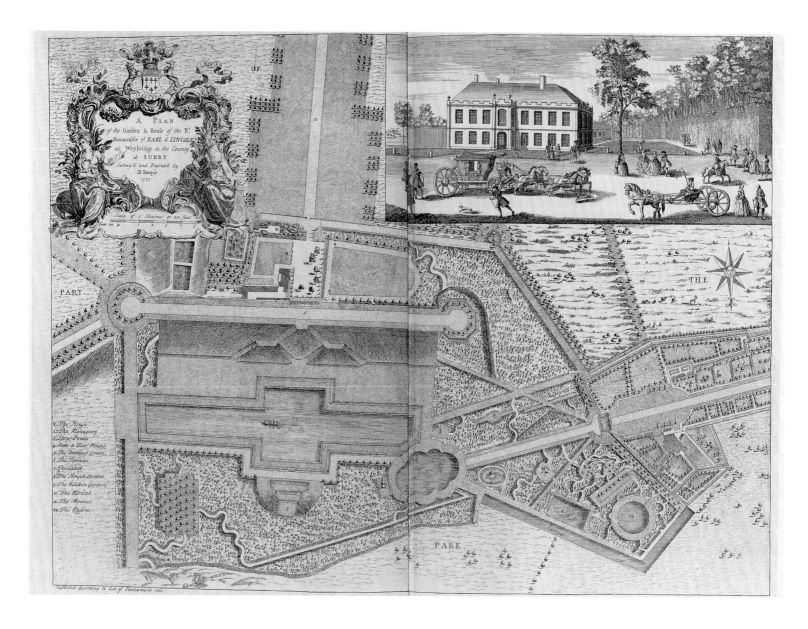

78. John Rocque, *The garden at Oatlands, Surrey*, before the 9th Earl of Lincoln's alterations, 1737. RIBA, London

architect earl, would make her fit neatly into Devis's circle of High Tory and Jacobite sympathisers. The painting also establishes that the idea of placing owners in the setting of their revolutionary gardens began with those who created them.

Devis must have visited the locations he depicted and there was clearly a desire on the part of sitters to see their gardens recorded as emanations of their particular sensibilities. Lady Burlington was interested in the garden at Chiswick for Kent designed a flower garden for her.[82] But Devis's canvas indicates that she may have had an input into the Orange Tree Garden suggesting indeed that the garden as a whole should be seen more as a joint venture than as the expression solely of her husband. Such a picture strengthens the likelihood that, although we do not as yet have the evidence, the Palladian garden buildings and sheets of water we see in portraits such as that of Mrs Travers (1751) (77) must have existed.[84] Together these pictures capture the tide of enthusiasm for this last phase of the formal style before its dissolution with the advent of Brown in the 1760s.

A more detailed examination of two more of Devis's most striking portraits

will bear out this hypothesis. Henry Fiennes Clinton, 9th Earl of Lincoln, later to become the 2nd Duke of Newcastle, was in his early thirties when he commissioned Devis to paint him and his wife, Catherine Pelham, whom he married in 1744, with their eldest son, George (79).[85] The boy was to die when he was seven in 1752 and, judging from his age, the picture must have been painted about 1750 or 1751. The composition always strikes the eye as unusual with these solitary figures arranged beneath a tree that rises from a swathe of green turf stretching into the distance and placed dead centre of the canvas. The setting is in fact an exact rendering of the most acclaimed feature of the earl's Thameside estate of Oatlands in Surrey.

Lincoln came into Oatlands at the age of ten in 1730 on the death of his brother.[86] He inherited a formal garden that is precisely recorded in an engraving of 1737 by John Rocque (78). Its most prominent feature was an enormous terrace, the one, having been revamped, on which we see the Lincoln family sitting. This ran east–west and looked down onto a large formal lake. At a distance from the house there was a wilderness with squiggly walks and other features. There were three acres of pleasure grounds and then parkland beyond

79. Arthur Devis, *Henry Fiennes Clinton, 9th Earl of Lincoln, with his wife, Catherine, and his son, George, on the great terrace at Oatlands, Surrey, c.* 1750–51. Private collection

80. Luke Sullivan, *View looking up towards
the terrace at Oatlands*, engraving, 1759

making in all, by 1788, five hundred and sixty acres. The house was sited high
above the Thames and the fame of the garden rested on the feature we see in
the picture and which was already there when Lincoln inherited, the view from
the terrace. From here could be seen one way up the Thames towards St Anne's
Hill, Cooper's Hill and royal Windsor (the direction in the picture) and the
other way towards to Walton Bridge, Sunbury, Harrow and Highgate.

Devis's canvas commemorates Lincoln's alterations to the garden during the
previous decade.[87] He returned from his Grand Tour which lasted three years
in 1741 having been the supreme object of Horace Walpole's affections. We
know that at least two people were certainly involved in re-laying out the garden at Oatlands. One was the cleric, Joseph Spence, who had accompanied
Lincoln on his tour, who was certainly responsible for much of the planting and
who also spent a great deal of his time supplying his friends with plans for their
gardens. In 1751 he actually wrote the rules he observed for garden making:
'the making of pleasure-grounds is an imitation of "beautiful Nature"'. Two
rules were absolute: 'To correct or conceal any particular object that is dis-
agreeable. To open a view to whatever is particularly agreable.'[88] Oatlands in
its new guise fulfilled both these criteria.

The other person involved was William Kent who designed a temple and may
also have been responsible for persuading Lincoln to include in his garden
scheme a gateway by Inigo Jones from Oatlands palace. Kent's connexion was
probably the earl's wife, Catherine Pelham, whose father Henry Pelham created
nearby Esher Place, regarded at the time as one of Kent's masterworks. Kent
had been working there since 1729. It seems therefore likely that he also had a
hand in the dissolution of formality at Oatlands. The old formal grass terrace
was not swept away, but the occasional tree on it must have been part of the
1740s restyling as there is no indication of any in the Rocque plan. Under one
there was a circular seat as the view from there was recognised as being particularly fine. Both the tree and the seat are recorded in an engraving of 1761 that
looks in the opposite direction from the picture, to the west. It could be that

81. Arthur Devis, *Philip Howard seated before a panorama of the river Eden at Corby Castle, Cumberland,* 1753. Private collection

this is the exact viewpoint in Devis's picture, the painter having dispensed with the seat (80). To visitors the breathtaking landscape panorama was always a source of amazement, caught, for example, in Dodsley's eulogy in *London and Its Environs Described* (1761): 'its majestic grandeur, and the beautiful landscape which it commands, words cannot describe, nor the pencil delineate so as to give an idea of this fine scene.'[89]

In the picture we see to the left part of the house, then a gravel walk followed by the grass terrace and finally the spectacular view. The old formal lake has gone, replaced by a naturalistic sheet of water three-quarters of a mile long and, although it actually terminated before it reached the Thames, it was designed to give the illusion that it was somehow a tributary and passed under Walton Bridge. Around that there was a dense planting of young trees. This was borrowed landscape on the grand scale and although Lincoln was to add a Temple of Venus and a spectacular grotto later nothing detracted from the dominance of the view.

Oatlands called for a short journey along the Thames, but to depict the garden at Corby Devis must have travelled as far north as Cumbria.[90] Philip Howard was twenty-three, about to marry and thirteen years into his inheritance of the Corby Castle estate in Cumberland in 1740 when he sat for his portrait (81).[91] The castle lies to the south-east of Carlisle above the river Eden which had been used by the sitter's father to create one of the earliest landscape gardens. Thomas Howard came into Corby in 1708 and the garden seen in the picture was already largely in place by 1729 making it coincidental with the early phases of Lord Cobham's Stowe (see Chapter three), but on a far more modest and provincial scale. The importance attached to the garden is reflected in the fact that the sitter has relegated himself to one side of the canvas so that the eye is drawn into the magical panorama of the river Eden meandering into

82. Survey of Corby made by G. Smith in 1752, including several improvements that were not executed. The view in plate 81 is from the twist in the river Eden, looking towards the long narrow island

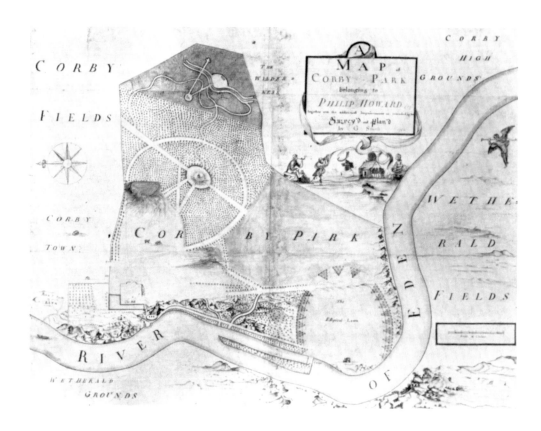

the distance. It is difficult not believe that this has been done to evoke the lines which inspired Thomas Howard to make the garden in the first place, ones which became almost a sacred text for the exponents of the new style, the description of Eden in Milton's *Paradise Lost*:

> Southward through *Eden* went a River large,
> Nor chang'd his course, but through the shaggie hill
> Pass'd underneath ingulft, for God had thrown
> That Mountain as his Garden mould high rais'd
> Upon the rapid current, which through veins
> Of porous Earth with kindly thirst up drawn,
> Rose a fresh Fountain, and many a rill
> Waterd the Garden...
>
> (ll.223–33)

Howard was blessed with a terrain which matched Milton's poetic vision and indeed he was to use the cascade area for theatricals including a masque of his own derived from *Comus*. The viewpoint in the picture is close to the castle, which was high up on the left bank. From it a steep descent past a hundred-and-fifty-foot high cascade led to the river bank along which ran a walk flanked by primitive statuary of various mythological figures, including Polyphemus, to a classical pavilion, the Tempietta, which terminated the vista and which we see in the picture. In these allusions we see the usual conflation of the Christian paradise with the classical golden age. In the river is a narrow island and on the opposite bank the top of the gate-house of the old Benedictine priory of Wetheral can be seen floating above a planting of trees as a borrowed eye-catcher. Sir John Clerk of Penicuik described the experience of the garden at Corby soon after its creation in 1734:

a very agreable winding walk down to the River where there are some artificial grotos...on the River side is a large walk...beautified all along with grotoes, Statues of the rural deities. at the end of this walk next the house is a Cascade 140 feet high.[92]

Thomas's son Philip was of a scholarly cast of mind, a correspondent of the continental philosophers of the day and the author of a book on the scriptural history of man and the earth. He was also interested in gardening for he assisted the owner of nearby Netherby Castle in landscaping the park, the owner acknowledging his 'taste and judgment'. What we see in the picture must record his remodelling of an inherited domain for it is full of young trees which could only have been planted during the previous decade and indeed there is a survey (82) from the previous year which incorporates plans for substantial additions to the park in the form of an 'Elliptical Lawn' and an extensive wilderness. These apparently were never carried out, but little is known of the history of the garden. Philip Howard would hardly sit for his portrait only to celebrate his father's creation. It must celebrate his own contribution – alterations made during the 1740s – a further process of naturalising the terrain somewhat akin to Lincoln's work at Oatlands. No other picture more vividly evokes the role reversal in the dialogue between tamed and untamed nature than this picture. Its parallel image is Isaac Oliver's melancholy young man seeking the shade of the greenwood tree in contrast to the walled formal geometric garden (106). By the middle of the eighteenth century that division had not only been gradually dissolved but in this case gone.

Edward Haytley is another artist whose pictures shed light on the evolution of the early landscape garden.[93] Haytley was a portrait and landscape painter who was possibly born in the Preston area in Lancashire and who was patronised by the same people as Devis. He made his earliest appearance as a flower painter in 1740 and exhibited at the Society of Arts in 1760–1. About 1747 he presented two competent if somewhat mechanical views of the Chelsea and Bethlem Hospitals to the Foundling Hospital in London. Little is known about him and his work has only recently emerged with any clarity, consisting in the main of small-scale portraits and conversation pictures in the Devis manner which have the same naive charm, although Haytley is far less sophisticated. Simultaneously with Devis he began to place his single sitters in a garden ambience (83), bestowing attributes on them which clearly have meaning but probably never existed. However three pictures certainly enlarge our knowledge of gardens.

Haigh Hall, near Wigan in Lancashire, was the seat of the Bradshaigh baronets. In 1746, the year before he succeeded to the baronetcy, Sir Roger Bradshaigh IV and his wife, Catherine Bellingham, sat for Haytley wearing Van Dyck costume (84) with the historic mansion house of the family behind them.[94] There is a second version, with slight alterations in pose and other

83. Edward Haytley, *Miss E. Wandersford in an imaginary landscape garden*, 1753. Marble Hill House, Twickenham

84. Edward Haytley, *Sir Roger and Lady Bradshaigh, of Haigh Hall, Lancashire*, 1746. Wigan Heritage Services, Wigan Council

85. The garden at Haigh Hall before the alterations of the 1740s. From J. Kip, *Nouveau Théâtre de la Grande Bretagne*, London, 1716, New Haven, Yale Center for British Art, Paul Mellon collection

86. A celebration of Sir Roger Bradshaigh's alterations to the Haigh Hall gardens. Detail of plate 84

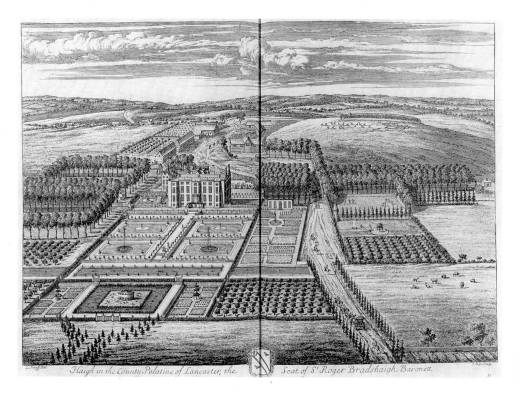

details, by Joseph Highmore which was painted for the novelist Samuel Richardson, for whom Lady Bradshaigh had a passion, and which can be seen hanging over the chimney piece in his portrait now in the National Portrait Gallery.[95] That version was painted four years later and can be discounted as evidence. In the original Bradshaigh and his wife stand in an up-to-date garden, a series of geometric ordered terraces descending away from the house leading, via a Bramantesque double staircase, to a formal pond on which a party is boating. On a hill to the right there is a ruined Gothick eye-catcher in the manner of that major designer of ruins and follies, Sanderson Miller. Everything would point to a picture celebrating a re-fashioning of the ancestral domain but it is not quite as simple as it seems.

Haigh Hall was a house in the manner of Robert Smythson. It does not survive, being demolished in 1827.[96] Our knowledge of its appearance only goes back to 1707 when it appears in Kip's *Britannia Illustrata* (85). It shows that the fenestration in the Haytley painting has been updated. However the greatest discrepancy lies in the garden for what we see in the print is a spectacular formal garden projecting out from the façade with grass parterres and fountains which bears no

87. Edward Haytley, *The Brockman Family and Friends at Beachborough Manor: The Temple Pond looking towards the Rotunda*, 1744–6. National Gallery of Victoria, Melbourne

resemblance whatsoever to the garden in the picture. That formal garden was the creation of the sitter's father Sir Roger Bradshaigh III who succeeded to the estate in 1684 and died in debt in 1747, having already handed the Wigan estate over to his son in 1742, the year before his marriage. We can, therefore, pin-point this revamping of the garden to the years 1742–6. But seeing is not always believing, for in the case of his other two major garden pictures Haytley painted a garden still in the making. The same could be true here for we are presented with a mature garden, the complexities of the old formality swept away in favour of an arrangement of geometric banking with close-cut grass and a formal pond for boating. Formality has in fact not been dissolved here, only radically simplified. The garden stretches out from the house in an exactly symmetrical way and straight lines are every-

where in evidence. It would be interesting to know whether this scheme was that of a professional improver or an *ad hoc* revamping by the owner as in the case of Beachborough Manor, the subject of Haytley's other two major garden pictures.

Beachborough Manor was situated in a park of three hundred acres between Folkestone and Hythe in Kent. In 1743 Haytley was commissioned to paint two views of a garden then only in the planning stage, including in it the family and friends of the owner, James Brockman (87, 88).[97] The project was to take three years in all and its inception and the garden's is recorded in a letter of December 1743 from Mrs Elizabeth Robinson to her daughter Elizabeth Montagu. No other document sheds such an illuminating light on both a garden project and the painting of two pictures to commemorate it:

88. Edward Haytley, *The Brockman Family and Friends at Beachborough Manor: The Temple Pond looking from the Rotunda*, 1744–6. National Gallery of Victoria, Melbourne

Mr Haytely is come back from my neighbours where he has been drawing a landskip from ye life it is a view of his pond & his Temple that is to be built & ye neighbouring fields & hills, with some figures to adorn it principle of which are ye Squire & Miss Molly. She is set on a Stool and drawing & he is fishing near her & smiling very graciously on her. Then at some distance is Miss Hymore & ye Parson & Miss Betty and Miss Hinkle. & there is to be added Mr & Mrs Hinkle; all that is to be put into a Picture painted by Mr Haytely. he wants some better name than that of a pond for his water which puzzles him very much for he fears it is too small to call a Serpentine River; but thinks that of a pool wou'd Sound (bettr) than a pond, your father proposes he shou'd call it ye Temple Pool or Sacred Pool, pray if you or Sally as you are great readers Shou'd findout any bettr name for it send us it and we will transmit it to him.[98]

From this we learn a number of details: that originally only one picture was planned, the identity of the sitters, the agony experienced by the owner in framing his newfangled garden and that the painting was underway before the temple was even built. There is something comically Pooteresque about all of this, and it is this that makes these canvases so engaging for they are a rare glimpse into the repercussions of the change of garden style on provincial people lower down the social scale. One is reminded of Lady Catherine Burgh's withering comment to Miss Bennet about her father's very small park.

In the first picture we are presented with a view to the temple across an asymmetrical but still formally landscaped pond. In the centre foreground there is the small figure of a river god reclining before a walkway which acted as a damn to the water. The squire of Beachborough Manor advances towards the water, not fishing as in the letter, but raising a hand in salute to his niece (who acted as a housekeeper), Molly or Mary Brockman. She is seated on a stool having almost finished a sketch of the temple. Behind her is a second female figure, Mrs Hinkle, whose husband is the man on the left walking along the bank with a book in his hand. On the right there is a fishing party, a lady and a child, 'Miss Betty [Elizabeth Brockman] & Miss Hinkle', and two more beyond, the Reverend Edmund Parker and 'Miss Hymore', probably Susannah, the daughter of the painter, Joseph Highmore.

In the other picture the time of day has shifted. In the twilight men are fishing with a basket to hand for the catch, reminding us that for all its pretence at being a garden in the new fashion it fulfilled its time-honoured function as the manor's fish pond supplying the house. The sitters are not identifiable but clearly belong to the same circle of family and friends. The telescope on the table emphasises the temple's role as a viewing point.

No other pictures capture so vividly the part played in Georgian social life by the garden. It was of course a vehicle for display, but was equally a setting for the new discourse of polite society. It was also designed to provide recreation. North wrote in *A Discourse of Fish and Fish Ponds* (1713): 'Young People love Angling extremely: then there is a Boat, which gives Pleasure enough in summer...'[99] The latter can be seen moored close to the temple in the second picture. To the left Mr Hinkle, book in hand, is a rare depiction of the tradition of meditation in a garden, still going strong in the fifth decade of the eighteenth century. In 1714 a clergyman called John Laurence produced *The Clergy-Man's Recreation* which ran to no fewer than six editions by 1728. He extolled the virtues of a garden which 'by Walking and Meditation, has help'd to set forward many useful Thoughts upon more divine Subjects'. He added to the book a little treatise recommending its use to the gentry, for there 'all the best and noblest Entertainments are...There a Man may converse with his God, by contemplating his Works of wonder in each flower and in every Plant: And then the devout Admirer cannot but lift his Eyes and his Heart in praise to the great Creator of all Things.'[100]

In stylistic terms we witness the ripple effect of the great innovative gardens created by Charles Bridgeman and William Kent laid out two decades before on modest country gentry. That is caught in the reference to the fact that Brockman's pond was 'too small to call a Serpentine River', perhaps an allusion to Bridgeman's Serpentine in Kensington Gardens, begun in 1730. The temple topped by the figure of Mercury must surely have been inspired by Kent's temple for Queen Caroline in Richmond Gardens (72) which also was set upon a mount and designed for prospects, in its case up and down the Thames. Squire Brockman clearly acted as the Bridgeman and Kent of his own garden works in the same way that hundreds of Georgians must have done.

At Beachborough the temple is part of an inexpensive essay in borrowed landscape, for young trees have been planted to frame a view to Hythe and beyond that they lead to the white chalky cliffs of the Kent coastline. A telescope sits on the table in the temple so that ships at sea could be viewed in the distance. Beachborough is a provincial pre-Brownian landscape garden on a tiny scale, still preserving the demarcation between garden and country with retaining walls, geometry and clipped grass. It was an accessible style that welcomed in the working landscape as the cows nearby indicate. All that was to change after 1760 when that demarcation disappeared.

89. George Romney, *Sir Christopher and Lady Sykes strolling in the garden at Sledmere*, 1786. Private collection

GARDEN INTO PARK

The process of the erosion of formality was completed in the work of 'Capability' Brown. The garden quickly gave way to the age of the landscape park, an open undulating green domain punctuated by a major lake and dotted with clumps of trees. In this new scheme of things the turf came right up to the walls of the house. This was the age of the private elysium, a verdant paradise in which the country house was set like a jewel to catch the eye of the visitor as he sped along the carriage drives of the parkland. Geometry and any sign of rural labour were banished. The flower garden survived, but it was discreetly tucked away behind walls far from the mansion house.

The garden therefore vanishes from the portrait, although its successor, the park, is ever present. In Romney's portrait of Sir Christopher and Lady Sykes, painted in 1786, the latter leads her husband out to survey his park at Sledmere (89).[101] In the distance we glimpse a planting of exotic conifers and on an eminence there is an eye-catcher. Such portraits are representations of 'men of feel-

90. Alexander Nasmyth, *The Family of Neil, 3rd Earl of Rosebery, in the grounds of Dalmeny House, West Lothian, c.* 1787. By permission of the Earl of Rosebery

ing' in the new era of sensibility which marked the decades before the French Revolution when a philosophical and sentimental enjoyment of nature and the countryside was considered a desirable attribute. In this new dispensation women increasingly occupied a more central position embodying the genius of the place.

The final glimpse, however, of the garden in eighteenth-century portraiture is an ironic one. Rousseau's *Emile*, published in 1762 and translated into English the following year had a huge influence on the upbringing of boys. In England it resulted in what can only be described as a charade of egalitarianism in which boys were made to undertake manual labour, including, in particular, gardening. Indeed the cultivation of a small patch of land where the little labourer might see the fruits of his own work was a fundamental concept for Rousseau and his followers. An early instance of this is caught in a portrait painted about 1770 of the future fourth baronet, Sir William Clayton.[102] Immaculately dressed in wildly inappropriate clothes for gardening, including a white shirt and fine white stockings (admittedly he has put his smart jacket and hat to one side), he gingerly wields a spade harvesting root vegetables which are piled into a wheelbarrow. In the distance the mansion house floats amidst a Brownian parkland.

In Alexander Nasmyth's portrait of the family of the third Earl of Rosebery (90), painted in 1787, we are presented with a panorama of pride of possession

91. Joshua Reynolds, *Master Henry Hoare as 'The Young Gardener'* 1788, Toledo Museum of Art, Ohio; gift of Mr and Mrs George W. Ritter

on the grand scale.[103] But the heir, Archibald John, later the fourth earl, is depicted clutching a child's rake. Behind him is a miniature wheelbarrow with a diminutive spade. These he has used to cultivate the flower garden to the right and his younger brother and two sisters stand among the blossoms he has cultivated. In the following year Reynolds was to cast Henry Hoare, member of the fabulously rich banking family, as 'The Young Gardener' rather pathetically trying to push his tiny spade into the earth (91).[104] In these pictures in which the aristocratic and gentry classes are re-cast as common labourers we witness a role reversal which would have astonished their ancestors.

II

A PARADISE OF DAINTY DEVICES

The Emblematic Garden

About the year 1400 an English illuminator who signed his name as 'Johannes' depicted a king and queen at chess in a garden setting (93).[1] The castle walls and a wooden fence form an enclosure and within it the two chess players are seated on that quintessential feature of the late medieval garden, turf benches. Along the wooden fence there is a raised border and both it and the greensward are dotted with flowers. Beyond it there is a second garden with another raised flower border where a gardener is busy trimming shrubs.

This illumination is the only representation we have of a medieval garden from an English source, scholars of the subject otherwise relying entirely on continental ones. The miniature was executed at precisely the time when the royal gardens were becoming increasingly elaborate, although not as yet places of regal display so much as ones of private relaxation.[2] The particular kind of garden recorded here is an *herbarium*, a grassed enclosure that had been a feature of English royal gardens since the thirteenth century when Henry III had ordered benches to be made around his great *herbarium* at Clarendon. In this case they were made of stone, but more usually they were of turf as Chaucer describes in the *Legend of Good Women*: 'a litel herber that I have, that benched was on turves fresh y graven'. According to the descriptions, English medieval royal gardens could be quite elaborate, with vine-covered walks, summerhouses, ponds and fountains, but we have no way of knowing their appearance and, as a consequence, no way either of tracing any development in garden style.

The impulse to depict actual gardens was no stronger in the rest of Western Europe. Instead we have a plethora of pictures of gardens, which gradually reflected an increased reality, marrying with what can be garnered from archival and archeological sources, but whose point of departure was either religious or literary. Nevertheless it is these pictures which are the direct antecedents of the garden paintings of the seventeenth century and beyond. Although, at first glance, they seem very distant from the elysiums of the English eighteenth-century aristocracy as recorded in the lyrical canvases of Zoffany or Devis, both the line of descent and their meaning are closer than might initially appear.

Symbolic Gardens

The urge to depict the garden came from the Christian image of Paradise, the Garden of Eden in the Old Testament, that enclosed space where both the Tree of Life and the Tree of Knowledge grew, watered by the four rivers of Paradise

93. Johannes, *King and Queen playing at chess in a garden*, c. 1400. Bodleian Library, University of Oxford. MS. Bodley 264f.

92. A unique depiction of a Jacobean garden, with raised walks and compartments filled with geometric clipped hedges. Detail of plate 121

94. Oberrheinischer Meister, *Hortus Conclusus of the Virgin Mary*, c. 1410, Städelsches Kunstinstitut, Frankfurt am Main

95. Master of the View of Sainte-Gudule, *Virgin and Child, a Female Donor and St Mary Magdalene*, c. 1470, with a garden view beyond. Musée d'art religieux et d'art mosan, Liège

and tended by Adam and Eve.[3] The Fall of Man signalled his expulsion from that garden and his Redemption spelt his return. To the lost vision of Eden a second garden from the Old Testament can be added, the one in the Song of Songs which describes the walled enclosure of a Persian royal garden filled with fruit trees, aromatic herbs, flowers and shrubs and also with fountains.

In the New Testament Christ's agony and betrayal took place in the public Garden of Gethsemane, his tomb was in a garden and in Mary Magdalene's first glimpse of him after the Resurrection he was mistaken for the gardener. In the Christian scheme Paradise was equated with Eden before the Fall. Christian iconography was thus to provide an abundance of horticultural imagery.

This series of biblical scenes called for artists to depict gardens, but, as the Middle Ages drew to their close two subjects predominate, giving us glimpses of gardens of a kind we know to have existed. The first are representations of Paradise, the second pictures stemming from the Song of Songs as a prefiguration of the *hortus conclusus* of the Virgin Mary. Paradise was enriched by its fusion with the classical tradition of the *locus amoenus*, that lovely place which occurs in both Hellenistic and Roman literature. It was always described as a flower-bedecked meadow through which ran a babbling brook, where it was forever spring, with gentle breezes rustling the leaves on the trees. In this garden there was also a reflection of another classical topos, that of the Golden Age in which, in the words of Ovid's *Metamorphoses*, 'it was a time of everlasting spring, when peaceful zephyrs, with their warm breath, caressed the flowers that sprung up unplanted.' To represent these visions of paradise artists painted what was in effect a version of the medieval herbarium.

Images of the *hortus conclusus* of the Virgin Mary record more precise developments in late medieval garden-making.[4] The Virgin Mary came to be identified with the enclosed garden of the Song of Songs, for she was not only the

96. Attributed to the Master of the *Juvenal des Ursins*, 'Jardin d'amour', from *Le Roman de la Rose*. Bibliothèthque nationale de France, Paris. MS fr. 19153 fol. 7r

'new Eve', but also the Beloved, the Bride of Christ and the Christian Church. Around 1400, at the same time that Paradise began to make its appearance as a flowery *locus amoenus*, pictures depicting the Virgin and Child sitting within a walled or fenced garden begin to appear (94). The garden itself is usually filled with her attributes – the fountain and the portal – along with symbolic flowers such as the lily and the rose. In fifteenth-century Flemish painting in particular the opportunity is taken to place the Virgin in a walled town-garden of the kind that must have existed in every Flemish town of the period, with raised beds spot planted with flowers and herbs, plants trained into topiary, a fountain and benches upon which to sit (95). Nonetheless the pictures themselves remain firmly imaginary, however often they are used by scholars today to illustrate features of contemporary garden-making.

As well as Paradise the *locus amoenus* evolved into the other garden image that was to haunt not only the medieval but also the renaissance mind, the *jardin d'amour* as it was envisioned in the thirteenth-century love poem the *Roman de la Rose*.[5] The narrative of the *Roman* concerns the admittance of the Lover into a garden in search of his beloved figured in the rose. The poem in fact contains little descriptive detail about the garden itself, beyond walls, a gate and a fountain, but this was not to impede the long series of illuminated manuscripts which evoke for the viewer the most spell-binding of all visions of the medieval garden (96). These illuminations give us a very different set of garden images: amorous and courtly ones that belong solidly to the present world, ones in which the focus is on the joys of the senses – the sound of trickling water and birdsong together with the radiant beauty of trees and flowers. We see the garden as a setting for music and singing, dancing and love-making. With the Renaissance this *jardin d'amour* was to don a more classical mantle, as a paradise presided over by a Venus or Flora and later the

97. School of Simon Benning, *The Month of March*, *Hours of the Virgin*, Bruges, *c.* 1520, New York, The Pierpont Morgan Library

98. *Populus alba* from Andrea Alciati, *Emblemata* 1584

style of the garden itself developed through mannerist and baroque phases.

Gardens impinge in other areas of medieval art. Representations of the months often brought tangential garden images like a man holding a flower, but these only developed into fully fledged garden pictures in late medieval Books of Hours. These included calendars of the feast days arranged by month and the borders provided an opportunity for including garden pictures that were appropriate in particular to the season of spring and the months of March and April (97).[6] Margins were filled with exactly observed plants and flowers in what were some of the earliest essays in botanical illustration.[7] Both reflected a metamorphosis in illuminations initiated by members of the Ghent–Bruges School who replaced their formerly stylised treatment of plants and flowers with ones that aimed at total realism of observation.

Books that dealt with the practicalities of gardening were another source of garden imagery. Apart from classical agricultural treatises like Columella's *De re rustica* (which includes one book devoted to gardening), the earliest text available in Western Europe was a work by the thirteenth-century Bolognese lawyer, Petrus Crescentius, *Liber ruralium commodorum* (*c.* 1304–9), which was copied, translated and printed innumerable times.[8] Two sections of this book deal with gardening and versions from Flemish fifteenth-century workshops provide us with another series of garden images, both of small intimate gardens where lovers linger and also of larger park-like ones with trees and a flowery mead. Crescenzi's book was certainly known in England and Edward IV owned an illustrated copy in French written for him in Flanders between 1473 and 1483.[9]

GARDENS IN IMPRESE PORTRAITS

Virtually all of these traditions of garden image making so far have been symbolic and the advent of the Renaissance intensified that through the revival of the repertory of pagan antiquity and through the universal cult of emblems and *imprese*.[10] The fashion for the latter expanded, elaborated and consolidated the inherited tradition of hidden meanings typified by the allegorical interpretation of the Song of Songs. Allegory was revitalised by a passionate belief that a pre-Christian tradition of secret wisdom transmitted by myth and symbol had existed. This was reinforced by the publication of the *Hieroglyphica* (1505), a book supposedly written by an Egyptian priest which gave meaning to hieroglyphics. The principles that this embodied were translated into a more popular idiom in 1531 by Andrea Alciati in his *Emblemata*, which precipitated a torrent of such publications (9). In these emblems the visible world was presented as a thin veil hiding deep philosophical truths, and in this new pantheon the natural world of trees and flowers occupied a prominent place, directly affecting how people must have looked at their gardens. By the middle of the century this had been codified in one large volume, Piero Valeriano's *Hieroglyphica* (1556), which went into many editions and was translated into French and Italian. The world of plants occupies eight long chapters, opening with the symbolism of the palm and the laurel and ending with the onion and various herbs.

99. Garden emblem, from Henry Peacham, *Minerva Britanna*, 1612

This approach to the elements of the garden and indeed the garden itself was reinforced by the all-pervasive Neoplatonism and hermeticism of an age that also found expression in *imprese,* a revamping of the devices of medieval chivalry. The taste for *imprese* provoked a flood of books that continued until the eighteenth century. The natural world – trees, flowers, fountains, even whole gardens – were pressed into service to form aggregate images, which, accompanied by a motto, expressed the ideals and aspirations of a particular person.

By about 1545, the date of the royal family group with the garden of Whitehall Palace glimpsed behind it (4), the Reformation had already happened and iconoclasm was shortly to follow. From then on the garden iconography of Catholic piety lost its visual expression and was transferred to a new life in prose and poetry. Images of religious gardens now existed only in the mind. But that loss by no means diminished the role of the garden as symbol, for sixteenth-century England devoured foreign books of emblems and *imprese* and indeed made its own modest contribution in works like Geoffrey Whitney's *A Choice of Emblems* (1586) or Henry Peacham's *Minerva Britanna* (1612), both filled with meaningful plants and flowers.[11] A single emblem of a garden from Peacham's book must serve to illustrate this approach (99). It depicts a garden surrounded by tunnel arbours with pavilions at the corners from which sprout shaped trees.[12] The garden comprises an arrangement of raised beds, gillyflowers in pots and one planted at the centre, towards which a hand extends to pluck a blossom. The verse opens:

A garden thinke this spatious world to be,
Where thou by God the owners leaue dost walke,

100. Artist unknown, *Lord Edward Russell*, 1573. By kind permission of the Marquess of Tavistock and the Trustees of the Bedford Estates.

And art allow'd in all varietie.
One only flower to crop from tender stalke...

That flower represents some 'honest course wherein to leade thy life' or 'the heedie choosing of thy wife'. The moral is that God allows only one choice in such matters and that choice must be a wise one, or 'to thy ruine ever after, erre'. The motto is *Vnum, et semel* (Once and once only).

Imprese were assiduously cultivated, above all they were employed at the great tournaments staged on the anniversary of the accession day of the monarch throughout most of the reigns of Elizabeth and James I. Knights who appeared on these occasions presented their sovereign with a pasteboard shield bearing an *impresa*; these were displayed in the Shield Gallery of Whitehall Palace where they were much visited and studied.[13] There were several hundred of them, providing an extraordinary index to the imagery apotheosising the crown. In them plants, if not gardens, abound. The Earl of Montgomery, for instance, presented to James I a shield with a beautiful garden on it filled with all sorts of flowers with the motto: *Ridet favonio flante* (It smiles when the west wind blows). The garden represents both the donor and the kingdom, the wind the beneficence of the king. For Elizabeth I there was a plethora of flower *imprese* like the one which depicted a rose garden with the motto: *Dulce decus meum* (My sweet glory); or another with a rose just above which the sun rises: *Dum splendes Floreo* (While you shine I flourish).

The chaste ladies of these *impresa* portraits, bearing their branches of laurel, and enclosed in their gardens, are typical of the Elizabethan portrait aesthetic in which rank was the prime preoccupation. Any further meaning was conveyed through the use of signs and symbols designed to be read only by the *cognoscenti*. The result was something which can be designated the *impresa* portrait in which likeness was embellished with symbolic attributes, inscriptions and mottoes to express a sitter's circumstance or aspirations.[14] An *impresa* consisted of a picture (the body), and a motto (the soul), which were interdependent. Just as masques were a corporate expression of the era's obsession with 'remov'd mysteries', the *impresa* was their individual equivalent.

A rudimentary example of the garden as *impresa* is the inset scene in a portrait dated 1573 called Edward, Lord Russell, eldest son of Francis Russell, 2nd Earl of Bedford (100).[15] His wife was referred to as a widow the previous year, making the identification questionable. The *impresa*, inset without concern for any logical spatial relationship to the figure, shows a gentleman, presumably the sitter, standing in the middle of a turf maze. This is one feature of a garden compartment with geometric plats and trees enclosed with a hedge through which there is an entrance. The trees appear to have been shaped into tiers and the maze, albeit small, is of a kind known to have existed at Richmond Palace earlier in the century. Designs for unicursal mazes appeared in Serlio (1537) and were planted in every royal or aristocratic garden during the sixteenth century; designs for square and circular ones appear in Thomas Hyll's *Most Breife and Pleasaunt Treatise* (1558).[16] Below this tableau is the motto, *Fata viam invenient* (The Fates will find a way) from the *Aeneid*, III, l.95 and X, l.113. The *impresa* is taken from Claude Paradin's *Devises Héroïques* (1557) (101), a collection which was widely studied in England, where it is explained that the maze signified that the bearer must commit himself to the grace of God to guide him through the dangerous labyrinth of the world.[17]

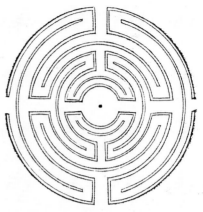

Fata viam inuenient.

Par la Deuiſe du Labyrinthe que porte le Signeur de Boiſdauphin, à preſent Arceueſque d'Ambrun, ſe pourroit (poſsible) entendre, que pour rencontrer la voye & chemin de vie eternelle, la grace de Dieu nous adreſſe:nous mettāt entre les mains le filet de ſes ſaints

101. Garden with a turf maze. Detail from plate 100

102. Maze device from Claude Paradin, *Devises Héroïques*, Lyon, 1557

103. Artist unknown, *Portrait of Sir George Delves with a Lady bearing a branch of myrtle*, 1577. Board of Trustees of the National Museums & Galleries on Merseyside (Walker Art Gallery)

104. A huge garden deployed as an emblem of the seduction of court life. Detail of plate 103

Four years later a member of a Cheshire gentry family commissioned a far more complicated portrait (103).[18] Sir George Delves was a younger son of Sir Henry Delves of Doddington, Cheshire.[19] Through his family connexions he obtained a place at court in 1561 as a gentleman pensioner. Much of his career, however, was spent in Ireland, where he acquired both land and a castle. Returning to England in the 1570s he became a member of parliament in 1572 and eventually received a series of minor appointments in a career that fell far short of his ambitions. The portrait, a full-length (rendering it remarkable for the period), is something of a pictorial lament on that particular point. Delves presents himself hand-in-hand with a lady, who is only partially seen; both figures are set against a distant panorama of a stupendous garden. A motto in Italian, ALTRO NO[N] MI VAGLIA, CHE A[MOR], [E], FAMA (I value only Love and Fame) explains the composition. The Fame that Delves seeks is represented by the victor's laurels that shower downwards to the right; the mysterious lady whose face is concealed behind the large sprig of myrtle – the attribute of Venus – that she carries, is Love. She wears a contemporary costume in black, the colour of constancy, but her full meaning remains obscure.

Two sets of rhyming verses concern other attributes in the picture. The verse at the bottom, in proximity to a pile of armour, explains how the sitter's pursuit of arms HAETH. WAST. MI. WEALT[H] and has also consumed time with little to show for it but WOE. AND. PA[IN]. More important is the second verse inscribed across the sky; this fleshes out the significance of the garden scene:

THE[E]. COURT. WHOES. OVTWRD. SHOES
SET[S]. FORTH. A. WORLD. OF. JOYES
HA[E]TH. FLATTERED. ME. TO. LONG
TH[A]T. WANDRED. IN. HER. TOYES
W[H]EAR. SHOVLD. THE. THIRSTI DRINK
BVT. WHEAR. THE. FOVNTAYN. RON
THE. HOEP. OF. SVCH. RELEEF
H[A]ETH. ALMOST. ME. VNDON.

The background is clearly an emblem for 'The court whose outward shows/Set forth a world of joys' and among whose 'toys' Delves has lingered unrewarded all too long. The court is identified as a place of hoped-for advancement: 'But where should the thirsty drink/But where the fountain runs?' This is the garden as site of seduction, a world of sensual delights, one which has its prime classical exemplar in the garden of the evil enchantress Circe, who enslaved men, turning them into beasts. In the portrait of Delves we are looking at a precursor of Jones's opening scene to *Tempe Restored* (134) in which Circe presides over her magical garden of the senses.

It has been estimated that, if scaled-up, Delves's garden would have extended to 2.7 acres, an area only matched by Hampton Court and Theobalds. However, enough is known about both those gardens to eliminate the possibility that either is represented. Nonetheless this is the most comprehensive representation of a large garden from the period and it must reflect the sitter's expectation of what such a place should be like. It is compartmented in the same way that Hampton Court and Theobalds were. In the case of what seems to be the kitchen garden with bee skeps and espaliered fruit trees the compartments are contained by walls, and in the others by tunnel arbours with arches for access and pavilions at the corners. These were hugely expensive garden features and the interiors are also palatial in concept. The central enclosure contains a large circular maze probably of turf or some low-growing herb, a second garden is laid out in plats, but with a large central fountain of a type that existed at Whitehall Palace, and another garden comprises some kind of interlacing knot pattern. Shaped trees are dotted along the broad gravel walks.

The painter is certainly not English but Netherlandish and the nearest parallel is found in the gardens that appear in contemporary Flemish paintings, where the bird's-eye-view was first exploited. This suggests that the artist may have drawn on an engraved source of the kind seen, for example, in an engraving after Martin de Vos from his series *Circulus vicissitudinis rerum humanarum* titled 'Wealth brings forth Pride' (105).[20] Here the background is filled with a large castle surrounded by pleasure gardens that include an alfresco banqueting house, a trick fountain and a tree house. Vredeman de Vries was paint-

105. Karel van Mallery after Martin de Vos, *Wealth brings forth Pride*, from *The Cycle of the Vicissitudes of Human Affairs* (*Circulus vicissitudinis rerum humanarum*). Museum Boijmans Van Beuningen, Rotterdam

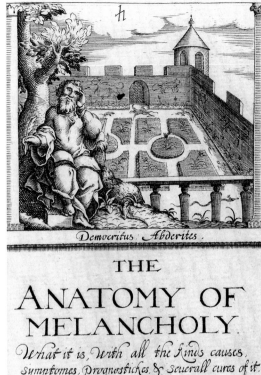

ing pictures of this kind that the artist could have seen. But the garden in the Delves portrait anticipates by a few years those in De Vries's hugely influential *Hortorum Formae...* (1583), which established the bird's-eye garden-view as a format and gives a whole sequence of compartmented gardens with mazes and geometrically patterned beds.[21]

More than a decade later Isaac Oliver employed a similar juxtaposition of figure and garden in a large-scale miniature of an unknown young man in the guise of a melancholic (106).[22] De Vries's book had been published a decade earlier and the garden speaks of Oliver's familiarity with it (107). We see the usual garden compartment held in on the outer side by a brick wall and, on the inner, by a long gallery of carpenters' work. Within it is laid out with a symmetrical pattern of turf beds planted with flowers. The garden represents the antithesis of the greenwood tree in the shade of which the young man sits. The message is not so different from that of the Delves portrait; again a young man turns his back on worldly matters in pursuit of a life dedicated to arcane contemplation. The allusion here is to those born under the sign of Saturn, who are naturally drawn to the shady groves that melancholics seek out for solace.[23] The repertory was to be described so graphically by Milton in *Il Penseroso*. The sitter's clothes and attributes all pertain to melancholy. He wears black, a floppy broad brimmed hat, has his arms folded and sits in what was known as a 'dump' or 'muse', exactly in the manner satirised by Sir John Davies:

> See yonder melancholy gentleman,
> Which, hood-wink'd with his hat, alone doth sit!
> Thinke what he thinks, and tell me if you can,
> What great affaires troubles his little wit.[24]

The *locus classicus* of melancholy, Robert Burton's *The Anatomy of Melancholy,* was published in 1621, but the 1628 edition used a new titlepage, containing inset vignettes of melancholics (108). Democritus of Abdera, the laughing philosopher, sits on a bank beneath a tree outside a walled formal garden meditating on 'the vanity and fripperies of the time, to see men so empty of all virtuous actions.'[25]

Henry Percy, 9th Earl of Northumberland, the so-called 'Wizard Earl', is another melancholic of the same generation, this time recorded in a miniature

107. Doric garden from Hans Vredeman de Vries, *Hortorum Formae...*, Antwerp, 1583

108. Democritus of Abdera seeking the shade of the greenwood tree outisde a formal garden. Detail from Christof le Blon, Titlepage of *The Anatomy of Melancholy*, by Robert Burton, 1628. British Library, London

106. Isaac Oliver, *Unknown Young Man with a garden view*, c.1590–95. The Royal Collection © HM Queen Elizabeth II

109. Nicholas Hilliard, *Henry Percy, 9th Earl of Northumberland, c.* 1590–95, he reclines in a hedged garden compartment on a summit. Rijksmuseum, Amsterdam

by Oliver's master, Nicholas Hilliard, in which he seen reclining full length in some form of garden (109).[26] The date is the early 1590s, almost certainly before 1593 when he received the Order of the Garter which it was mandatory to wear. Here again are the same negligent clothes, black and somewhat dishevelled, with shirt and doublet undone and gloves and book tossed to one side on the greensward. Recent research has shown that the riddling device – a globe and a feather balancing each other – that hangs from a tree is an illustration of one of the simpler propositions in Archimedes's treatise *De Aequeponderantibus*. It demonstrates that 'unequal weights all balance at unequal distances, the greater the weight being at the lesser distance'.

But what role does the garden play? On first encounter it would seem to be a rectangular hedged enclosure set on an eminence from which mountains can be glimpsed from afar. Within the clipped hedge is a narrow gravel path, then a stretch of grass, in which the earl reclines, followed by an upward slope on which is set a second rectangular hedged enclosure. This hedge has five trees set within it. The year Northumberland was made a Knight of the Garter a minor poet, George Peele, celebrated the event with a poem which contains a clue. He describes the earl as one of those who:

…following the auncient reverend steps
Of Trismegetus and Pythagoras,
Through uncouth waies and unaccessible
Doost passe into the spacious pleasant fieldes
Of divine science and Phylosophie…[27]

At this period the earl was closely involved with the mathematician and astronomer, Thomas Hariott, one of his three 'magi'. The function of this garden is surely diagrammatic; at that time the diagram was seen not only to demonstrate a mathematical argument, but also to have another function as a hieroglyph with an occult and mystical meaning. In this context it is pertinent that the square is the symbol of secret wisdom and an attribute of the god Hermes Trismegetus to whom Peele refers. Hilliard's mastery of perspective was never complete so it is conceivable that these rectangular hedges are in fact meant for squares, the miniature being a celebration of Northumberland's quest for arcane wisdom.

Northumberland died in 1632 and sometime in the next eight years his son commissioned Van Dyck to paint a posthumous portrait incorporating many of the elements seen in the Hilliard miniature.[28] The earl is posed differently, but in what is still a classic melancholic stance, his clothes are again somewhat dishevelled and also black. On a piece of paper on which he rests his elbow is the same tantalising device of the balance, but the garden is missing. We have already seen a similar iconographic shift in Van Dyck's portraits of women where gardens no longer figure. Here Van Dyck has had to come to terms with a programme dictated to him that was still in the tradition of the Elizabethan *impresa* portrait, an assembly of often wildly discrepant images as attributes to one person. So successful has he been in absorbing them into his composition

110. British School. *William Style of Langley* 1636, with a garden of the de Vries, *Hortorum Formae* type behind (see plate 107). Tate Gallery, London

that we have to look twice to realise that this picture represents a voice from another age.

The sophisticated imagery of the new muted baroque court portraiture would take time to percolate and the old style lingered on. William Style was one who belonged firmly to that earlier era. Like George Delves, he was a younger son, but in later life he inherited the family estate at Langley, Kent (110).[29] Style was born around 1600–3 and educated at Oxford, proceeding to

111. Frontispiece to William Style's translation of J. M. Dilherr, *Contemplations, Sighes and Groanes of a Christian*, 1640. British Library, London

112. Christ leads his faithful bride into the new garden of the church. Engraving from I. David, *Paradisus sponsi et sponsae*, 1618, British Library, London

the Inner Temple, where he was called to the bar in 1628. It is conceivable that he travelled abroad for there is a record in the register of English visitors at Padua of a 'Mattia Styles inglese' which just could be him. Apart from a number of legal works, his only other book was a translation in 1640 from the Latin of a devotional handbook by the Nuremberg humanist and theologian Johann Michael Dilherr entitled *Contemplations, Sighes and Groanes of a Christian*. The frontispiece to that is the prime clue as to the meaning of the quite extraordinarily complex *impresa* portrait of himself which he commissioned in 1636 in which a large garden figures in the background.

The engraving which forms the frontispiece to *Contemplations* (111) shows the author, clasping a book and with his eyes cast to the heavens with, before him, set on a table, objects symbolising various temptations to the senses – a vase of flowers for smell and a lute for hearing. Behind him stretches an enclosed formal garden of a kind we have seen before, a *hortus conclusus*, which Dilherr uses as an analogue for the Church. This arrangement is more or less repeated in the portrait. Style turns his back on a window bearing his coat-of-arms and a table on which there are books for study, writing-tools and a dancing-master's violin with the motto 'I will rest from the too much desire of knowledge'. His cloak and hat rest on a chair with a second motto, 'O vaine mantles, O lamentable coverings!' With his cane he points to an image of the world contained within a flaming heart with the inscription: 'The microcosm (or heart) of the macrocosm (or man) is not filled (even) by the megacosm (or world).' In other words the human heart cannot be satisfied even if offered the whole world but only with its creator.

The garden beyond beckons: a path leads like a perspective vista into the distance, drawing the viewer in towards an arch. This is part of an elaborate tunnel arbour that holds in railinged and hedged gardens on both sides; within they are laid out in much the same manner as those in the Oliver miniature. Perspective is used in part but not the whole of a picture's surface in order to emphasise the emblematic function. A direct compositional parallel is found in the two portraits of Thomas Howard, Earl of Arundel, and his countess (54), painted by Daniel Mytens in 1618, eighteen years earlier.[30] In the Arundel portraits the perspective scenes show off the sculpture and picture galleries of Arundel House. In the case of Style's portrait perspective emphasises the garden in its prime role as an emblem of the Church, one not so far distant from the holy horticultural visions of Henry Hawkins and Henrietta Maria although on the opposite side of the theological divide (125). A comparison may be made between this garden and an engraving in I. David's *Paradisus sponsi et sponsae* (1618) in which the Garden of Eden, site of man's fall, is set against Christ leading his faithful bride towards the new garden of the Church, just such a railinged and hedged enclosure with geometric beds in the De Vries manner but onto which have been embroidered the instruments of the Passion (112). In the Protestant context of William Style these would have been omitted.

OUR SEA-WALLED GARDEN

The presentation of the Tudor dynasty as the union of two roses, the red of Lancaster and the white of York to form the double Tudor rose made it inevitable that the garden should be employed as a metaphor for the kingdom. In a volume of music presented to the young Henry VIII in 1516 England is depicted as a medieval *hortus conclusus*, a crenellated, walled island set within a sea (113). From four towers flutter banners, one with the royal arms, another with those of Castile and Aragon and two with the red cross of St George. Within, the royal heraldic beasts crouch around a castle gateway.[31] Otherwise we find ourselves inside a medieval herber besprinkled with flowers and with a pomegranate tree representing the queen, Catherine of Aragon. The branches of a huge rose bush support the red, white and Tudor roses, the latter crowned and bearing in addition fleurs de lys.

Five years later when the Emperor Charles V entered London he was greeted with a tableau that employed similar imagery: a silver sea within which there was an island full of mountains and woods 'and dyuers maner off trees herbys and flowers as roses, dayses, gyluffloures, daffadeles and other[s]…' Within this enclosure the Emperor in a castle and Henry VIII 'in an herbar with rosys' were depicted.[32] This image had currency enough at the end of the century for Shakespeare to give it its most enduring expression in *Richard II*, when the gardener instructs his two assistants to 'Cut off the heads of the fast growing stays; / That look too lofty in our commonwealth…' and they complain about their task:

When our sea-walled garden, the whole land,
Is full of weeds, her fairest flowers choked up,
Her fruit-trees all unprun'd, her hedges ruin'd,
Her knots disorder'd, and her wholesome herbs
Swarming with caterpillars?

(III, iv, ll.43–7)

It is into this context that we need to place the allegorical presentation of Elizabeth I, who attracted horticultural imagery of unbelievable complexity.[33] The rose, the eglantine, the pansy and lily were all absorbed as aspects of her cult, portraying her as a secular substitute for the Virgin Mary presiding over her symbolic *hortus conclusus*. As Astraea, the Just Virgin of Virgil's fourth *Eclogue*, Elizabeth ushers in the new Protestant state seen in terms of an eternal golden-age, flower-bedecked springtime. In the famous *Rainbow Portrait* at Hatfield House, painted at the very close of her reign, for example, her bodice is embroidered with flowers, among them pansies, honeysuckle and gilly-

113. Tudor badges in a *hortus conclusus* of the Tudor dynasty, 1516. By permission of the British Library, London. MS. Royal 11.E.xi, fol.2

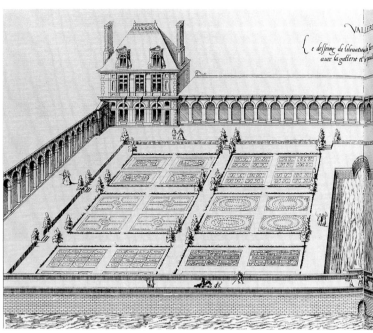

114. Unknown artist, possibly after Lucas de Heere, *Allegory of the Tudor Succession (The Family of Henry VIII)*, *c.* 1590–1600. New Haven, Yale Center for British Art, Paul Mellon Collection

115. Part of the garden at Vallery, from Androuet du Cerceau, *Les Plus Excellents Bastiments de France*, 1576. The compartments filled with circular hedges are close to those in plate 116

flowers. These are resolutely English flowers, ones associated with aspects of Elizabeth's own complex horticultural imagery.

These are commonplaces of the cult, but what of the garden itself? The earliest appearance of a garden in her portraiture is in the allegorical group attributed to Lucas de Heere called *The Family of Henry VIII*, a picture almost certainly given by the Queen as a gift to her secretary of state, Sir Francis Walsingham, in gratitude for his part in negotiating the Anglo-French treaty of 1572.[34] A second version from the 1590s exists in which the Queen's dress has been updated, but the garden remains identical (114). Elizabeth is seen leading Peace with her olive branch by the hand, Plenty manages to bear her train and balance a cornucopia of fruits (116). All three figures enter from a garden which is railed and within which low hedges are planted and trimmed into diminishing circles set within gravel or sand. The architecture in the background is early Tudor with elements that suggest some allusion to Whitehall Palace, the circular building on the left resembling Henry VIII's Cockpit. The garden however bears no relation to what we know of the Great Garden, which was studded with posts painted white and green topped by heraldic beasts and filled with topiary; it resembles far more closely ones recorded in Androuet du Cerceau's *Les Plus Excellents Bastiments de France* (115), a compartment infilled with clipped shrubs arranged in a symmetrical pattern. Its role must surely be symbolic of the queen's peace and perhaps may be compared with a passage in Henry Lyte's dedication to the Queen in his translation of Robert Dodoens's *A Niewe Herball* (1578):

> Blessed is the task, and worthy to bear thy name, O mighty Elizabeth, by whose moderation alone joyous Peace with her Olive so flourish in England that the British people may walk at random in the sunlight and gather safely fragrant blossoms.[35]

That association of the kingdom with a garden recurs in the entertainments presented to the Queen on progress during the final years of her reign and it was

transmitted on to her succcessor. The mythology of the Tudor dynasty is passed on to the Stuarts in James I's entry into London in 1604. In the arch entitled *Hortus Euporiae* (117), Plenty's Bower, Gloriana's garden is bestowed on the Solomonic king.[36] Sylvanus bad him 'walk into yonder garden', a huge arbour of carpenters' work entwined with 'apples, pears, cherries, grapes, roses, lilies, and all other both fruits and flowers most artificially moulded to the life.' Within it sat the familiar figures of Peace (*Eirene*) and Plenty (*Euporia*) flanked by the muses and the seven liberal arts. Again the monarch's advent signals spring:

> O this is Hee!
> Whose beames make our Spring,
> Men glad, and birdes to Sing,
> Hymnes of praise, joy and glee.

Vertumnus, in clothes 'fit for a gardener', welcomes James in the name of Peace and of the governors of the City, 'who carefully prune this garden, weeding out all hurtful and idle branches that hinder the growth of the good...'

In his celebrated essay 'Of Gardens' (published 1625), Francis Bacon wrote: 'God Almighty first planted a Garden and indeed it is the purest of human pleasures...and a man should ever see that, when ages grew to civility and elegancy, men come to build stately sooner than to garden finely, as if gardening were the greater perfection.'[37] It is precisely in that capacity that the garden appears so

116. Queen Elizabeth I leads in Peace and Plenty from a garden. Detail from plate 114

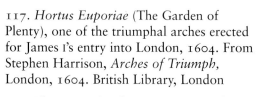

117. *Hortus Euporiae* (The Garden of Plenty), one of the triumphal arches erected for James I's entry into London, 1604. From Stephen Harrison, *Arches of Triumph*, London, 1604. British Library, London

118. Flower garden from Crispin van de Passe, *Hortus Floridus*, 1614

frequently in those archetypal entertainments of the Stuart court, the masque. In the Caroline ones the garden becomes the supreme symbol of the new civilisation made possible by Charles I and his Queen. His reign is presented as a golden age reborn, a return to a primordial paradise in which man has mastered not only himself but also his environment. Indeed the garden is the most potent and recurring of all the images deployed to evoke the peace and plenty of Charles's rule.

It was not a vision confined to the masque stage. William Marshall's engraving of the royal family (119) was issued shortly after the birth of the king's third daughter, Anne, in 1637. A year later the masque *Luminalia* presented the island kingdom as a garden Parnassus, offering shelter to the wandering muses.[38] The royal couple and their offspring stand on a stage, twisted Solomonic columns establish the divinity of this kingship, behind them wooden balustrading encloses a garden to which a gate lies open. If the garden is a familiar one it is hardly surprising, for Marshall has adapted it from Crispin van de Passe's famous picture in his *Hortus Floridus* (1614) (118). The kingdom as a garden is an equation that was still firmly fixed in the mind of Andrew Marvell in the 1650s when he wrote 'Upon Appleton House', lamenting the desecration that the Civil War had brought:

> O thou, that dear and happy isle,
> The garden of the world erewhile.
>
> (ll.321–2)

In this context it should perhaps be mentioned that, although Van Dyck

119. William Marshall, *Charles I and Henrietta Maria and their children*. The garden is lifted from de Passe's *Hortus Floridus* Engraving, *c.* 1637. British Museum, London

replaces the garden with luscious vistas of the English landscape in his representations of the king, the meaning remains the same.

THE VIRGIN IN THE GARDEN

One garden image which could not immediately be transferred to the incoming dynasty was the *hortus conclusus* of the Virgin Mary, elements of which had been deployed for the Virgin Queen. That had to await the arrival of Charles I's queen, Henrietta Maria, who practised a moderate form of Counter Reformation Catholicism, Devout Humanism, in which piety and pleasure overlapped and intertwined. In this scheme the *jardin d'amour* could be a line of ascent to a contemplation of the Marian *hortus conclusus*.[39]

Henrietta Maria's gardens all occur in the series of spectacular court masques over which she presided during the 1630s. I shall come to a fuller discussion of these later in the chapter, but it is sufficient at this point to say that these spectacles were a series of visual emblems, realised by Inigo Jones. Articulated by speech, music, song and dance their end was to make the audience conscious of the divinity of royalty. In the case of Henrietta Maria gardens came to occupy a central place in these entertainments. Her masque gardens are of two kinds: the garden of sensual desire of the kind that formed the opening scene of *Tempe Restored* (see p. 114), in which men lose their virtue and valour and degenerate into beasts; and the garden of love and beauty as in *Chloridia* or *Luminalia*, over which the Queen herself reigns as a chaste Neo-Platonic love goddess. Jones's task was therefore to present her in a series of essentially painterly visions in which the imagery of a garden and flowers also just happened largely to coincide with the attributes of the Virgin Mary.

120. Emblemtic garden of the Virgin Mary from Henry Hawkins, *Partheneia Sacra*, 1633

Whether or not these visions of the Queen of England in her allegorical garden of Love and Chastity might have led the audience to associate the imagery with Marian gardens, leading on to their conversion, as has been suggested, is arguable. However, gardens undoubtedly figured largely in the cult of the Virgin which had found fresh vigour in the post-Tridentine era. The emblem book *Partheneia Sacra* (1633), 'Sacred Virginity', was written by the Jesuit Henry Hawkins for the use of a secret recusant Sodality of the Immaculate Conception (120).[40] Hawkins, who came from a Catholic Kentish gentry family, entered the English College in Rome in 1609 and was ordained priest in 1614. Banished from England for four years he returned to this country and remained twenty-five years. Although printed in Flanders, the engravings in *Partheneia Sacra* were executed by a Netherlander working in England, following what must have been very detailed instructions from Hawkins. The book is virtually a series of garden emblems in which the medieval *hortus conclusus* of the Virgin is revivified and combined with the renaissance cult of emblems in the service of Counter-Reformation Ignatian methods of contemplation.

The image of the Virgin in the garden was one employed on both sides of the theological divide. The Song of Songs in which the vital text appeared ('A garden enclosed is my sister, my spouse, / A spring shut up, a fountain sealed') was also interpreted by the reformers as a reference to the Virgin and to Christ's espousal to the Church. The garden writer Gervase Markham, who was stoutly Protestant, adopted it without hesitation in his version of the Song, *The Poem of Poems* (1596):

O fountaine of the garden, and her flowers,
O blessed Well, whence lyving waters flowe...[41]

In this the medieval image of the Virgin in her *hortus conclusus* lived on in Protestant England in word if not image.

Some of the most puzzling of Jacobean and Caroline portraits are of ladies, who are shown against a background of gardens and symbolic trees. They provide us with some of the earliest images of the English garden, whether real or imaginary. Most of these women are virgins for they wear their hair unbound as was customary for brides, suggesting that the context for most of these pictures must be marriage. The earliest, painted about 1610 some five years after Inigo Jones's first court masque, is a lady of the Hampden family (121) wearing what could be a masque costume. These pictures could not have been painted without the simultaneous development of the court masque and its use of allegorical costume and emblematic setting. However, as has been pointed out, these portraits are less direct records of a particular masque appearance than masques in themselves.[42] The lady of the Hampden family stands on a grassy platform looking down onto a traditional garden compartment, a railinged enclosure, her unbound hair adorned with a jewelled garland, her dress embroidered with flowers and with a pink mantle looped over it. She is placed between four trees, two palms and two laurels, all of which have symbolic meaning.

The laurels must allude to the sitter's chastity, perhaps a double allusion both to the Ovidian myth of Apollo and Daphne and to Petrarch's Laura. There are a number of precedents for this portrait; it may be compared to a device of Lucrezia Gonzaga in which a white hind stands beneath a laurel tree with a

121. Robert Peake, *Portrait of a Lady of the Hampden Family,*
c. 1610–15. Museum of Art, Rhode Island School of Design.
Providence, Rhode Island, gift of Miss Lucy T. Aldrich

122. Laurel tree device of Lucrezia Gonzaga from Battista
Pittoni, *Imprese di diversi Principi, Duchi, etc.*, Venice 1566

motto from Petrarch: *Nessun mi tocchi* (Let no one touch me) (122).[43] An
impresa carried at the Accession Day Tilts shows Cupid pointing to a laurel tree
beneath which a knight-at-arms reclines with the motto *Heu subumbra*
Daphnes (Alas, under the shade of Daphne), where the knightly lover has been
vanquished by his lady's chastity.[44] The portrait's symbolism might also be
compared to the Apollo and Daphne legend as used in the entertainment laid
on for the Queen by Lord Chandos at Sudeley Castle in the autumn of 1592.[45]
On that occasion Apollo mourns the loss of Daphne beneath a laurel tree, from
which she bursts forth to seek succour at the hands of the Virgin Queen: 'I stay,
for whither should Chastety fly for succour, but to the Queene of Chastety.'

This combination of a female sitter, a garden and laurel occurs in other portraits. In one, dated 1611, the sitter, traditionally Agnes, daughter of Sir George

123. Artist unknown, attributed to Marcus Gheeraerts, *Portrait of a Lady, traditionally known as Agnes Fermor*, 1611, with a turf garden behind in the manner of plates 30–33. Private collection

124. Artist unknown, *Jane Shirley, Baroness Holles of Ifield*, 1630. Reproduced by permission of the Marquess of Bath, Longleat House, Wiltshire

Fermor, has a large sprig of laurel in her hair (123). She stands against a background of classical architecture that includes an arch giving on to a garden view, again with a crenellated wall but the garden itself being of geometric grass plats. The second, about 1625–30, depicts Jane Shirley, later Baroness Holles of Ifield (124). She holds a branch of laurel with her right hand and extends her left up into the tree behind her. In the distance there is an old-fashioned garden – of the type never used by Jones in the masques – with knots, one of which has flowers. A portrait of Lady Elizabeth Pope by Robert Peake, painted to mark her marriage in 1615, shows her as a virgin bride with her hair unbound; she is placed within the embrace of a laurel tree but this time there is no garden.[46]

Virtually all these portraits celebrate the chastity of the sitter, using the enclosed garden and the laurel in what was in effect a post-medieval secular adaptation of the Virgin in her *hortus conclusus*. A parallel for this can be found in Thomas Campion's masque for the marriage of Lord Hay in 1607. The action centred on a 'hill hanging like a cliff over the grove below, and on top of it a goodly large tree was set, supposed to be the tree of Diana'.[47] At the climax the masquers went in procession to lay tribute at it:

> About her tree solemn procession make,
> Diana's tree, the tree of Chastity.[48]

The species of tree is not given but it must have been laurel. In the case of the lady of the Hampden family the two palms call for explanation and that can be given by turning to Hawkins's *Partheneia Sacra* (125):

> They are so amorous one of another, as they wil hardly liue without the socie-
> tie of each other, and yet so chast, as they breed and bring forth without
> contaction...Among *Palmes*, there are Male and Female; and the Female
> neuer brings forth fruits, but standing opposite her Male; and hence it is, that
> two *Palmes*, being planted by two banck-sides of a riuer, are the Hieroglifick
> of Nuptials...[49]

Without doubt the Hampden lady's palms allude to her chastity, a reference also found in *Love's Triumph through Callipolis*, Inigo Jones's first masque of the years of Charles I's Personal Rule. In the midst of the final scene, a *jardin d'amour* of the celestial Venus, there suddenly sprang up 'a palm tree with an imperial crown on the top' which the goddess describes in a valedictory song:

> Beauty and Love, whose story is mysterial,
> In yonder palm tree and the crown imperial.
> Do from the rose and lily so delicious
> Promise a shade shall ever be propitious
> To both the kingdoms...[50]

Here the palm tree, the emblem of chastity and chaste love in marriage, joins hands with the palm of victory presiding over a garden prospect that stands for the kingdom. Unlike the emblematic repertory of the garden as kingdom, this bridal iconography is abruptly abandoned by Van Dyck. In his female portraits roses, the flowers of Venus, replace the laurel and the garden gives way to arcadian landscape.

MEDITATION IN THE GARDEN

So far garden images have been preoccupied with celebrating a regal paradise, in the apotheosis of virgin brides and as an emblem for a louche life to be shunned, or, on the contrary, God's Church beckoning the sinner to redemption. William Style's garden (110), unlike those in either the Delves portrait or the melancholy young man (104, 106), is empty of humanity. William Style will pace in that garden alone. This is a feature unique to English gardens, setting them apart from their continental counterparts.[51] Whereas the French went into their gardens primarily for social intercourse, the English wended their solitary way, prayer-book in hand, seeking a dialogue with God as revealed in Nature. That quest was unknown in the sixteenth century, but it was most definitely in place by the third decade of the seventeenth. It is a key factor by the middle

125. The palm as an emblem of chastity from Henry Hawkins, *Partheneia Sacra*, (1633)

years of the century when gardens move centre stage in human sensibility.
Literary historians have long recognised the importance of gardens and plants
in the interpretation of the poetry of George Herbert and Henry Vaughan, not
to mention that of Andrew Marvell.

The revival of the practice of meditation within the Anglican tradition led to
a new function for gardens, which were to be the prime places for such religious
reflection. This was to have a profound impact on the English use of and attitudes to gardens throughout the seventeenth and into the eighteenth century. In
effect it meant that the emblematic way of looking at gardens was revitalised –
a fact that must be taken into account in the emergence of paintings of gardens.

One book, Francis Quarles's *Emblemes* (1635), had a particularly widespread influence.[52] In 1639 over two thousand copies of this and of his *Hiero-
glyphicks of the Life of Man* were sold when they appeared as a joint edition.
At least three thousand more were sold the following year and the *Emblemes*
were to appear in edition after edition until the middle of the eighteenth century. Quarles, drawing on Jesuit sources, adapts the emblematic method for
Protestant meditative ends in a series of allegorical tableaux in which the soul,
Anima, journeys towards the heavenly city. Garden motifs figure quite prominently in this voyage – the sundial, the bowling green and the maze – in addition to visions of Christ crucified on the branches of a tree (126, 127). In the
emblem of the maze, for instance, we see Anima attired as a pilgrim battling her
way through the troubles of the world.

Quarles was hugely popular but he was not alone. In the same year, 1635,
George Wither produced *A Collection of Emblemes Ancient and Modern* (128,

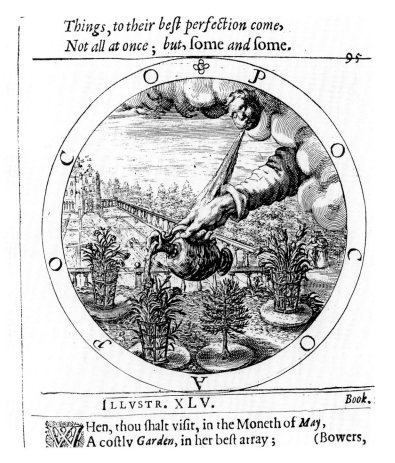

Things, to their beft perfection come,
Not all at once; but, fome and fome.

95

ILLVSTR. XLV.   Book.

Hen, thou fhalt vifit, in the Moneth of *May*,
A coftly *Garden*, in her beft array;   (Bowers,

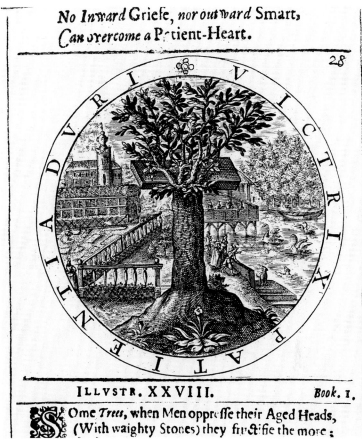

No Inward Griefe, nor outward Smart,
Can overcome a Patient-Heart.

28

ILLVSTR. XXVIII.   Book. I.

Ome *Trees*, when Men oppreffe their Aged Heads,
(With waighty Stones) they fructifie the more:

128, 129. Garden emblems from George Wither, *A Collection of Emblemes Ancient and Modern*, 1635, pp.28, 107

129) some two hundred of them re-using plates engraved by Crispin van de Passe for Gabriel Rollenhagen's *Nucleus Emblematum Selectissimum* (1611).[53] Although Wither's purpose was instructional and moral rather than devotional many of the emblems include plants, flowers and views of gardens (rather old-fashioned ones in fact for the 1630s but he was aiming at a middle class audience) interpreted in a pious light.

Nor was this approach limited to one side of the theological divide as *Partheneia Sacra* bears testimony. E. M.'s *Ashrea* (1665) was probably written by the Jesuit Edward Mico.[54] The title, the author explains, means 'a wood or grove' in Hebrew and he represents each of the Beatitudes by a tree, in addition to which he links this system of spiritual meditation to one derived from the art of memory. The Catholic tradition never quite lost the notion of the garden as a place of spiritual succour. St John of the Cross introduced the habit of solitary meditation in the friary garden and it was a course of action also recommend by St Francis de Sales. Its revival within the Anglican tradition was owed chiefly to Joseph Hall, Bishop of Exeter and later of Norwich, in two books which aimed to encourage Protestant meditation, his three volume *Meditations and Vowes, Divine and Morall* (1605) and his hugely popular *The Art of Divine Meditation* (1607).[55] Both called for solitude and saw the garden as a place where that could be achieved. Hall was a major influence in reviving the use of the medieval Biblical Book of Nature, re-casting it for a Protestant audience. In his meditations occasioned by the sight of gardens and their contents, he aimed to achieve a series of ascents to the divine, by means of visible elements that were of God's and not man's making. Before the Reformation such ascents

A Treatise of
FRVIT=TREES
*Shewing the manner of Grafting, Setting, Pruning, and Ordering of them
in all respects : According to divers new and easy Rules of experience;
gathered in y̆ space of Twenty yeares.
Whereby the value of Lands may be much improued, in a shorttime, by
small cost, and little labour
Also discovering some dangerous Errors, both in y̆ Theory and Practise
of y̆ Art of Planting Fruit:trees
With, the Alimentall and Physicall vse of fruits.
Togeather with
The Spirituall vse of an Orchard: Held forth in divers Similitudes be:
tweene Naturall & Spirituall Fruit:trees: according to Scripture & Experiēce.*
By RA: AUSTEN.
Practiser in y̆ Art of Planting

A Garden inclosed is my sister

pleasant fruits : Cant 4 12 13

my Spouse: Thy Plants are

Oxford printed for

Tho: Robinson 1653

130. Title page to Ralph Austen, *A Treatise of Fruit-Trees*, 1653

would have been made by way of holy images in the parish church or at home by holy images in illuminated or printed Books of Hours and other devotional works. Under Hall's aegis the garden brought back images into religion in a way which did not offend Puritan sensibilities at precisely the time that Laudianism, with its reintroduction of ritual and painted and carved images into churches, actually did.

By 1621 John Melton could walk into his walled garden and be overwhelmed with every sign of his spiritual need and his hope of salvation:

> But as I was seriously looking over this Æden of delight, my eyes took notice of a withered banke of flowers, hanging downe their weather-beaten heads, that not seven dayes before had flourished in their full prime; intimating unto Man, that the beautie of all Mundane and Earthly pleasures have no perpetuitie.[56]

For Melton every flower spoke of death and resurrection, every tree breathed a biblical thought.

So in England the garden became a surrogate Bible, resulting in even such extreme Protestants as William Prynne seeing it as purveying the truths of Scripture in a 'more sweete and lively wise,/ Then all the Pictures Papists can devise.'[57] In the garden man assumes an allegorical guise as the gardener, a type of Christ, tending the care of his own soul, subduing his will in preparation for union with the divine:

> But this is nought to those Soule-ravishing,
> Sweete, heavenly Meditations which doe spring
> From Gardens, able to rap and inspire
> The *coldest Muse*, with *Coelestiall fire*;
> You melt the flintiest Heart, and it advance
> Above the Spheares in a delightfull Trance.[58]

Ralph Austen, a proctor of Oxford University and Registry of Visitors there, is perhaps an even keener touchstone of the increasing pervasiveness of this attitude to the garden.[59] His two books, *A Treatise of Fruit Trees* (1653) and *The Spirituall Use of an Orchard* (1653), marry practicalities with mysticism (130). The latter opens with a flurry of biblical quotations on the subject of plants and gardens and then in 'A Preface to the Reader' Austen opens up his scheme of things:

> The *World* is a great *Library, and Fruit-trees* are some of the *Bookes* wherein we may read & see plainly the *Attributes of God his Power*, *Wisdome*, *Goodnesse* &c and be instructed and taught our duty towards him in many things even from Fruit-trees for (in a Metaphoricall sence) are *Bookes*, so likewise in the same sence they have a *Voyce*, and speake plainely to us, and teach many good lessons...
>
> We must be content to stoope to their way and manner of teaching, as the *Egyptians* and others in former times, who were instructed by *Characters* and *Hyeroglyphiques*, by something represented to the eye, Notions were conveyed to the understanding...

The Ancients were skilled in this kind of Learning, in teaching by SIMILI-
TUDES, and one of them observes, that God sent us the *Booke of Nature*,
before he sent us the *Book of the Scriptures*.[60]

DELICIOUS PROSPECTS

The designs by Inigo Jones for garden scenes in the Stuart court masques form
the earliest large corpus of images of gardens to be made in England.[61] These
drawings, together with the often-extensive descriptions given in the masque
texts, provide us with an unmatched cornucopia of garden images. The fact that
garden pictures make their first appearance in quantity as what was essentially
stage scenery is, as we shall discover, revealing. The masques came at a moment
when visual imagery was reasserting itself more forcefully after the iconoclasm
of the Reformation. They began in 1605 when Jones, in association with the
poet Ben Jonson, staged *The Masque of Blackness*. For the next thirty-five years
these spectacular court entertainments, staged at Epiphanytide or on the occasion of a dynastic marriage, offered a richness of avant-garde visual experience
unmatched by any other art form. In them royalty and aristocracy appeared in
allegorical guise as their ideal selves, Platonic ideas personified, descending on
clouds to banish darkness with light or to bring a flower-decked springtime in
the midst of winter. The garden is a recurring *leitmotif* and it runs the whole
gamut of meanings. Not only do the masques give us a profound insight as to
how gardens were viewed in the four decades before the Civil War but, at the
same time, they take us back to how gardens were pictured in the previous century. Jones's stage gardens have a novel element untrue of their predecessors, for
he uses the garden picture not only to act as symbol, but, for the first time, to
promote a new style.

Inigo Jones's scenery for the court masques was motivated by exactly the
same principles as Ben Jonson's texts for them. They mingled 'profit & example'.[62] The audience was presented with new styles in garden design in what
were in effect a series of pictures. At the same time these pictures were emblems
to be read and, as such, vital to the action of the masque. Through them we
recapture the meaning of the garden as an image, indeed we are able to tap into
the motive underlying the need to picture the garden at all.

These garden pictures conjured not reality but aspiration, gardens whose
source was Italy tempered by France. During the four decades before the Civil
War England underwent a horticultural revolution under the aegis of the new
queen, Anne of Denmark, and her eldest son, Henry, Prince of Wales, and, later,
under her successor, Henrietta Maria.[63] To them one can add members of the
aristocracy and gentry: Sir Henry Wotton; Lucy Harington, Countess of
Bedford; Sir Henry Danvers; the Earl of Arundel; Philip Herbert, 4th Earl of
Pembroke; and Sir Arthur Capel. Together they effected a transformation introducing to England the principles of Italian renaissance garden design in all its
fullness, with its dependence on symmetry, deploying space in terms of perspective and also working from a design premise of proportions which would
reflect the microcosm-macrocosm in the same way as Renaissance architecture,
art forms that were direct expressions of a cosmology rooted in the belief that
God had constructed the universe on mathematical principles. This revolution
brought with it terracing; balustrading; statuary, both antique and modern;
grottoes and fountains; it also introduced the use of plant material such as

131. Crispin van de Passe the Elder after Maerten de Vos and Georg Hoefnagel, *Spring*. Engraving. Rotterdam, Museum Boijmans Van Beuningen

132. Garden cast into quarters, from Gervase Markham, *The English Husbandman*, 1613

cypresses and new garden forms like the *parterre de broderie* to re-create a classical and Italianate effect. And the desire to do this was triggered at least in part by the stage pictures by Inigo Jones in exactly the same way as his deployment on stage of the classical orders was meant to precipitate an architectural revolution.

Jones's contribution to developing perceptions of the garden came chiefly in the latter part of his career. All his surviving designs for gardens date from the 1630s, the period of the personal rule of Charles I. Grottoes appear earlier and one garden scene, *Tethys' Festival* (1610), revealed Anne of Denmark and her ladies seated *en tableau* in a grotto of the kind the French hydraulic engineer, Salomon de Caus, was constructing for her and her son, 'caverns gloriously adorned' with scallop shells, tritons, sea-gods and 'ornaments...of mask-heads spouting water, swans, festoons of maritime weeds, great shells and such like...'[64] The masque closed with Anne and her ladies reappearing as themselves 'within a grove/And garden of the spring addressed to Jove'. It is regrettable that no design for this has survived and all we are left with is the description: 'a most pleasant and artificial grove'.[65] The scene must have been derived from an image of Spring from a series depicting the Seasons and the likelihood is that the source was a Netherlandish print (131), since *Tethys' Festival* pre-dates Jones's extended Italian visit by three years.

The earliest major garden picture on the masque stage for which a full description exists was in a spectacle paid for by Francis Bacon as part of the festivities marking the marriage of the king's favourite, the Earl of Somerset, to the notorious Frances Howard in 1613.[66] *The Masque of Flowers* was not designed by Inigo Jones; its theme was how the presence of the king had brought spring in the midst of winter in the form of 'a garden of glorious and strange beauty'. The garden was rectangular or square, with espaliered fruit trees trained against the walls. Within it was divided into quarters, with a fountain nine feet high at the centre. Each quarter was delineated with hedges of juniper and cypresss and filled with knots laid out in herbs. The perimeter was railed with balusters and pedestals topped by 'personages' or royal heraldic beasts like unicorns and lions. At the far end was a thirty-foot high arbour of carpenters' work in which the masquers were discovered as flowers.

This is not an Italianate garden but one which might have been lifted straight out of Gervase Markham's *The English Husbandman* (132) published two years before, where he describes a square quartered with 'a Standard...Dyall, or other Piramid' at its centre and each of the four quarters treated differently to the 'infinite delight of the beholders'.[67] Even as he was writing Markham was aware that change was in the air, leading him to go out of his way to defend knots and mazes 'at this day of most use amongst the vulgar though least respected with great ones, who for the most part are wholy given over to novelties.' In this comment he was thinking of the gardens of the queen, Prince Henry and people like Lady Bedford.

Inigo Jones returned from Italy the same year that *The Masque of Flowers* was staged. His earliest full-blown garden picture – the bower of Zephyrus –

came two years later in Ben Jonson's *The Vision of Delight* (1617). During this period Jonson suppressed virtually any description of the scenery, the appearance of which has to be divined from the poetry, fleshing out the minimal indications given by the poet:

> Behold!
> How the blue bindweed doth itself enfold
> With honeysuckle, and both these entwine
> Themselves with bryony and jessamine,
> To cast a kind and odiferous shade![68]

These plants would have been supported by an arbour of carpenter's work, a reworking of *The Masque of Flowers*, but with a difference because it was must have been set at the close of a perspective vista.

Jones's garden pictures were essentially one aspect of his use of landscape, a new genre which he deployed in his very first masque, *The Masque of Blackness* (1605).[69] At that date landscape was a novelty and the text explains to the audience what such a thing was, anglicising the Netherlandish term for it. By the description of that front curtain, which depicted a hunt in a wood, it must have been in the Flemish mannerist style of painters like Gillis van Coninxloo or Joos de Momper, who produced dramatic asymmetrical vistas with a foreground of trees giving way to rugged terrain, winding rivers and misty craggy peaks beyond. A Netherlandish print would have been a likely source. By the 1630s Jones's landscapes were very different. He edits his engraved sources, often still of the Flemish mannerist kind, introducing the renewed classicism seen in the landscapes of Annibale Carracci and in the later work of Paul Bril.

Jones applied the same principal to his garden sets, where all mannerist asymmetry and superfluous clutter was removed. His late stage technique of receding pairs of side wings and shutters to close the scene, an arrangement that facilitated any number of changes, also encouraged a rigid symmetry of vision. For that he drew on a tradition of staging first formulated at the Medici court at the close of the sixteenth century by Bernardo Buontalenti. Indeed the latter established the garden picture on stage in the *intermezzi* of 1589,[70] the print (133) of which may well have been the inspiration for the tableau in *The Vision of Delight*, as well as his first garden scene of Henrietta Maria as Chloris, goddess of flowers, in *Chloridia* (1631). Buontalenti's garden picture was also symbolic of Spring. That scene in *Chloridia*, however, was preceded by another garden – the climax to the king's masque, *Love's Triumph through Callipolis*, for which no design survives. All that can be garnered is that it was an edenic vision of the king's peace and, at the same time, a *jardin d'amour* in homage to the idyllic marriage of the royal couple, for Venus enthroned descended to preside over it.[71]

There is no design for the garden in *Chloridia* but it clearly re-used the familiar format of the arbour:

> a delicious place figuring the bower of Chloris, wherein an arbour feigned of goldsmiths' work, the ornament of which was borne up with terms of satyrs beautified with festoons, garlands and all sorts of fragrant flowers.[72]

But Jones was far more under the spell of Buontalenti's successor, Alfonso

133. Garden setting by Bernardo Buontalenti for the second *intermezzo*, 1589. Engraving by Epifanio d'Alfiano, 1592

134. Arbour work in the opening scene of Aurelian Townsend's *Tempe Restored*, 1632, design by Inigo Jones. Devonshire Collection, Chatsworth, by permission of the Duke of Devonshire and the Chatsworth Settlement Trustees

Parigi, whose set designs for Medici spectacles were relentlessly plagiarised by the architect, naturalising a whole succession of Italianate garden pictures into England. For the opening scene of the Queen's next masque, *Tempe Restored* (1632), for which the design does survive (134) he copied the side wings from the scene *Il Giardino di Calipso* from the third intermezzo of Parigi's *Il Giudizio di Paride* (1608) (135).[73] Although arbour work was certainly a feature of Elizabethan and Jacobean gardens nothing quite like this would have been seen before: 'a prospect of curious arbours of various forms' composed of marble pilasters, grotto-work, statues, fountains and a second story 'of silver work mixed with fresh verdures' entwined with grapes.[74]

Parigi's sets fitted in with Jones's classicism and his relentless emphasis on perspective in the garden must have affected the way in which audiences viewed their own gardens. Until the 1630s the English response to the Renaissance reorganisation of space in the garden had been to introduce geometric compartmentalisation – a series of squares and rectangles – each containing different garden experiences like a maze, a fountain, a mount or a knot. Jones always stresses the ensemble, re-casting the elements as a totality orchestrated in terms of vista. That concern for reordering his sources in accordance with his new ideals is caught in one of his cut-out tableaux, or what were referred to at the time as 'scenes of relieve', in the queen's pastoral, *The Shepherds' Paradise* (1633) (136).[75] Yet another arbour is the focus, this time inspired by an engraving after Paul Bril of the months of May and June.[76] It is placed absolutely centre, the centrality emphasised by an arch of trellis work supported by terms whose form is virtually identical to that in Buontalenti's 1589 garden set.

GIARDINO DI CALIPSO INTERMEDIO TERZO

135. Set designed by Giulio Parigi depicting the Garden of Calypso, the third intermezzo in *II Giudizio di Paride*, 1608. Etching by Giulio Parigi

136. Inigo Jones, 'Love's Cabinet' in *The Shepherds' Paradise*, 1633. Devonshire Collection, Chatsworth. By permission of the Duke of Devonshire and the Chatsworth Settlement Trustees

137. Inigo Jones, Sketch for the arrangement of the masquers in a 'delicious arbour' in *The Triumph of Peace*, 1634. Devonshire Collection, Chatsworth. By permission of the Duke of Devonshire and the Chatsworth Settlement Trustees

One more stage arbour completes the story, this time in *The Triumph of Peace* performed by members of the Inns of Court in 1634. The masquers came as the Sons of Peace and were discovered sitting on a terraced hillside encompassed by 'a delicious arbour with terms of young men...These bore up an architrave...interwoven with branches through which the sky was seen.'[77] All that we have is a sketch placing the performers, but the arbour architecture is clearly of the type seen in the Queen's pastoral (137).

In *The Shepherds' Paradise* Jones presents the court with another novelty, the *parterre de broderie*, a contracted version of Callot's engraving *Le Grand Parterre de Nancy* (1625) (138, 139).[78] Immediately before *The Shepherds' Paradise* appeared on stage the royal gardens at St James's Palace had been redesigned by André Mollet, whose family had been responsible for the development of the embroidered parterre at the French court during the opening years of the century. The St James's Palace parterre probably preceded those laid out at Wilton by Isaac de Caus and it is described as being 'of different figures, bordered on every side with a hedge of box'.[79] In adapting Callot's parterre Jones has added a small central fountain and simplified the Bramantesque terracing, introducing a row of cypress trees. The arrival of the *parterre de broderie* was to separate aristocratic garden style from general practice where the old formula of the knot continued. No knots appear in any of Jones's garden pictures.

That sense of the deliberate promotion of new courtly ideals was never more strongly stated than in *Coelum Britannicum*, the king's own masque for 1634 (140). This spectacle embraced the whole of British history from 'the rude/ And old abiders here' (the Picts), down to the apogee of the present day expressed by a scene:

showing a delicious garden with several walks and parterres set around with low trees, and on the sides against these walks were fountains and grots, and in the furthest part a palace from whence went high walks upon arches, and above them open terraces planted with cypress trees, and all this together was composed of such ornaments as might express a princely villa.[80]

Jones's source for the scene is an engraving of the month April after Antonio Tempesta (141). Once again symmetry is reinforced, the tunnel arbour and low lattice fencing on one side being duplicated on the other to replace an architectural arcade.[81] His rearrangement is anticipated in the titlepage of Daniel Rabel's *Theatrum Florae* (1622) (142), suggesting that Jones may have seen this, although it is odd that he did not include Rabel's updating of Tempesta by introducing *parterres de broderie*. Rabel was a leading designer at the French court, specialising in costumes for the *ballet de cour*, and Henrietta Maria would certainly have known both him and the book.[82]

The two final garden scenes were also both associated with the Queen. The

138. Inigo Jones, Garden scene in *The Shepherds' Paradise*, 1633. Devonshire Collection, Chatsworth, by permission of the Duke of Devonshire and the Chatsworth Settlement Trustees

139. Jacques Callot, *Le Grand Parterre de Nancy*, 1625, engraving

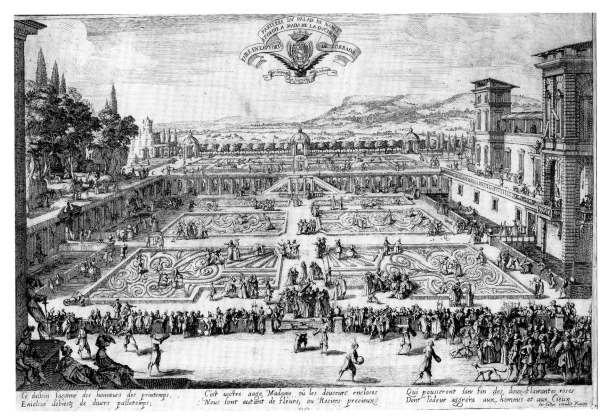

140. The garden of a princely villa. Inigo Jones's design for the climax of *Coelum Britannicum*, 1634. Devonshire Collection, Chatsworth, by permission of the Duke of Devonshire and the Chatsworth Settlement Trustees

first was for her pastoral, *Florimène* (1635) where it was one of four *intermedii* of the seasons, the garden being for Spring: 'a spacious garden, with walks, parterres, close arbours and cypress trees...' (143)[83] Again the source is Tempesta rearranged, anything which might detract from the almost austere classical perspective being suppressed (144). Far more important must have been his garden setting in *Luminalia: The Queen's Festival of Light* (1638). Its plot tells how the Muses, driven out of Greece and 'out of Italy by the barbarous Goths and Vandals', find refuge in Britain and a haven under the aegis of Henrietta Maria cast as a *Reine Soleil*: 'the scene where this goddess of brightness was discovered was styled the garden of the Britanides, or muses of Great Britain, not inferior in beauty to that of the Hesperides, or that of Alcinous celebrated by Homer.' The actual set is described as 'a delicious prospect, wherein were rows of trees, fountains, statues, arbours, grottos, walks, and all such things of delight as might express the beautiful garden

141. Antonio Tempesta, *April*

142. Daniel Rabel, *Theatrum Florae*, Paris 1627, detail of the frontispiece. British Library, London

of the Britanides.'[84] This must have been by far the most ambitious of all Jones's garden pictures and it cannot have looked so very different from Alfonso Parigi's Garden of Venus in *Le Nozze degli Dei* (1637), a source which Jones certainly drew upon for scenes in the last masque of 1640.[85]

So far we have approached these stage garden pictures as evidence of aspiration expressed in a new English garden style. As part of the visual argument of a court masque they acted as components of a series of emblems that dissolved one into the other. Masque pictures play a vital part in the emergence of a desire to picture the garden. Jones employs all the sources which were to lead to the birth of garden painting: the garden as Paradise and Eden returned; as the symbol of spring, of the island kingdom, as the enclosed garden of the Virgin – the *hortus conclusus* – as much as its opposite, the sensuous garden of forbidden delights presided over by a Venus or Circe.

Although the Civil War was to sweep away the garden as the image of the

143. Inigo Jones, Design for the second intermedium, 'Spring', in *Florimène*. 1635. Devonshire Collection, Chatsworth, by permission of the Duke of Devonshire and the Chatsworth Settlement Trustees

144. Otho Vaenius after Antonio Tempesta, Scene from the *Historia Septem Infantium de Lara*, 1612. British Museum, London

king's peace, it was only to reinforce its role as a prime source of spiritual nourishment and consolation. Clutching his prayer book the devout Puritan was to pace his garden, orchard and wilderness rapt in holy contemplation. In the same way Anglican royalist gentry of the type of John Evelyn were also to turn for solace to the cultivation of their gardens seeking to find in them a return to a lost Eden. In the latter the religious currents of the age joined hands with another motivating force which was to elevate garden, the cult of the country estate.

III

PORTRAIT OF A PLACE

The Garden Picture

Up until now we have glimpsed gardens in the backgrounds of portraits or as settings in which sitters have chosen to display themselves in fullness of pride of possession, and we have seen gardens deployed as vehicles for symbol and allegory. But we have not as yet encountered a detached view of a garden which actually existed. By that I mean a topographical view of a place, although the earliest of these pictures depicted both house *and* garden and only occasionally the garden on its own. By the eighteenth century these images were to multiply into sets of paintings and engravings, taking the viewer on a tour of a single creation. These are considered in Chapter IV, but here I intend to confine myself to outlining the evolution of the garden picture and then pursue in greater depth some specific examples of what it can represent in terms of evidence for the period preceding the landscape style.

The subject of views of English country houses has already been substantially covered by John Harris in his pioneering *The Artist and the Country House* published in 1979. The exhibition he organised on the same subject in 1995 assembled a rich corpus of material from the Tudor to the Victorian period.[1] From time to time he touches upon the garden element in them, but his thesis focuses on the evolution of a topographical tradition concerned with recording the country house and its environs. So far the garden element has never been detached from the architectural and examined in its own right. In 1979 garden history was in its infancy and over twenty years of research now needs to be taken into consideration and projected onto the material Harris assembled. Each picture calls for detailed analysis employing a myriad of sources, an exercise far beyond the confines of the present study. This chapter outlines the emergence of the country house view with an emphasis on its garden aspect and then considers in detail two specific topics, flower gardens and town gardens, where visual evidence can provide vital, but otherwise unobtainable, information. But before that we must set developments in England against the backcloth of what occurred in mainland Europe.

The European Background

The notion of a portrait of a house and its environs emerges in the Renaissance. It is a child of the revival of an antique architectural format, the villa, epitomising the humanist division of *negotio* from *otium*, of political and business life from the one of leisure and philosophical contemplation, the former transacted in the city palazzo, the latter in the country house. Topographically accurate

145. Wollaton Hall, Nottinghamshire. The Elizabethan garden as it was remodelled for Sir Thomas Willoughby in the 1690s. At the bottom of the picture can be seen what must be the rear of an orangery overlooking a rare view of a small section of a formal flower garden. Detail from plate 173

146. Giralomo Muziano and students, *View of the gardens of the Villa d'Este, c.1568.* Villa d'Este, Tivoli

147. *The Villa Lante, Bagnaia, and its gardens 1574–78.* Palazzina Gambara, Villa Lante, Bagnaia

recordings of both house and garden had to await the invention of scientific perspective in which the natural world was reordered around man. By the fifteenth century perspective views of buildings were already being painted, but the earliest panorama of a great villa and its gardens is found in the frescoes painted by Girolamo Muziano and his pupils of the Villa d'Este at Tivoli in 1565 (146).[2] These form part of an iconographical schema celebrating the possessions of the garden's creator, Cardinal Ippolito d'Este. The main view is not as yet a bird's-eye one but rather looks straight on and upwards at the soaring terraces which rise towards the villa at their summit. In the foreground trees and undergrowth and then swags of flowers and columns frame the composition.

Their successors come a decade later in the two views of the Villa Lante at Bagnaia (147) and the Villa Farnese at Caprarola in the Palazzina Gambara at Lante, dating from 1574–8.[3] This is the first bird's-eye view of a property, the whole orchestrated in submission to recessionary perspective. Both paintings celebrate what was to be a continuous theme until the advent of the landscape style in the eighteenth century, the conquest and taming of wild nature. The viewer is asked to admire a terrain hewn out of uncultivated landscape that has been reordered by the hand of man according to Renaissance rules of harmony and proportion. The division between the realm of Nature and that of man is sharply emphasised by containing walls, the garden within being an exercise in geometry, a symmetrical pattern of squares, rectangles, triangles, ovals, circles and squares. At about the same time Jacopo Zucchi recorded the villa and garden of Cardinal Ferdinando de'Medici in Rome (148).[4] Again we hover over the garden, looking down on the neatly ordered space firmly held in by walls and divided within into com-

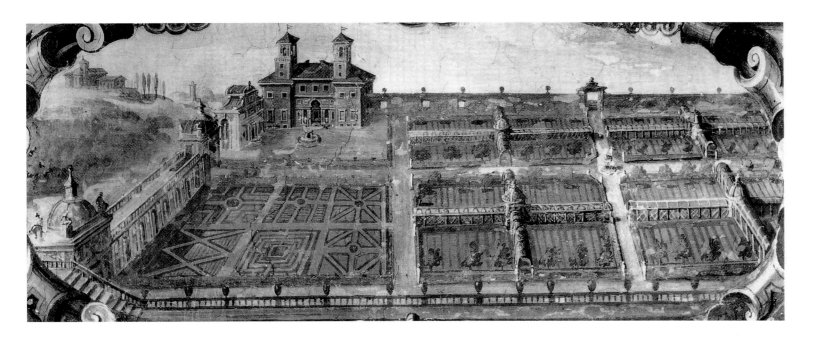

partments with patterned beds and criss-crossed with *berceaux*. By 1599, when the Flemish artist Giusto Utens painted his celebrated series of lunettes for the Villa Artimino for the same patron, now Grand Duke of Tuscany, the format was fully established.[5]

By now engravings of gardens had also begun to appear. Their origin can be pinpointed to 1573 when the Frenchman Etienne Dupérac issued his view of the Villa d'Este (149).[6] Rather than adopting the precedent set by Muziano's fresco this engraving follows the frescoes of Bagnaia and Caprarola. By 1573 Dupérac would also have been familiar with the bird's-eye garden views of Vredeman de Vries, which were already being issued in the 1560s. Dupérac states that he had

148. Jacopo Zucchi, *Garden of the Villa Medici, Rome, c.* 1576. Villa Medici, Rome

149. Etienne Dupérac, *Tivoli, Villa d'Este,* engraving, 1573

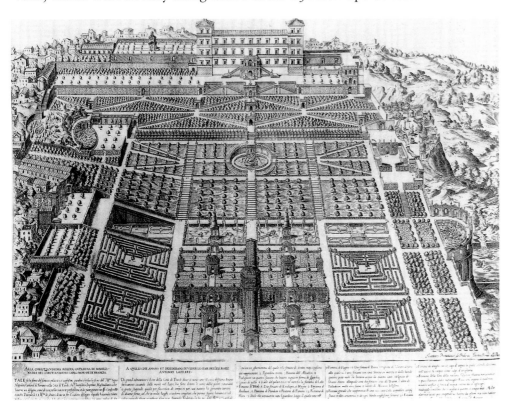

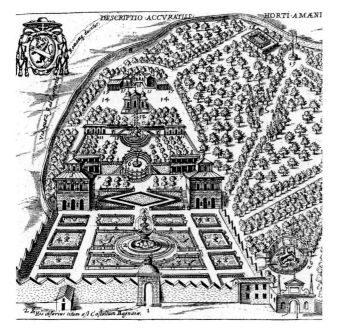

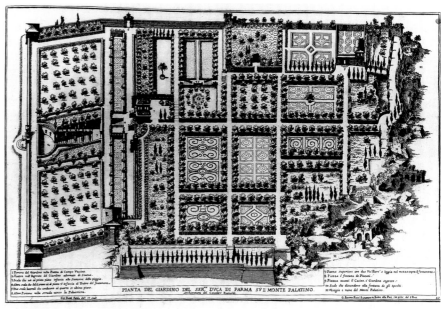

150. Detail of the Villa Lante, Bagnaia; from Giacomo Lauro, *Antiquae urbis splendor*, 1612–28

151. Giovanni Battista Falda, *The Gardens of the Villa Farnese, Rome*. Engraving, 1675

been sent by the Emperor Maximilian II to draw the garden and he dedicated the print to Catherine de'Medici, Queen of France. In his view Dupérac improves on the reality to convey an ideal order. This engraving is the fount of a long line of engraved views of the famous villa gardens of Renaissance and Baroque Italy which stretches down to Piranesi, who caught these majestic creations in their crumbling decay.[7] Dupérac's engraving was to be copied and re-issued time and again for the next two centuries influencing the way in which artists depicted such gardens. The desire was always to look down from above conveying in detail a garden's extent and lay-out, but not giving any notion of the visitor's experience on foot which would have been one of constant wonder and surprise.

As we move into the seventeenth century such engravings multiply, meeting the ever escalating demand from travellers as the Grand Tour gained momentum. The great publishing houses of de'Rossi met the demand by commissioning etched and engraved copper plates directly from graphic artists. Such prints were sold both separately and bound up as books and needless to say they were endlessly reworked until too worn to produce clear impressions. Giovanni Battista Falda was among the artists in greatest demand (151), his most famous work being the illustrations executed for the first two volumes of *Le Fontane di Roma* issued by Giovanni Giacomo de'Rossi in 1675.

That these and earlier engravings must have reached England can be deduced by turning to one of John Evelyn's drawings of a garden he designed for his brother in the early 1650s (152).[8] This was executed shortly after his return from the continent, a trip that had included an intensive study of Italian gardens. The drawing is inscribed: 'Wotton in Surrey / The house of Geo: Evelyn Esq r: / taken in perspective from / the top of the Grotto by / Jo: Evelyn 1653.'

Such a topographical rendering presupposes knowledge of a print like Lauro's view of the Villa Lante in *Antiquae urbis splendor* (1612–28) with its head-on bird's-eye viewpoint to emphasise the central axis and geometric symmetry (150). Equally the endearingly naive rendering of the Italianate garden laid out by Mutton Davies at Llanerch, Denbighshire (153), painted in 1662, must stem from a similar source brought back to Wales by Davies, who was in Italy from 1654 to 1658.[9] Davies must have purchased Greuter's engraving of the villas of Frascati (154) or a comparable image, and asked some luckless provincial artist to record his own creation in just such a manner, thereby precipitating the earliest oil on canvas bird's-eye perspective of a country house and its gardens in British painting. Nothing else could account for this extraordinary aesthetic aberration in the fastnesses of Wales.

By the 1660s the English were familiar with engravings of Italian gardens and they were well acquainted with those produced North of the Alps. The Elizabethans were certainly familiar with Jacques Androuet du Cerceau's *Les Plus Excellents Bastiments de France* (1576–9).[10] Du Cerceau had been to Italy in the 1540s to study antiquities and he had already begun work on his book in the 1560s. The garden element in these views is always rich and ornamental, much of it of his own invention. He was also an architect, who, in 1576 had published *Leçons de perspective positive* in which he demonstrated the principles of the bird's-eye view as applied to architecture. This was in part a response to Vitruvius's reference to *scaenographia* as one of the three types of architectural drawing, the other two being the plan and the elevation.[11]

Du Cerceau's work had no successors until the following century, due to the religious wars. Garden views re-emerge as part of the campaign to restore the prestige of the monarchy in prints such as that by Alessandro Francini dated

153. Artist unknown, *The House and Gardens of Llanerch, Denbighshire,* as laid out by Mutton Davies between 1658 and 1662, 1662. New Haven, Yale Center for British Art, Paul Mellon Collection

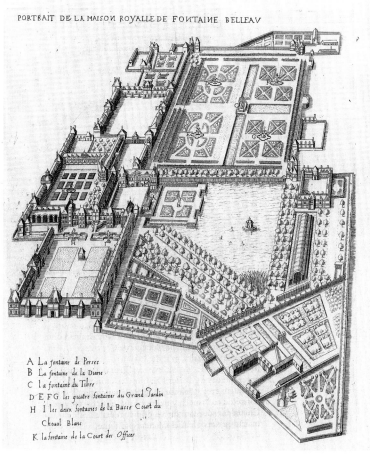

154. Matthias Greuter, *Villa Belpoggio, Frascati*. Detail from an engraving, 1620

155. The Gardens of Fontainebleau as laid out by Alessandro Francini, 1614

1614 of the gardens laid out for Henri IV at Fontainebleau (155). This heralded a long series of engravings expressing the glorification of the crown and acting as disseminators of French garden style as it rose to European ascendancy in the work of Le Nôtre.[12] These prints were produced in vast quantities, the work in the main of two men, Adam Perelle but, first and foremost, Israel Silvestre. Their work dominated the second half of the seventeenth century, recording every transformation of Versailles and the other royal palace gardens, besides those of the nobility like Vaux-le-Vicomte, André Le Nôtre's first great masterpiece. In 1662 Silvestre became official draftsman and printmaker to Louis XIV.

Remarkably, neither the Italian, nor the French traditions, spawned a school of topographical painters. However, in the Low Countries not only a vigorous print tradition but also one of painted views of great houses and their surrounding domain emerged. These pictures are the direct source of the efflorescence of view-painting in England in the last quarter of the century.[13] The Netherlandish garden view had its roots in De Vries's *Hortorum Formae* in the 1580s, as well as in depictions of spring, and in the taste for scenes of elegant company disporting themselves in gardens (157). All of these we have already encountered but the innovation in the seventeenth century was to produce views of actual gardens. As in the case of France the driving force was dynastic; this was summed up in one of the earliest prints, Balthasar Florisz. van Berckenrode's isometric rendering of Frederik Hendrik of Nassau's great garden laid out by André Mollet at Honselaarsdijk (156).[14] The print can be dated to about 1640 and it was to be the ancestor of a long series of topographical pub-

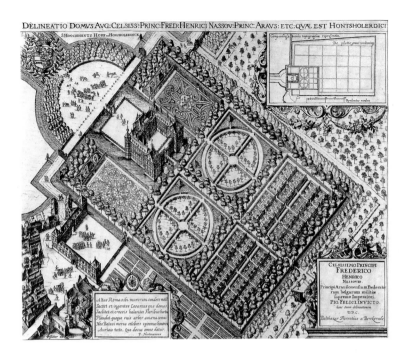

156. Balthasar Florisz. van Berckenrode, *Honselaarsdijk*, *c.* 1640, Haags Gemeente-archief

157. Netherlandish School, *A jardin d'amour*, *c.* 1590; Amsterdam, Rijksmuseum

lications that were to flood the book market, above all during the 1690s and the first decade of the eighteenth century. These depicted the gardens of the stadholder and those of members of his court. William III's garden at the palace of Het Loo was to be engraved more than any other, an index that this out-pouring was part of the Dutch propaganda war against France, produced with the intention of eclipsing the equally numerous series of Versailles and the other royal gardens by Perelle and Silvestre.[15] In the same way, the long series of engravings of English royal palaces, country houses and gardens published in

158. Willem Schellincks, *Munnikenhof,* 1659, Middelburg, Het Koninklijk Zeeuwsch Genootschap der Wetenschappen, Zeeuws Museum

159. Gardens in the area of Moorgate and Bishopsgate, a section of the so-called 'Copper-plate' map of London, *c.* 1553–9. Museum of London

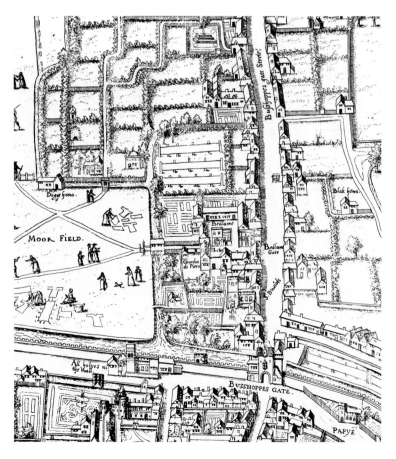

1707 as *Britannia Illustrata* presented the *mise-en-scène* of the British monarchy and of members of its ruling classes as equal to or hopefully outshining those of the enemy, France.

More significantly the Low Countries established a tradition of country-house view-painting that was to be exported directly to England. Schellinks's panorama of Munnikenhof (158), dated 1659, records the enlargement of a medieval house and the embellishment of its gardens by its owner, Frederik van Roubergen.[16] This composition has in place already all the elements which were to be repeated again and again in the long series of English country house views which were to span the late 1670s and spill over into the first two decades of the following century. The view is a bird's-eye one. In the foreground a coach, always a status symbol, has just deposited its occupants. They and the others arriving on foot are richly dressed, again emphasising the social ambience of the owners. The house, rather old-fashioned, is recorded in the distance, but the main focus is on its extensive gardens which are also old-fashioned for the 1650s, being divided into separate enclosures with gaily painted wooden gates, bridges and seating alcoves. Fourteen years after this painting was made the forty-four-year-old Jan Siberechts was to arrive in England effectively initiating country house and garden view painting in this country.

THE ORIGIN AND DEVELOPMENT OF THE COUNTRY HOUSE AND GARDEN VIEW IN ENGLAND IN THE SIXTEENTH AND SEVENTEENTH CENTURIES

The indigenous topographical tradition in England never extended beyond the cartographic. The earliest views of London from the 1550s and 1560s (159) include crude renderings of gardens that are still medieval, later there are bird's-eye plans of the City by Franciscus Hogenberg for Braun and Hogenberg's *Civitates Orbis Terrarum* (1574) and Peter van den Keere's in Norden's *Speculum Britanniae* (1593).[17] More revealing for London is William Faithorne's map, surveyed in 1643–7 and published in 1658, which contains vivid evidence of the stylistic developments during the decades before the Civil War. Even more detailed in the case of gardens is the only surviving unfinished plate by Wenceslaus Hollar of the west central district, between the City and Whitehall, part of a projected giant map of London executed between 1660 and 1666 but rendered obsolete by the Great Fire.[18] That was not to be eclipsed until John Rocque's survey of 1741–5 *Twenty Miles Round London*, published in 1746. It is a veritable goldmine of information on the ground-plans of gardens of the great houses surrounding the metropolis such as Cannons or Osterley Park besides of more modest ones in villages like Wimbledon (160).[19] To these we can add maps of cities such as those engraved by Augustine Ryther of Oxford and Cambridge issued in 1588 and 1592–3 (161) which are rich in garden detail.[20] These provide peripheral, accidental, garden evidence.

Within this tradition only two images give us some substantial notion of the appearance of an Elizabethan garden. Part of the Privy Garden at Nonsuch Palace as it was laid out by John, 1st Lord Lumley, in the 1580s is inset into Jodocus Hondius's map of Surrey published in Speed's *Theatre of the Empire of*

160. The gardens of Wimbledon Village from Rocque's survey *Twenty Miles Round London* 1741–5; pub. 1746. British Library, London

161. Gardens in late Elizabethan Cambridge, from the bird's-eye plan of Cambridge, by Augustine Ryther after John Hammond, 1592–3. British Library, London

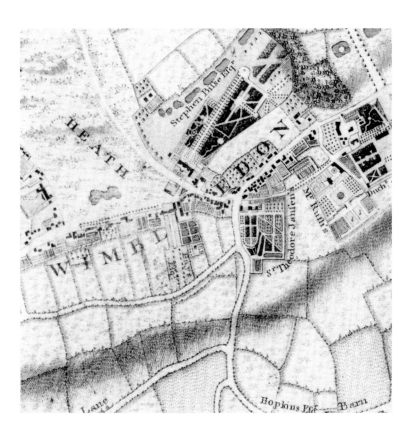

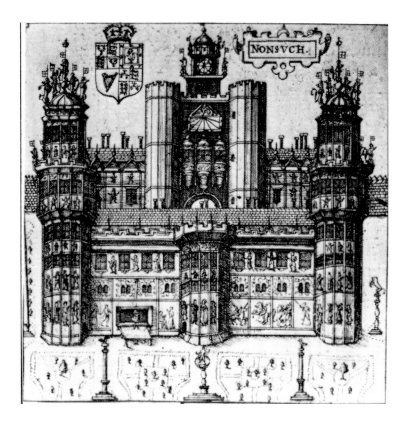

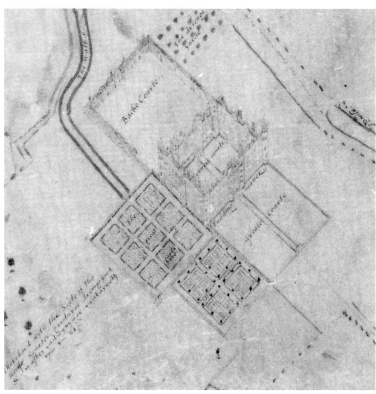

162. *The Privy Garden of Nonsuch Palace*, detail from Jodocus Hondius's *Map of Surrey* in John Speed, *Theatre of the Empire of Great Britaine*, 1611–12

163. Ralph Agas, *Bird's-eye view of Toddington Manor, Bedfordshire*, 1581, showing the ambitious garden created by Henry, Lord Cheyney between 1559 and 1581. British Library, London. Add MS 38065H

Great Britaine (1611–12) (162). This includes garden ornaments that are illustrated in an inventory of the palace in 1590.[21] The second image is an overlooked and far more important one, the bird's-eye view by Ralph Agas dated 1581 of Toddington Manor, Bedfordshire, a house that no longer exists (163).[22] Henry, Lord Cheney inherited this estate in 1559; he was created baron in 1572 and died in 1581, the year of the drawing. The garden is shown in quite extraordinary detail. It is a huge garden, duplicating in its arrangement Lord Burghley's Theobalds, and like it having a great garden of nine compartments and a second or little garden which is quartered and each compartment quartered again.

The views of Nonsuch and Toddington are the nearest we get to a topographical delineation of an actual garden apart from the drawings by Anthonis van den Wyngaerde, which constitute our major visual for source for the gardens of the Tudor royal palaces. Wyngaerde, it is now thought, came to England in 1557 in his capacity as Painter in Ordinary to the future Philip II of Spain, one of the prince's entourage on the occasion of his marriage to Mary Tudor.[23] Dates on some of the drawings indicate that he must have continued to shuttle between England and the Low Countries from 1558 until 1562. I have already touched on the drawings of Whitehall and Richmond (7, 17), but the most important by far is that of the great garden laid out by Henry VIII at Hampton Court (164), two of which are dated 1558.[24] This was created from 1532 onwards, occupying a large triangle of land along the river front below the King's privy lodgings. The main garden is clearly delineated, a rectangular, walled, plot with the space within divided absolutely symmetrically, a French Renaissance influence, into two groups of ten plots with walks around and a central walk dividing them. There are the painted and gilded posts 'of the Kynges and quenys beestes' of exactly the same type as in the painting of Whitehall. What cannot be seen is any detail of the internal planting beyond the shrubs surrounding the perimeter of the

164. Anthony van den Wyngaerde, *View of the Privy Garden, Pond Garden and the Mount at Hampton Court*, 1558, Ashmolean Museum, Oxford

165. Wenceslaus Hollar, *Spring*, 1643, British Museum, London

166. A glimpse of what may be the garden of Tart Hall, laid out in the 1630s. Detail of plate 165

garden. Just behind the river gatehouse can seen the walk lined with the king's beasts leading up to the banqueting house.

Nothing of a similar nature appears for almost one hundred years, when Wenceslas Hollar engraved Spring clasping a bunch of tulips in 1643 (165). It has been suggested that the garden records the residence of the Countess of Arundel, Tart Hall, close to the site of the present Buckingham Palace (166).[25] The house had gone up in the 1630s, certainly by 1638. To the left of the foreground figure there is a garden in the new Italianate manner: quartered, with a fountain in the middle and what looks like an embroidered parterre with a flight of steps leading to a terrace from which to look down on the pattern. Such a view should be considered in the context of the garden visions conjured up by Inigo Jones on stage in the court masques during the 1630s (140). Both depend on the discovery of scientific perspective as it was understood by the theorists of Renaissance Italy.

The series of no less than twenty-six plates of different types and sizes, known collectively as *Wilton Garden* are fully discussed in Chapter four where the evidence is presented for dating the publication to the years 1645–6.[26] However, the large folding plate (228) which contains the first bird-eye engraved panoramic view of an English garden belongs here. The second edition is firmly dated 1654, when the plates were in the hands of Peter Stent. This garden was laid out between 1632 and 1638 by Isaac de Caus for Philip Herbert, 4th Earl of Pembroke. It was a major creation, synthesising French, Italian and indigenous traditions, many of the features suggesting a substantial input by Inigo Jones. The original drawing for this plate, in the possession of Worcester College, Oxford, has an early annotation 'Wilton by Callot'. This garden view does relate directly to Callot's famous plate of *Le Grand parterre de Nancy* (139), but it does not necessarily mean that we are looking at a

Callot engraving.[27] The artist died in 1635 three years before the garden at Wilton was finished and there seems to be no reason to dismiss the evidence of the engraved plate 'Isaac de caus Invent'. The view of Wilton shamelessly plagiarizes Callot for its staffage trees and lifts elegant figures from the Lorraine court at Nancy and deposits them strolling along the paths of Wilton. An even more important precedent for the Wilton plates is Theodore de Bry's series in Salomon de Caus's *Hortus Palatinus* (1620), which includes a large folding plate of the garden created by de Caus for the Elector Palatine and his wife, Elizabeth, daughter of James I (226). It would certainly have been familiar in England.

The bird's-eye garden view was to dominate depictions of house and garden until well into the following century. There are a number of reasons for its popularity. In the case of Wilton the reception of Renaissance garden principles involved the superimposition of symmetrical geometry on a terrain, only fully visually appreciated if seen from above. The desirability of an aerial view was reinforced by the introduction of the extended axis. The Wilton scene only hints at this, for beyond the grotto and the closing terrace wall we can see the start of a central avenue; other evidence suggests that it continued to the top of the hillside opposite the façade of the house. The principle of the extended axis was central to André Mollet in his book *Le Jardin de Plaisir* published in 1651. Mollet was working in England in the 1630s and again at the Restoration, after which the book was translated into English.[28] The bird's-eye view developed in tandem with the golden age of the great formal garden, in England represented above all by the work of George London and Henry Wise. It allowed the many parts of a garden to be displayed to full advantage in an architectural and horticultural composition that encompassed the countryside around by means of avenues radiating out in all directions to the distant horizon.

The *Wilton Garden* format was to find rich expression after 1660 in the long series of illustrated county histories, which included plates of country houses with their environs. In David Loggan's volumes on the two universities, *Oxonia Illustrata* (1675) and *Cantabrigia Illustrata* (1690), college gardens are depicted that must have been laid out before 1642 and continued to include even knots (167).[29] Tucked into these views of colleges are rare records of the modest small gardens of some of the fellows, tiny parterres of turf cut into the usual symmetrical patterns and inset with vertical evergreens. Detached engravings of country houses appear for the first time although the majority come in the outpouring of county histories, such as those by the Dutch engraver Michael Burghers for Robert Plot's *Staffordshire* (1686) and *Parochial Antiquities Attempted in the History of Ambrosden* (1695). To these we can add John Drapentier's twenty-nine views of country houses in Sir Henry Chancy's *Historical Antiquities of Hertfordshire* (1700), those by Jan Kip for Sir Robert Atkyns's *Gloucestershire* (1712) and those by Thomas Badeslade for Dr John Harris's *History of Kent* (1719) (168). Suddenly there is a plethora of visual evidence on country house gardens, ones which include not only the latest in garden fashions but features like mounts and mazes left over from earlier periods.

167. Detail of New College Garden with the Tudor mount as it was remodelled in 1647. From David Loggan, *Oxonia Illustrata*, 1675. British Library, London

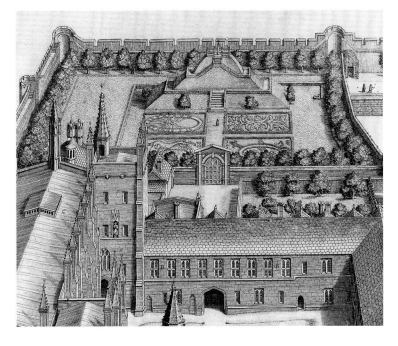

168. Knole, Kent, and its gardens, as updated by George London after 1698 for the 1st Duke of Dorset. Detail of an engraving from John Harris, *History of Kent*, 1719

169. Bretby, Derbyshire, the spectacular garden created from 1669 for the Earl of Chesterfield. Detail of an engraving from Jan Kip, *Nouveau Théâtre de la Grande Bretagne*, London 1716. New Haven, Yale Center for British Art, Paul Mellon Collection

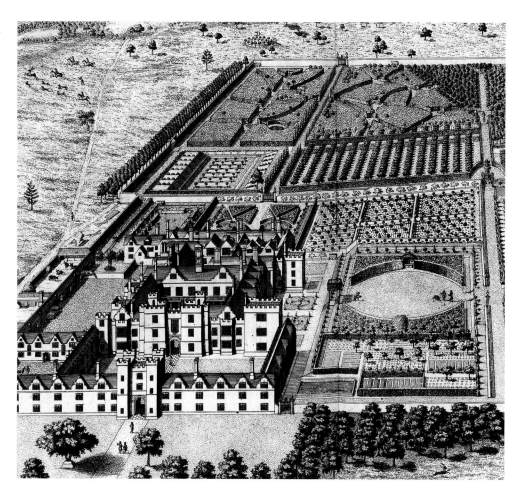

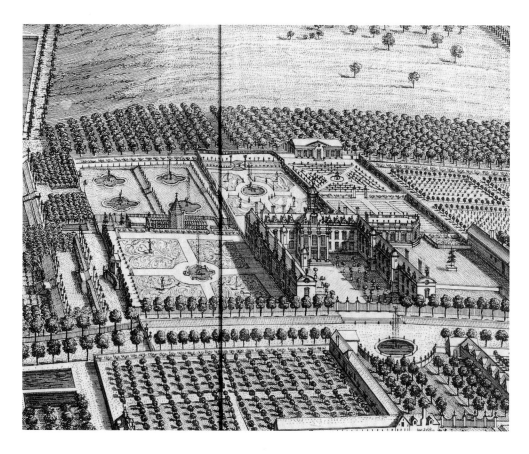

More important than all of these was the collaboration of Jan Kip and Leonard Knyff which led to the publication in 1707, the year of the Act of Union with Scotland, of *Britannia Illustrata*. A second volume appeared in 1715, the year before David Morier's *Nouveau Théâtre de la Grande Bretagne* (169). This reprinted the whole of *Britannia Illustrata* and went on to include all kinds of miscellanea including county maps,[30] marking the transition from the age of the baroque into the neo-Palladian generation. Together these books provide us with a rich resource covering all the major gardens of the age of George London and Henry Wise.

And, finally, country-house and garden view-painting arrived. Leonard Knyff's brother, Jacob, painted views which could include some garden detail.[31] Of these by far the most important is that of Durdans, Surrey, signed and dated 1679 (32) which anticipates his brother's format by twenty years. An elevated perspective looks down upon a house, embracing not only the building and its gardens but going on to include the activities of the estate around.[32] In the case of Durdans we are provided with a precious glimpse of a garden which is likely to date from the 1630s, laid out probably at the same time that Sir Robert Cooker built the classical wing recorded to the right in the painting. The garden is virtually identical to the Countess of Arundel's at Tart Hall as recorded by Hollar (165).

Leonard Knyff and his Netherlandish colleague, Jan Siberechts were at the forefront of the new style. Knyff came from Haarlem sometime after 1676 but there is no painting certainly by him before 1697.[33] No more than seven or eight country-house canvases can be attributed to him with some certainty. These include paintings that have long been recognised as key documents, providing us with detailed panoramas of some of the greatest formal gardens. Two

The North Prospect of
Hampton Court With y
Park & Decoy By Mr Knife

171. Leonard Knyff, *The North Prospect of Hampton Court, Herefordshire*, 1699, showing the gardens created for Thomas, Lord Coningsby, by George London in the 1690s. New Haven, Yale Center for British Art, Paul Mellon Collection

172. Leonard Knyff, *Clandon Park*, 1708, a view of the spectacular gardens designed in the 1690s for Richard, 1st Baron Onslow. National Trust, Clandon Park

oils of Hampton Court, Herefordshire (one dated 1699) (171) record the gardens laid out by George London for Thomas, Lord Coningsby; one of Hampton Court, Middlesex (Royal Collection; *c.* 1702) captures William III's garden works by London and Wise at their apogee; finally, one of Clandon Park, Surrey (dated 1708) (172) records the *furor hortensis* of Richard Weston. The view of Clandon shows the thousands of recently planted, regimented trees, the astonishing canal pushing its way into the fields and the complicated baroque parterre close to the house.

Jan Siberechts arrived in England in 1673, reputedly brought over by George Villiers, 2nd Duke of Buckingham.[34] His pictures are by far the most dazzling panoramas of late Stuart country houses and their surrounding domain. For his two major patrons, Sir Thomas Thynne and Sir Thomas Willoughby he was to paint several versions of their houses, Longleat, Wiltshire, and Wollaton Hall, Nottinghamshire (173). The three of Longleat are dated 1675, 1676 and 1678, that is before Thynne became 1st Viscount Weymouth and embarked on the spectacular garden recorded in *Britannia Illustrata*. Of the three Wollaton

173. Jan Siberchts, *Wollaton Hall, Nottinghamshire*, 1695, the gardens were created in the 1690s for Sir Thomas Willoughby. Collection Lord Middleton, Birdsall, Yorkshire

174. Unknown artist, attributed to Jan Siberechts, *Chatsworth*, c. 1707–11, view of the garden laid out by Henry Wise for the 1st Duke of Devonshire between 1687 and 1706, with the Cascade House, bottom right, designed by Thomas Archer and built in 1703. Private collection

views, two are dated 1695 and 1697, all record the ambitious garden transformation by Sir Thomas Willoughby of the old Elizabethan gardens. Siberechts's last picture, of The Grove, Highgate, provides a rare view of a vegetable and fruit garden in a modest domain.

These painters are at the summit of a genre which spawned a host of largely unattributable country-house views. These are often of beguiling naivety, like that of Denham Place, Buckinghamshire, with its quite extraordinary display of sculpture[35] or of prime historical importance as the one recording Henry Wise's great masterpiece at Chatsworth (174). A range of minor artists such as John or Jan Stevens, Thomas Smith, Jan Griffier, John Setterington, John Harris the Younger, Adrian van Diest and others were active at this time. Some of them also produced sets of views of the same garden that are discussed in Chapter IV. Collectively they belong to the heyday of the genre which had run its course as the landscape style triumphed. That no longer called for observation from above but at ground level and the line between landscape painting and the bird's-eye country-house view dissolved.

Between about 1670 and 1730 we have a quite unprecedented glut of garden pictures or rather pictures which include detailed delineation of gardens, ones which mercifully record the gardens which were to be felled by Brown and his followers. No other garden paintings are of such documentary importance for the historian. Through them one can explore two types of garden – flower gardens and town gardens – about which all too little is known, assembling the visual evidence in an attempt to reconstruct their evolution during the seventeenth and into the early eighteenth centuries.

THE RENAISSANCE AND BAROQUE FLOWER GARDEN

The flower garden evolved as a consequence of the plant explosion of the late sixteenth century, the result of renewed contact with the Levant in the aftermath of the establishment of a Turkish Empire whose capital was Constantinople. Diplomatic ties between the courts of Western Christendom and that of the Sultan resulted in a phenomenon concisely summed up by William Stearn:

> Never before or since has there been such an astonishing influx of colourful strange plants into European gardens, when in the second half of the sixteenth century, importations of unpromising onion-like bulbs and knobbly tubers from Constantinople brought forth tulips, crown imperials, irises, haycinths, anenones, turban ranunculi, narcissi and lilies.[36]

Within a century twenty times as many plants entered Europe as in the preceding two thousand years. It gave an enormous impetus to the renaissance exploration of the natural world, typified in the case of England by the plant drawings of Jacques Le Moyne de Morgues and Alexander Marshall as well as the activities of John Gerard, the herbalist, and the plant-collecting John Tradescant.

In Italy during the Renaissance and Baroque periods flowers were found mainly in the *giardino segreto*, a walled enclosure reserved for the use of the owner and his family.[37] In Rome these newfangled private floral areas can be seen in many of the views recorded in Falda's *Li giardini di Roma...* (1680). Flowers were incredibly expensive and needed protection from theft, hence the walls and gates. One need only recall the Dutch tulipomania of the late 1630s at its maddest, when the price of a single bulb would have bought a house. Such private gardens were laid out in the same geometric manner as the main area, that is in compartments. Serlio, in the fourth book of his *Architettura* (1547), prints lay-outs (175) that must have been intended as designs for flowerbeds. They were the ancestors of a long line of designs for flower gardens that were still being laid out in England and Scotland at the close of the seventeenth century. However, it was only at the very end of the sixteenth century that flower gardens in which to display the new exotic bulbous and tuberous flowers seriously developed.

So far, detailed information has only emerged for two Italian flower gardens. One is the garden of the Cardinal Antonio Barberini, nephew of Pope Urban VIII, a small area attached to the Barberini Palace on the Quirinal Hill (176).[38] This was a creation of the 1630s and was geared to provide a spectacular display achieved by forcing or retarding flowers which were grown in pots and plunge-planted to create a pattern of colour predominantly in shades of yellow and white. The Barberini were passionate plant collectors and paid for the engravings in Giovanni Battista Ferrari's *De florum cultura* (1633) in which he includes several designs for flower gardens in the Serlian manner, (177). Among the designs in Ferrari's *Flora overo cultura di fiori distinto* (1638) is one of the four compartments of the second garden about which most is known, that

175. Compartment designs from Robert Peake's 1611 translation into English of Serlio, *Architettura*

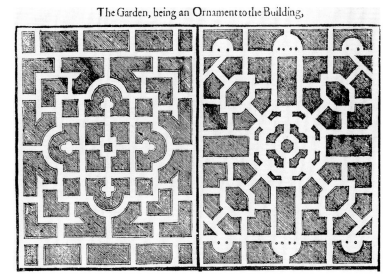

The Garden, being an Ornament to the Building,

176. Cardinal Barberini's flower garden, Plan of the *giardino segreto* at the Palazzo Barberini. Biblioteca Apostolica Vaticana, MS. Barb. Lat.4265

177. Flower garden design, G. B. Ferrari. *De florum cultura*, 1633. British Library, London

178. The flower garden of Francesco Caetani, Duke of Sermoneta, near Cisterna. From G. B. Ferrari *Flora overo cultura di fiori distinto in quattro libri*, Rome, 1638. British Library, London

179. Design for a compartment with a combination of interlacing and separate beds. From Charles Etienne and Jean Liébault, *L'Agriculture et Maison Rustique*, 1564

laid out by the Duke of Sermoneta at Cisterna (178). By 1651 this garden contained over 62,000 plants and each of the four compartments was dominated by a single colour.

Turning to Northern Europe, pictures of gardens of the Serlian type as reinterpreted by Vredeman de Vries show only turf punctuated by shaped trees and shrubs. Crispin van de Passe's *Hortus Floridus* (1614) with its two prints of the same garden, a flower garden, in spring and in summer is a landmark (118). The plants, among them tulips, hyacinths, auriculas, tulips and crown imperials, are widely spaced, emphasising their cost and rarity, and they are clearly planted not in turf but in earth beds held in by some variety of edging plant like germander or box. Representations of flower gardens of this kind recur in Netherlandish and Flemish art throughout the sixteenth century, depictions of enclosed areas devoted exclusively to the cultivation of flowers. The arrangement in them is always the same, a hedged, railed or walled enclosure with a geometric pattern of beds edged and filled with flowers.[39]

Both Italy and the Netherlands had an impact on England, and so, as the century progressed and particularly after 1660, did France.[40] Advances in botany, the arrival of new species and the cultivation of new varieties stimulated the

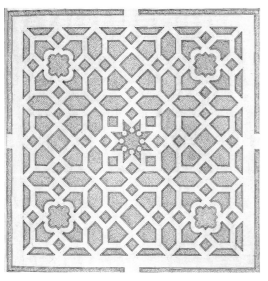

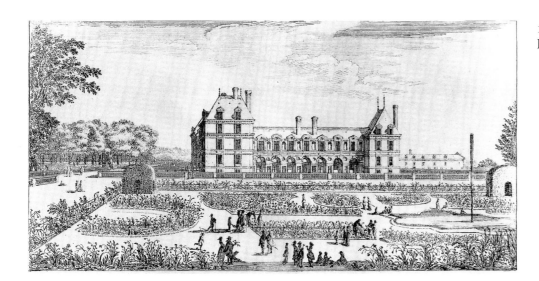

180. The flower garden at Liancourt, 1654. Engraving by Israel Silvestre

development of the flower garden. The most important sixteenth-century treatise was *L'Agriculture et Maison Rustique* (1564) by Charles Etienne and Jean Liébault which was translated into English in 1600. In it aesthetics move to the fore even in the case of a modest country house: 'The most pleasant and entertaining part of the small French farm is the flower garden...'[41] This was to be divided into two with one half for flowers for cutting and the other in the main for those grown for their scent. The designs are of three kinds: the first patterns for interlacing knots (of the kind we have encountered in the portrait of Lettice Newdigate; see plate 20); the second what the authors call a 'parterre de carreaux rompu', that is a symmetrical arrangement of separate beds for flowers; and a third which was a mixture of the two (179). Of these three the second is the flower garden proper and it continued to feature despite the rise to dominance of the parterre as it was evolved by members of the Mollet family and Jacques Boyceau and subsequently by André Le Nôtre.

In a parterre flowers were relegated to encompassing borders, known as *plates-bandes*. Engravings, however, of the great French gardens indicate that the separate flower garden continued to have a life of its own. A vast garden at Liancourt was laid out in the 1630s by Roger de Plessys. Close to the house was a *parterre à fleurs* with a *jet d'eau* at its centre. There were geometric beds filled with flowers, two old-fashioned arbours and the whole surrounded with a flower border close to the kind of *plate-bande* laid out around a box *parterre de broderie* (180).[42] This flower garden, unlike its Italian and Netherlandish prototypes, is not enclosed by walls or a hedge or carpenters' work. It is also distinguished by the absence of shaped trees, which were seen to suck the ground of the nourishment necessary for the flowers. The driving force behind the garden design was the owner's second wife, Jeanne de Schomberg, who worked on it throughout the 1630s, reinforcing the association of the cultivation of flowers with women. That preoccupation was further strengthened in France by the *précieuses*, ladies of letters who developed a highly complex language of flowers as part of their love etiquette.[43]

Shaped trees are also absent from the flower garden at Vaux-le-Vicomte (181), André Le Nôtre's first great masterpiece laid out for Louis XIV's minister of finance, Jean Fouquet. The archetype for all French gardens in the classical

181. Detail of the flower garden at Vaux-le-Vicomte, 1665. Engraving by Israel Silvestre

The maner of watering with a Pumpe in a Tubbe.

182. Garden from Thomas Hill, *The Gardener's Labyrinth*, 1577. The layout is close to that in plate 92

style, it incorporates a series of different garden experiences into an overall grid scheme that stretched out from the château like a series of rectangular floating islands.[44] This is a flower garden that is well on the way to being subsumed into the many kinds of parterre, becoming what Dézallier d'Argenville calls a 'Parterre de pieces coupées pour les fleurs'. The apotheosis of that format was to be the flower parterres in the *Jardin du Roi* of the Grand Trianon at Versailles. Saint-Simon records that the flowers were changed daily and that in six months in 1687 over 125,000 plants were consumed in an excess of floral recklessness, which must have fuelled the reaction which led to the adoption of *le jardin anglais*.[45]

In England the Elizabethan evidence is scanty. Thomas Hill's *The Gardener's Labyrinth* (1577) contains a number of woodcuts of gardens. One is of a single compartment enclosed by a lattice frame as seen in the illumination of Henri d'Albret (12), but the beds within suggest familiarity with the designs in the *Maison Rustique*. A second (183) shows a rectangular hedged enclosure with a raised balustraded walkway looking down onto geometric compartments. A third illustration is of a gardener planting flowers into raised beds in a garden which is still resolutely medieval (183). To this meagre repertory we can add the portrait of Lady Holles from the 1620s (124), where flowers can be seen planted into what was technically known as a closed knot, closed because the flowers closed it. An open one, in contrast, was filled with sand and coloured earths.

183. Garden from Thomas Hill, *The Gardener's Labyrinth*, 1577. The herber is close to that in plate 92

Two pre-Civil War Flower Gardens
Newburgh Priory, Yorkshire

By far the most important country house portrait from the point of view of supplying a unique record of two pre-Civil War flower gardens is that which gives a bird's-eye panorama of the south or garden front of Newburgh Priory, Yorkshire (184).[46] The painter is anonymous and the picture is one of a pair, the other depicting the north or court-entrance side of the house. A date of around 1700 is usually assigned to them, but they could be ten years earlier than that. They certainly cannot be later than 1720, for a survey of that year records that these gardens had already been swept away.

Newburgh was the seat of the Belasyse, or Bellasis, family, which had built up its vast estates in the North in the aftermath of the Dissolution.[47] Newburgh, which had been an Augustinian priory, was acquired by the family in 1540 and six years later came into the possession of William Belasyse who built much of the manor house we see in the picture. He was, like his successors, politically cautious, being in fact Catholic in sympathy but establishing a pattern followed by several of his descendants, in which the head of the family and the eldest son conformed and the rest remained Catholic.

William died in 1604 and was succeeded by his son, Henry, who was knighted by James I on his journey south and created a baronet in 1611. By then the Belasyse family was one of the two wealthiest in the county, Sir Henry maintaining a large household and dispensing lavish hospitality. He sat as member of parliament for Thirsk and served on the Council of the North for almost the entire reign of James I. His son Thomas, who succeeded him in 1624, seems to

184. Artist unknown, *The South Front of Newburgh Priory*, late seventeenth century, with the Jacobean garden next to the house and the Caroline one in the foreground. Private collection

have been even richer with an annual income of £4,000 p.a. and progressed further up the social pyramid, being created Lord Fauconberg in 1627. There was bitter rivalry, however, with another up-and-coming Yorkshire family, the Wentworths, on such a scale that it landed both father and son in jail in 1631. When the Civil War broke out in 1642, the Belasyse family was firmly on the side of the crown. Fauconberg was rewarded for his loyalty by being ennobled, but in the aftermath of the battle of Marston Moor he was forced to flee to the continent. The parliamentary Committee for Compounding set out to seize the Belasyse assets, an attempt at which they cannot have been wholly successful, for when Lord Fauconberg died in 1653 large sums were still owed.

It is to these two men that the gardens must relate. The history of the house during this period is obscure, but Henry's elevation to baronet in 1611 must have triggered improvements to the old Elizabethan house.[48] A handsome chimney-piece by Nicholas Stone dated 1615 provides a clue that alterations were then underway. A survey of 1605 makes it clear that the two huge bay windows running the height of the south front were not there then and must have been part of the enhancement of the old house. These virtually duplicate windows at another Yorkshire house, Burton Agnes, which was built to a design by Robert Smythson during the opening decade of the century for a fellow member of the Council of the North, Sir Henry Griffiths.

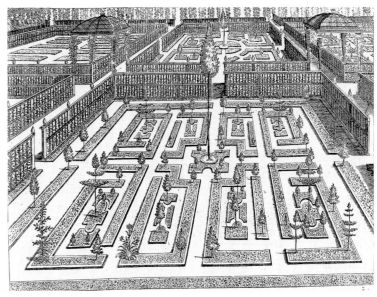

The garden lying immediately below the south front must relate to this phase (185). It is the kind of garden we have seen already lurking in the background of Oliver's miniature of a melancholy young man dating from the 1590s (106). The Newburgh one can be closely paralleled among those in Vredeman de Vries's *Hortorum Formae*, a symmetrical recti-linear pattern of grass plats and beds (186). That book first appeared in 1583 but there is little evidence that gardens were laid out in this manner before the nineties. The Newburgh garden is notable for its concern with the relationship of the house to the garden, reflected in the broad path that runs from the entrance porch the whole length of both gardens. The fact that this entrance was not exactly central is somehow skirted around in an otherwise perfectly symmetrical composition. It is a also a hugely expensive garden fully reflecting the family's financial resources, for instead of cheap hedges framing it there is costly carpenter's work of a complex kind with a forest of finials and elaborate entrance arches. The basic outline and structure of this garden is surely completely unchanged from the second decade of the seventeenth century, although it is likely that the central fountain with its *jet d'eau* and the balusters supporting flower pots are later additions. Originally the plats would have probably contained shaped trees and flowers in the medieval manner, the narrow rectangular borders holding in the grass plats would seem to have been converted to more modern *plates-bandes* with box hedges to hold displays of flowers.

185. The Jacobean garden beneath the south front of Newburgh Priory. Detail of plate 184

186. Garden of the same type, from Vredeman de Vries, *Hortorum Formae*, 1583

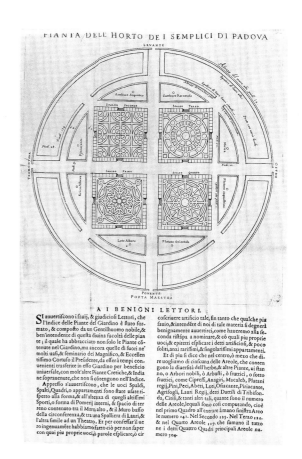

187. Knot design from William Lawson, *The Country Housewifes Garden*, 1617

188. Knot design from John Marriott, *Certaine excellent and new inuented knots and mazes, for plots for Gardens*, 1618

189. Knots from John Parkinson, *Paradisi in Sole*, 1619

190. The ground plan of the *Horto dei Semplici*, published by Girolamo Porro, 1561, British Library, London

We have encountered this type of garden already but the second garden nearer the spectator is a quite unique record of a type that stemmed from the renewed influence of Serlio and also the spreading interest in flowers which marked the Jacobean and Caroline periods (191). Editions of Serlio were of course known in Elizabethan England and he was drawn upon, for example, by Sir Francis Willoughby, when planning Wollaton Hall, Nottinghamshire, in the 1580s, but there is no evidence that his patterns for flowerbeds were ever copied during this period.[49] Robert Peake's English translation, which appeared in 1611, must have widened the knowledge of Serlio. We find it reflected almost at once in Sir Charles Cavendish's little castle at Bolsover.[50] Serlio's patterns for compartments in gardens appeared in an English translation at precisely the moment when there was an increasing passion for plants and flowers typified in the plant-hunting of John Tradescant and in the boom in the new spring bulb industry. These trends demanded a new type of knot and the Serlian patterns set a style visibly different from those of de Vries.

The earliest patterns for the Newburgh type of flower garden occur in the work of William Lawson in *A Country Housewifes Garden* (1618), a book directed at women. He includes among his repertory of knots one called 'Lozenges' which is Serlian in inspiration (187). The year after John Marriott in his *Certaine excellent and new inuented Knots and Maze, for plots for Gardens* gives two more (188), these were pirated and reprinted in the anonymous *The Expert Gardener* (1640). Very little is known about Lawson apart from the fact that he was a Yorkshireman and that he tells us that he had had forty-eight years experience as a gardener, which would take us back to 1564. What has

not been noticed is that his *A New Orchard and Garden*, also published in 1618, was dedicated to Sir Henry Belasyse in acknowledgement of his 'delight-full skill in matters of this nature' and for 'the profite which I receyued from your learned discourse of fruit-trees...Last of all, the rare workes of your own in this kinde.'[51] Although it cannot be proved that the picture represents a Lawson garden, it is certainly a possibility.

John Parkinson provides six patterns for flowerbeds in his *Paradisi in Sole: Paradisus Terrestris* (1629) (189). The first book that, although it also deals with the orchard and kitchen garden, focuses on 'The ordering of the Garden of Pleasure', an area devoted to the cultivation of flowers solely for aesthetic delight. If Lawson represents the beginning of a move away from knots and French prototypes in favour of Italian ones, that move is total here. Of the six designs Parkinson prints, four are copied from the groundplan of the *Horto dei Semplici* at Padua published by Girolamo Porro in 1561 (190). One of the other two designs is virtually identical to the plan of a quarter of the flower garden of the Duke of Sermoneta at Cisterna (178).[52] That was not published until 1633 by Ferrari which means that somehow garden plans crossed Europe, for in Parkinson we see the introduction of the Italian renaissance flower garden, albeit unacknowledged.

It is Parkinson's delightful book which reflects to the full the motivation behind the Newburgh garden: 'Let every man therefore...take what may please his mind, or out of these or his own conceit, frame any other to his fancy, or cause others to be done as he liketh best...'[53] It was important, he writes, to see that the allies and walks were spacious, as they indeed are, in order to preserve what were valuable plants from harm. He then proposes two methods of outlining such knots, one using hard artefacts like tile or bone or lead and the other evergreen plants – the option used at Newburgh. He lists thrift, germander, hyssop, majo-ram, savory, thyme and cotton lavender giving their drawbacks and recommend-ing strongly, despite its smell, box: 'This...I commend and hold to bee the best and surest herbe to abide faire and greene...'[54]

Parkinson's book was clearly prompted by a spreading interest in plants, par-ticularly spring ones that extended the flowering season by several months:

191. The Caroline garden at Newburgh Priory. Detail of plate 184

192. The Rev. Walter Stonehouse's plan of the rectory garden at Darfield, Yorkshire, 1640. Magdalen College Library, Oxford

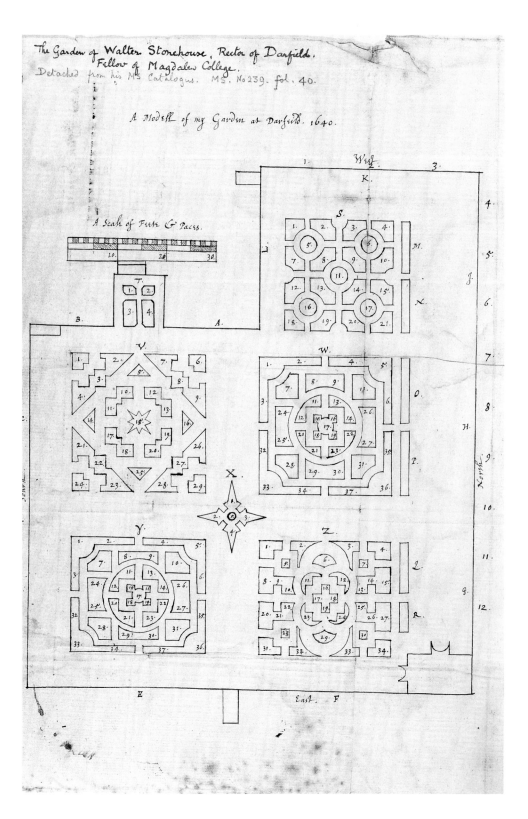

Daffodils, Fritallaries, Iacinths, Saffron-flowers, Lillies, Flowerdeluces, Tulipas, Anemones, French Cowslips, or Beares eares…are almost in all places with all persons, especially with the better sort of Gentry of the Land, as greatly desired…for that the most part of these Out-landish flowers, do shew forth their beauty and colours so early in the yeare, that they seeme to make a Garden of delight euen in the Winter time, and doe so giue their flowers one after another, that all their brauery is not fully spent, vntil that Gilliflowers, the pride of our English Gardens, do shew themselues.[55]

Parkinson had a friend, the Rev. Walter Stonehouse, who was appointed Rector of Darfield in Yorkshire in 1631 where he created a celebrated garden of which he drew a plan in 1640 (192).[56] Although it eschews the symmetry of Newburgh, it is nonetheless a flower garden of the same variety with five different knots in complicated patterns in which were displayed his collection of eight hundred and sixty-six plants. The effect would have been more or less the same. Gardens of this type were still current in Europe in the 1650s. Indeed the Newburgh garden may usefully be compared to that laid out for Count Johann of Nassau-Idstein in the immediate aftermath of the Thirty Years War in 1658, although by that date the rhythms of the design are far more baroque (193).[57]

Conceivably Newburgh was laid out after Belasyse's elevation to Lord Fauconberg in 1627, an action which would fully reflect Parkinson's comment: 'Gentlemen of the better sort and quality, will prouide such a parcel of ground to bee laid out for their Garden...as may be fit and answerable to the degree they hold.'[58] It must have been complete before 1642, but one needs also to ask how did these early gardens survive virtually unaltered for so long? Firstly the family was in the main Catholic and therefore conservative. Nothing would have been done during the Civil War, and when at last the first viscount did die in 1653 the estate passed directly to his grandson who was twenty-five. He was to weather every political storm, marrying one of Oliver Cromwell's daughters, yet being one of those involved in bringing back Charles II and, in 1689, he was rewarded with an earldom by William III for his services the previous year. Evidence would suggest that Newburgh, the family home in the north atrophied for his career was in the south where he had a London house in Soho Square and country house at Chiswick. It must have been due to these factors that we owe the survival of these gardens and their fortunate recording later in the century.

193. The garden of Count Johann of Nassau-Idstein, laid out c. 1650–70. Miniature by Johann Walter executed 1653–61. Bibliothèque nationale de France, Paris

LATE SEVENTEENTH-CENTURY FLOWER GARDENS

Interest in flowers, already witnessed in the gardens of Newburgh Priory, was to be intensified by the Civil War. During the decade preceding the Restoration Royalists, like John Evelyn and Sir Thomas Hanmer, sought solace in gardening and in the cultivation of plants.[59] Hanmer's flower garden at Bettisfield in Flintshire was famous, but, one feels, exceptional. This was a florist's garden, the creation of someone with a deep horticultural commitment to the cultivation of flowers, a member of a network, club almost, which stretched out to his friend Evelyn, to whom he sent plants and gave advice, and on to John Rea. The latter's *Flora* (1665) was to be the most important book on the making of flower gardens before 1700 and Rea dedicated it to Hanmer, acknowledging himself only to be 'the humblest of your Faithful Servants.' From Rea the floral interest passes to his son-in-law, Samuel Gilbert, author of *The Florists vade-*

mecum (1682), later editions of which take us into the eighteenth century. In order to understand the pictures we have of late seventeenth-century flower gardens we need to set them into the context of our knowledge about those created by Hanmer and Evelyn.

It is not possible to reconstruct the appearance of Hanmer's flower garden. Although there is a long description entitled '1660. Flowers in the Great Garden, December, Bettisfield', it is impossible to make the journey from the written description to reconstructing a plan. We know, however, from that written account that it included 'four little boarded beds in the midst of the boarded knot'. There are references to the fact that it was quartered, that there were narrow borders along walls and also ones next to the house, that it included a 'grasse walk' and that the whole garden was enclosed by walls lined with espaliered fruit trees. There was also a 'little garden'. Hanmer, who was cupbearer to Charles I, had spent three years on the continent in the late 1630s returning to England in 1641 and departed again in 1644, this time with his family, returning two years later, his wife having died in Paris. It is evident that he must have been familiar with the development of the flower garden on the continent.

We learn most about the nature of his flower garden from a passage he wrote which was clearly designed as a preface to his *Garden Book*, written about 1653, which he never published.[60] There he describes contemporary garden practice which was 'much different from what our fathers used'. He proceeds to describe the elements of the French garden style that was to be the dominant influence in England after 1660. Instead of compartments being hedged about as they used to be he writes 'all is now commonly neere the house layd open and exposed to the view of the rooms and chambers'. First come 'knotts and borders upheld only with very low colour'd boards, stone or tile', then 'quarters or *Parterre*, as the french call them…often of fine turf…cut out curiously into Embroidery of flowers, beasts birds or feuillages and the small alleys and intervalls filled with severall coloured sands and dust with much art, with few flowers in such knotts and those such as grow very low least they debase the beauty of the embroidery.' Then come 'Compartments as they call them, which are knotts also and borders destined for flowers, yet sometimes entermixed with grasswork and on the outsides beautified with gilt flowers, potts on pedesells and very dwarf cypresses, firrs and other greens…' He is describing what was known, if it focused around cut grass work, as a *parterre à l'angloise*. All of this finally leads on to what contemporaries called the wilderness, 'labyrinths' as Hanmer calls them, a geometrical arrangement of compartments forming hedged alleys and walks.

Where, we may ask, is the flower garden in the midst of all this? That comes at the very end of the passage where he dismisses what has just been described as 'their publicke grounds, wherein all people of quality are admitted to walke' contrasting them to the arcana of the flower garden: 'a little private seminary or piece to sow and raise plants and trees in, and keepe such treasures as are not to bee exposed to every one's view and adjoining to which they have a wynter house for shelter of tender plants in cold weather.' This description makes it explicit that the flower garden was a separate and secret enclosure precisely in the vein of those Italian ones filled with valuable and expensive plants, access to which was reserved strictly to the initiated.

In the case of John Evelyn's flower garden we are fortunate, for he drew a

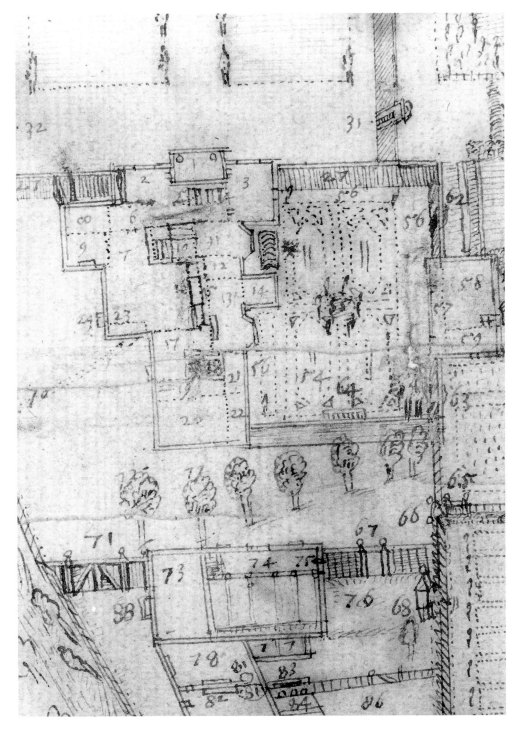

194. John Evelyn's flower garden, c. 1653, consisting of the walled area behind the house, top right, quartered into compartments. British Library, London

plan of of what he intended at Sayes Court, Deptford, in 1653 (194).[61] On his plan number 54 is labelled 'My Private Garden of choice flowers and Simples', a *giardino segreto* which ran along the whole of the back of the house and more. It was surrounded with 'Bricke walles 10 foote high with double gates' and within was quartered with a fountain at the centre. Number 56 draws our attention to 'The walkes or alleyes; at the end of one is an arbour under 2 tall elmes in the Corner. This Garden is walled about.' Sayes Court was a gabled Elizabethan house that was his wife's ancestral home and what Evelyn numbers as his private garden is the area of the old existing garden before he began his massive expansion of it. The lay-out in fact belongs to the 1630s, resembling,

for example, the quartered garden at Durdans, Surrey. It is certainly not of a Serleian complexity. How exactly this would have been planted it is impossible to know.

Evelyn's plan only serves to emphasise the extreme importance of any country-house view that records a florist's garden from the middle of the seventeenth century. One which certainly does is of a long-vanished house called Cheveley, near Newmarket, which was the seat of the Restoration rake, Henry, Lord Jermyn and later first Baron Dover.[62] His career is one long saga of debauchery and political disaster for, being Catholic, he backed James II and spent some time in exile before ending his life in retirement in England. In 1689 the house we see was stormed by a Protestant mob.

The picture, a sparkling work by Jan Siberechts, is dated 1681, a decade on from Jermyn's acquisition of the estate (196). The house and garden can therefore be dated very precisely as belonging to the 1670s. Vertue visited Cheveley in 1725 and although he got the date of the building wrong, 'about 1680', he does record that the house was filled with landscapes and also, more significantly, with 'flowers by Van Son & others'. [63] This suggests a particular interest in flowers, confirmed by the sale of the contents of the Jermyns' London house in 1727 which followed the death of his widow. There again Vertue records landscapes '& some flower pieces of Van Son... & others Herman Verelst –'.[64] Jan Frans van Son was the son of a famous flower painter, Joris van Son, and was an imitator of his father's work. Vertue records him as

a 'Flower fruits & fowles painter'.[65] Herman Verelst, brother of the portrait painter Simon, was likewise notable for his flower pieces.

This indicates that the spectacular flower garden in Siberechts's painting (195) was a reflection of someone who had a passion for flowers. This indeed is a glimpse into 'a little private seminary', although not that little. Whether it was Jermyn or whether, as is more likely, it was his wife, Judith, daughter of Sir Edmund Poley of Badley, Suffolk, it is impossible to tell. They married in 1675. There is no doubt but that this is an exceptional flower garden, the house being otherwise run-of-the-mill. The approach to the residence itself is by way of a quartered grass forecourt, giving access on one side to a kitchen garden (again a rare record), which is smaller than the flower garden that matches it on the other. Beyond that, beneath the other main façade of the house, there is the familiar pattern of grass plats being rolled by a gardener. Nothing, however, matches the flower garden, which must be about 300 feet square and is an explosion of late spring blossom.

The most detailed work to be written during this period on the making of flower gardens was by Sir Thomas Hanmer's friend, John Rea.[66] *Flora: seu, De Florum Cultura* was first published in 1665, although written earlier in the 1650s, and was to go into two subsequent editions. The delay in the initial printing was due to the cost of plates illustrating the plants, and when it did eventually appear it included only plans for the lay-out of flower gardens. Rea's description is so exact that it has been possible to reconstruct diagrammatically exactly what such a garden would look like (197).[67] A flower garden should be twenty yards square

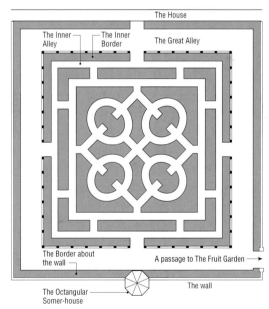

195. The walled flower garden. Detail from plate 196

196. Jan Siberechts, *Cheveley, Cambridgeshire*, 1681, Belvoir Castle

197. Plan for a flower garden, based on a description by John Rea, 1665

198. Flowerbed design from Rea's *Flora*, 1665

199. Sir William Blackett's house at Newcastle-upon-Tyne with a flower garden of the Rea type. Deatil from J. Kip, *Nouveau Théâtre de la Grande Bretagne*, London, 1716. New Haven, Yale Center for British Art, Paul Mellon collection

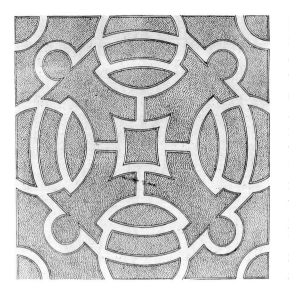

for a gentleman and thirty for a nobleman. It should be sited immediately beneath the south façade of the house and be a walled enclosure lined with espaliered fruit trees rising from narrow beds filled with flowers. Within, the enclosure was to be encircled by a wide sanded broad walk, the 'Great Alley', nearly nine feet in width and within which there was the flower garden proper laid out in what he called a 'fret'. This was a complicated symmetrical geometric pattern of narrow beds held in by boards or other

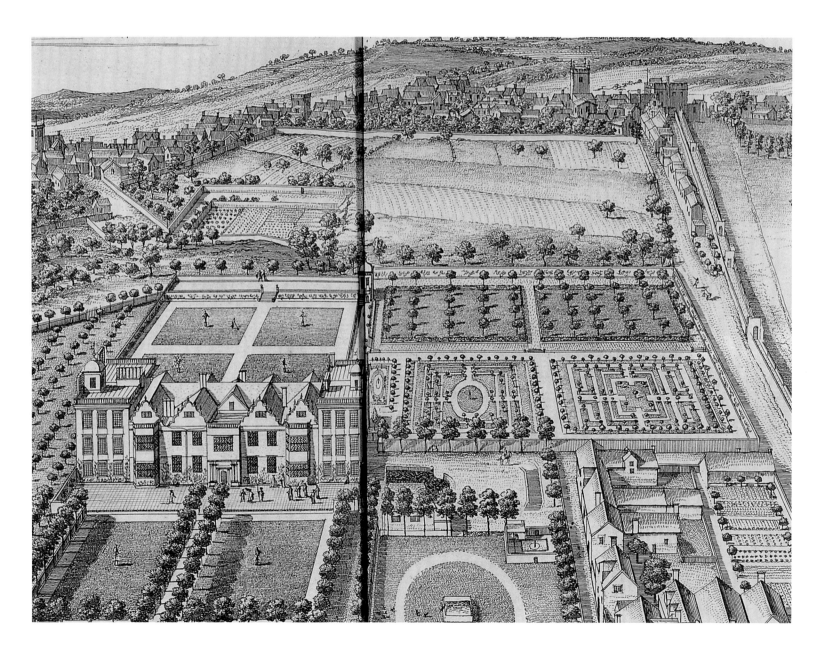

200. Yester, Midlothian, *c.* 1690 with flower gardens top left and right based on designs in Rea's *Flora*, Private collection

201. Designs for flower gardens from Rea's *Flora* (1665) close to those in the garden at Yester

edging, with a narrow walk around them the whole contained within a lattice-frame fence entwined with roses with a narrow bed within it filled with flowers and seasonal plants in containers.

Rea's designs (198), which continued to be published until the end of the century, were already old-fashioned by the time that they were printed, stemming as they did from Italian prototypes of the 1630s. But there is no doubt that gardens based on these designs were planted. Sir William Blackett's house on the edge of Newcastle-upon-Tyne as it appears in Kip's *Nouveau Théâtre* (1708) has a flower garden of precisely this kind (199) and two are identifiable in Scottish sources. A painting depicting the gardens laid out by John Hay, 2nd Earl and 1st Marquess of Tweeddale at Yester, East Lothian, in the 1670s and 1680s has two flower gardens with patterns matching those in Rea apparently cut into the turf (200, 201).[68] And a design probably from about 1690 for the gardens at

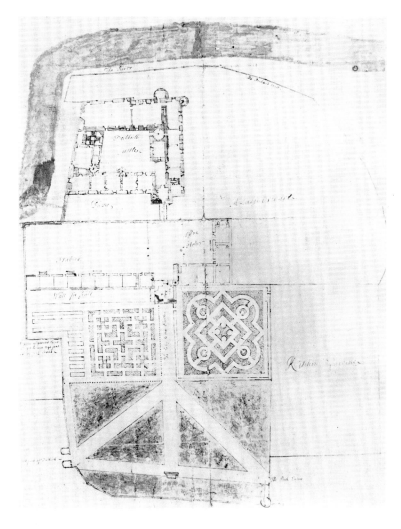

202. A plan for the formal garden at Dalkeith, probably laid out about 1690 with a flower garden, left, copied from Rea's *Flora*, 1935. By kind permission of the Duke of Buccleuch and Queensberry, KT

203. The flower garden design from Rea's *Flora*, 1665, used at Dalkeith

Dalkeith shows a Rea design adopted virtually unaltered (202, 203).[69] A fourth example appears in a drawing attributed to Leonard Knyff of a town garden in Old Palace Yard, Westminster (see below).

But how does Rea's description of a flower garden, and indeed the ones modelled on his designs, square with what can be seen at Cheveley? One is struck less by the similarities than by the differences. In terms of site it is in a quite different location, away from the house in contradiction of Evelyn and of Rea's instructions, although presumably facing south. The size must be about what Rea suggests as appropriate for a nobleman, some thirty yards square. The walls are covered with espaliered fruit and along one wall we can see a narrow bed beneath. But much of what Rea lists is absent. There is no great alley, nor central great 'fret' contained by a lattice-frame fence. Instead the beds would seem to have been cut into the green turf, as there is no sign of any sanded or gravelled walks of the kind visible in the garden beyond around the plats. The descent into the garden is down a flight of steps leading off a walk flanked by an avenue of containers. At the centre there are four identical square sets of beds and along two sides there are more flowerbeds that run directly to the walls. These long beds might be compared with John Evelyn's plan of a 'Coronary Garden' in *Elysium Britannicum*, which is certainly a plan of a flower garden and not one for a border around a parterre (204). The simple angular design of these beds is echoed in those provided by Rea and they compare closely to the many designs in another popular book, Leonard Meager's *The English Gardner* (1670).

The impressionistic nature of the painting technique precludes any precise analysis of the planting beyond the tulips that indicate that the season is late spring. Until the arrival of autumn flowering herbaceous plants from America in the next century gardeners were unable to extend the flowering season much beyond early summer. The extreme lushness of effect is achieved by means of flowers planted close to each other, not spaced apart, and allowed to tumble over the edges of the borders. The absence of topiary reinforces its role as a flower garden, for yew and box eroded vital nourishment from the flowers. The plants are arranged by height as recommended by Rea and the tulips are planted in the inner range of beds in a symmetrical display. As far as can be seen, the planting is not on some kind of rigid grid repeat system which was usual in the four- to six-feet wide flower borders or *plates-bandes* surrounding parterres. The painting by Robert Thacker of such a border around the great parterre at Longleat, recording its appearance a few years after 1684, exhibits a range of symmetrically planted clipped topiary and shrubs arising out of a profusion of flowers planted in repeat rhythms (205). It is impossible to be dogmatic about planting principles due to lack of evidence, although such borders in England, unlike France, were planted by the opening of the eighteenth century with a graduated range of flowers to cover the whole season.[70] In *New Improvements of Planting and Gardening* (1719), Richard Bradley states 'that an agreeable Mixture of Flowers may continually be founin

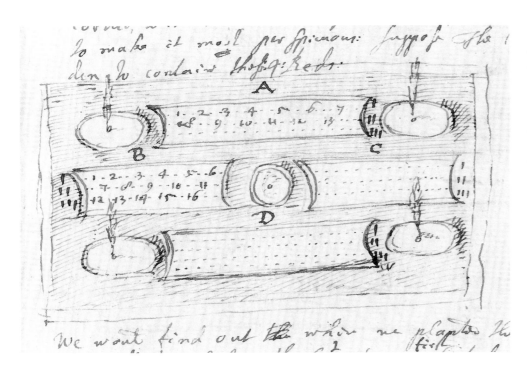

204. John Evelyn's 'Coronary Garden' from *Elysium Britannicum*, *c.* 1655, showing flowers in rows, British Library, London

205. Robert Thacker, *The Great Parterre at Longleat*, *c.* 1700, laid out by Moses Cook and George London from 1683 onwards for Thomas, 1st Viscount Weymouth. By permission of the Marquess of Bath, Longleat House, Wiltshire

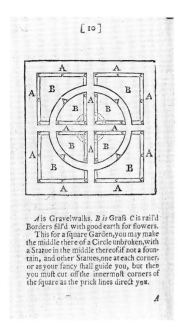

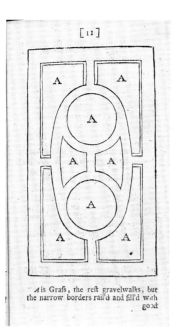

206, 207. Designs for flower gardens in Samuel Gilbert's *The Florists vade-mecum*, 1682, British Library, London

208. Robert Thacker, *The south side of Longford Castle with the flower garden*, 1680s. Engraving

the Garden, succeeding one another so long as the season will permit.'[71]

But what of the flower garden proper? John Rea's son-in-law, Samuel Gilbert, published *The Florists vade-mecum* in 1682, a book which was to go through three editions down to 1702.[72] Gilbert was a collector of auriculas and boasted also of having no less than a hundred varieties of tulip in his garden. Importantly, however, he provides two plans for flower gardens (206, 207), that are of a very different type from those in his father-in-law's book. At first glance we would categorise both as parterres, but he is specific in describing them as flower gardens. One is square and the other for a rectangular site, but the solution for both is identical, a broad, containing gravel walk around an area of green turf divided by cross-axis paths and further paths created by the imposition of a circle or oval. He suggests that such gardens could have a statue at the centre or, more grandly, a central fountain with four statues in the spandrels. Unusually the flowers are all contained within borders around the edges but inset within green turf. The effect is very different from the Rea type of flower garden where the flowers were within intricate patterns of narrow raised beds with sanded walks between. Indeed turf played an important part in this kind of flower garden. Immediately next to the gravel walk Gilbert recommends 'a foot or two foot according to the breadth of your Walk, with good Turf, from whence the heat of the Sun cannot be reflected as from the

Gravel to the prejudice of the neighbouring flowers, making them much sooner lose their beauty and leaves.'[73]

Not long after the publication of this book a garden which almost exactly matches these patterns was laid out at Longford Castle, Wiltshire. The latter had been built to a triangular plan in honour of the Trinity by Sir Thomas Gorges at the close of Elizabeth's reign. In 1641, Edward, 2nd Lord Gorges had sold the castle to Hugh Hare, 1st Baron Coleraine. During the Civil War it had become a royalist garrison so that by about 1650 it had been reduced to little more than a shell. Coleraine, who died in 1667, initiated its restoration and it was completed by his son, the antiquarian, Henry. Robert Thacker made a series of eleven engraved views of Longford sometime during the 1680s (he died in 1687), one of which bears the title: 'The Southside...with the Flower Garden' (208, 209).[74] Some connexion might be adumbrated between the laying-out of this garden and Coleraine's grand second marriage to the widowed Duchess of Somerset in 1682, although that was to end in disaster and they separated. The garden was still there in 1697 when Celia Fiennes visited it:

> you enter the garden on a terrass and that by stepps so to severall Walks of Gravel and Grass and to the Garden one below another with low walls to give the view all at once; here was fine flowers and greens dwarfe trees oring and lemon trees in rtows with fruite and flowers at once, some ripe, they are first the oringe trees I ever sawe...[75]

Turning to what we see of the garden in the engravings, there are no orange and lemon trees, so that the design must have been elaborated during the next

209. Robert Thacker, *View of Longford Castle at an angle with the second flower garden*, left, 1680s. Engraving

210. The Duchess of Beaufort's flower garden and rectangular flower beds similar to those in plate 209. Detail of engraving by J. Kip, from *Nouveau Théâtre de la Grande Bretagne*, London, 1716. New Haven, Yale Center for British Art, Paul Mellon Collection

decade and a half. But the garden exactly follows the plan Gilbert provides in his book. Handsome junipers provide vertical evergreen accents at the corners and there is a fountain in the middle with four statues in the spandrels, exactly as he recommends. The flower borders, which are raised and boarded, extend all the way around the turf areas and there is a series of wide flowerbeds around the central fountain. There is no box edging which accords with the view that it detracted from the nourishment of the flowers. The central beds must be about six feet in width, raised two or three inches, held in by boards and the soil within them level. The beds in the borders are narrower. They would have been planted with a mixture of perennials, biennials and bulbs either intermixed or in blocks. More puzzling is the glimpse of a second garden which consists of a series of rectangular beds that look as though they are filled with flowers. If this was also a flower garden it would link to an identical feature found in a garden belonging to one of the most renowned horticulturalists of the age.

In 1701 Leonard Knyff made a bird's-eye view of what was called Beaufort House which was subsequently engraved by Kip for *Britannia Illustrata* (210). We have encountered the house before when it belonged to Sir Thomas More (19). In 1681–2 it had been purchased by Henry, 1st Duke of Beaufort, whose wife was one of the two Capel girls glimpsed in the foreground of Johnson's great group depicting the garden at Hadham in the 1630s (plate 61). Gardening ran in the Capel blood: one brother, Arthur – created Earl of Essex at the Restoration – laid out a great garden at Cassiobury in Essex and Henry, Lord Capel of Tewkesbury, created yet another on the site of the future Kew Gardens. Both Beaufort House in Chelsea, and Badminton, the family seat in Gloucestershire, became paradises for exotics and flowers under the aegis of the duchess.

Flower lists were regularly sent to her from Beaufort House in the early

1690s so we have exact descriptions of the contents of each section of the Great Garden. It was walled and had flower borders everywhere, but the flower garden proper was sunken and surrounded by a raised walk with flights of steps giving access to it.[76] Within, it was quartered, with a fountain at the centre in the manner of Gilbert's designs, but otherwise unlike them for here were flowers in ducal abundance. Each of the four quarters was held in by a 'pole hedge', that is trees and shrubs bent over and tied onto a lattice framework. The engraving indicates that this incorporated standards rising from it at regular intervals. Within each quarter there were flowerbeds running north–south according to the Kip engraving. In the first quarter the beds were each devoted to one particular plant, crown imperials, anemones, jonquils, tulips and ranunculus. In the second there was a single bed of polyanthuses and others filled with carnations. The last two quarters each had four beds of stock gillyflowers, two each of polyanthus, narcissus and peonies and one each of white lilies and carnations. The walks, judging by the treatment by the engraver, were of grass and the plants were ranged in straight lines.

Due south, across a gravel walk, there was another different kind of flower garden, this time consisting of a series of short rectangular beds, twenty according to manuscript sources but less in the engraving. Seven were filled with gentianellas (felwort?), two mixed beds of auriculas, daffodils, hepaticas and snowdrops, one each of tulips, bachelor's buttons and lily-of-the-valley and four each of auriculas and hepaticas. One wonders whether this is not the same arrangement seen in the rectangular beds in the engraving of the Longford Castle garden.

This pictorial evidence establishes the variety of forms that a flower garden could take by the opening of the eighteenth century. Gardens corresponding to the patterns of Rea and of Gilbert existed simultaneously, but there could be

212. Artist unknown, *Temple and flowerbed in the garden of the Hon. Richard Bateman at Grove House, Old Windsor, Berkshire,* before 1740. Private collection

213. Detail from Thomas Robins, *The Hon. Richard Bateman's flower garden at Grove House, Old Windsor,* before 1748. Private collection

huge variations at the whim of the owner or in response to a site. They are united by their adherence to geometry and symmetry and that was to continue far into the eighteenth century as can be seen, for example, in Kent's design for Lady Burlington at Chiswick (211) in the 1730s.[77] Informality has crept in with the surrounding boscage which is neither a wall nor a clipped hedge but within all is symmetrical in a garden composition of great charm. A rustic temple is reflected in a circular pond that is surrounded by a series of narrow circular beds for the flowers.

An anonymous painting from the 1730s (212) contains the earliest representation known of a circular flowerbed at The Grove, Old Windsor, the home of the Hon. Richard or 'Dickie' Bateman.[78] The flowers are still graduated but the overall effect is of a cornucopia of bloom, a pool of scent and colour erupting as if by accident from an expanse of cool green grass. That was not the only signal of a new treatment of flowers in a new kind of flower garden. The painter Thomas Robins records Bateman's second flower garden (213), a *giardino segreto* in the form of a magical domain distant from the house in which flowerbeds in all kinds of different and wholly arbitrary shapes are cut into the greensward with all the frivolity of the rococo. This is what Horace Walpole was to describe as Bateman's 'kingdom of flowers' and was certainly in existence no later than the early 1750s. It represents the demise of the Renaissance and Baroque tradition as it had been transmitted to this country from Parkinson onwards and the dawn of a new age for the flower garden. In these records of Dickie Bateman's treatment of flowers we see the formula that enabled the flower garden, hidden from sight behind trees and shrubs, to survive the era of the landscape park to re-emerge in the Regency period under the aegis of Humphry Repton.

GARDENS OF THE URBAN RENAISSANCE: NOTTINGHAM AND SHREWSBURY

If pictures of country-house flower gardens are rare, those depicting any form of town garden, are even rarer. Only in the case of London is any more detailed information available. The gardens there were of course exceptional, embracing royal, aristocratic and city company gardens as well as those of the merchant and professional classes. Maps, however, give a vivid impression of just how numerous gardens were in the mid-seventeenth century, although the vast majority of houses had little more than a paved yard. Land within the City proper was to remain at a premium and available space was quickly built over. What increasingly militated against any form of horticulture was not so much the minute size of any garden but more the appalling air pollution due to the burning of coal fires. Such gardens where they existed, whether large or small, were situated in the innermost part of a house with the main reception room or parlour in proximity so as to enjoy the view. Long

214. Old Corney House, Chiswick, Middlesex, and its gardens, 1670s. Detail from the painting attributed to Jacob Knyff. Museum of London

215. A Fellow's town garden at Trinity College, Cambridge; from David Loggan, *Cantabrigia Illustrata*, 1690. British Library, London

galleries were often sited on upper floors affording panoramas of the garden below.[79]

Information as to their design and planting remains opaque, for in the case of most maps the treatment of gardens is schematic rather than the result of direct observation. The emphasis was certainly on produce, fruit and vegetables, rather than on creating a miniature pleasure ground. The earliest painted view of a London garden, albeit suburban rather than urban, shows the grounds of Old Corney House, Chiswick, in the 1670s (214).[80] The view is from the Thames. The garden is walled like that in Lockey's miniature of the More family from 1590s (19) and, although there is a garden house from which to enjoy the river view, the garden proper consists entirely of rows of vegetables in beds, flanking a central path with espaliered fruit trees against the walls. The gardens of Oxford and Cambridge seen in Loggan's *Oxonia Illustrata* (1675) and *Cantabrigia Illustrata* (1690) provide our only other detailed urban source, for they not only record the grand gardens of the colleges but occasionally also give a precious glimpse of the small gardens of the college fellows (215). They capture the conservatism of the garden designs, in style still in the main pre-Civil War. But even they are rare. Most had only a paved backyard.

In the metropolis urban garden design must have moved on, with changes of style and lay-out triggered perhaps by rebuilding after the Fire. A rare drawing by Leonard Knyff looks from one small garden across another towards Old Palace Yard with Westminster Abbey on the left (216).[81] It includes Nicholas Hawksmoor's Jewel Tower in its altered state – work that was carried out in 1718–19 – providing an approximate date. We see a flower garden with nar-

216. Attributed to Leonard Knyff, *Old Palace Yard Westminster*, after *c.* 1718–19, with a view of a garden. British Museum, London

row angular beds arranged in a pattern of the kind seen in Rea's designs. The borders are filled with standard trees and smaller evergreen topiary. In the centre what may be an urn forms a focal point. The house itself has climbers up its walls and two handsome bay windows afford garden views. In the garden from which we look the wall is covered with espaliered fruit, a reminder of the continuing importance of produce.

In this drawing we see the emergence of the urban garden as a place of elegant horticultural display. This only became the norm by the middle of the eighteenth century when fashionable town houses in Mayfair began to include long, narrow, rectangular back-gardens, for which some designs actually survive.[82] The fact that Knyff chose to draw this flower garden at all would seem to indicate that it was unusual. Indeed the town garden as we know it, a long rectangle stretching behind a terrace house was an innovation of the 1720s for upper-class housing. By the 1740s the format had spread to Bath.

Celia Fiennes on her travels in the 1690s leaves us in no doubt that there were town gardens and, occasionally, significant ones. Provincial towns afforded more space, especially on the perimeters, where there would be far less air pollution. These demonstrate the fundamental shift that occurred only after about 1650 that is usually summed up in the term, 'the urban renaissance'.[83] Until that date London alone had offered the aristocracy and gentry a round of pursuits for the fast emerging leisure class. Popular activities included theatre, music-making, promenades, pleasure gardens and opportunities to purchase luxury goods. In the second half of the century circumstances changed as provincial towns began in their turn to assume this kind of role independently

217. Artist unknown, *The garden of Pierrepont House, Nottingham, Nottinghamshire*, laid out in the 1690s for William Pierrepont. New Haven, Yale Center for British Art, Paul Mellon Collection

218. *The Prospect of Nottingham from the East*, with Pierrepont House and its garden on the right. From J. Kip, *Nouveau Théâtre de la Grande Bretagne*, London, 1716. New Haven, Yale Center for British Art, Paul Mellon Collection

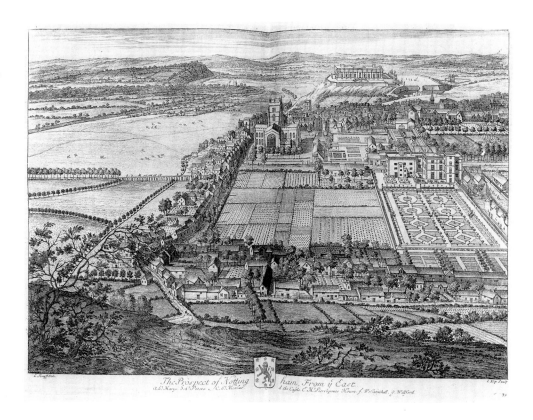

The Prospect of Nottingham From ij East

of the metropolis. The urban renaissance ran in tandem with a consumer revolution. Goods once only available in London could now be purchased in the major towns and cities. As a consequence a new kind of urban society emerged, composed of local gentry who resided part of the year in town, other gentry who preferred to live there permanently, rather than on their estates, and the emergent 'middling sort', members of the professional classes and wealthy tradespeople. All over England there was an urban building boom as town houses were updated in brick in the new classical style that replaced medieval and Tudor wood and plaster. At the same time gardens would have been updated.

Celia Fiennes singles out two towns, Nottingham and Shrewsbury, as being places which attracted the residence of those who she describes as 'persons of quality'. And it is precisely these two towns that provide us with the only paintings of gardens that must have been viewed as quite exceptional, places of parade for this new urban society. Nottingham in her view 'is the neatest town I have ever seen, built of stone and delicate large and long Streetes much like London and the houses lofty and well built...'[84] The oft-reproduced view of the garden of Pierrepont House (217) needs to be set within this context, one which is vividly brought to life in Kip's view of the town from the east where the house and its splendid garden dominates the foreground with the castle in its guise as the baroque palace of the Dukes of Newcastle crowning the hill beyond (218).[85] Nottingham is almost presented as a garden with a town attached rather than the reverse.

The Pierreponts were one of the great landed families of Nottinghamshire along with others like the Willoughbys of Wollaton. The builder of Pierrepont House was a younger son of Robert Pierrepont, 1st Earl of Kingston-upon-Hull and brother of Henry Pierrepont, 1st Marquess of Dorchester.[86] Although

Charles I had raised his standard at Nottingham, the city had passed into the hands of the Parliamentarians. The Pierrepont family like many others was divided in its loyalties. Francis Pierrepont became a Parliamentary colonel and it was he who erected the mansion we see in the 1650s, one of the first to be built in the prolonged rebuilding of town houses through the third quarter of the century.[87] Francis died in 1659 when the property passed to his son, Robert, who veered to the Royalist side, was elected to the Cavalier Parliament and married the heiress daughter of one of Charles I's grooms of the chamber. When he died he was succeeded by his son, another Francis, who was Whig, and on his demise, probably in 1694, the house passed to the creator of the garden, his brother William who sat as MP for Nottingham until his death in 1706.

This is a hugely expensive garden with raised brick terraces on all sides with balustrading near the house topped by statuary and four balustraded staircases descending into it. No less than fifty-seven glazed flower containers are dotted along the walls. There are espaliered fruit trees on the containing walls with narrow beds for flowers beneath and there are more espaliered fruit trees on the terrace walls below also arising from narrow beds for flowers and beyond that frames for plants that needed protection from cold. The upper walk must be of gravel but what material surrounds the flowerbeds below is more contentious; it may be another shade of gravel or some other compacted material. The beds themselves are likely to be stone-edged and there is a central statue forming a vertical focal point, perhaps of the goddess Flora. Any study of the beds as depicted in the engraving and in the picture reveals that the two are not compatible.

The picture surely more accurately records the mirror-image beds focusing on circles near the house and a duplicate arrangement at the opposite end, this time with squares at the centre. Patterns for beds similar to these appear in Meager's *The English Gardner* which, although first published in 1670, was into its eleventh and final edition as late as 1710 (219). The flowers in the narrow borders are planted in a pattern of red and blue. George London and Henry Wise's *The Retir'd Gard'ner* (1706), a translation of Louis Liger's *Le Jardinier fleuriste et historiographe*, describes what we see under an unillustrated section. This is headed 'Of plain compartments' and begins:

> Seeing all those, who are curious in raising Flowers, have not Parterres to put them in . . . such Persons content themselves with a middling Piece of Ground, which they divide into equal Squares, and then mark out Beds by the Line of a like Length and Breadth.
>
> They allow to these Squares, Borders of only Two Foot broad in case the Plot of Ground be little . . . and for greater Neatness sake edge the Beds with . . . flat Stones cut on purpose . . . It is no purpose to give here Designs of Plain Parterres, there being scarce any Gard'ner, tho' never so unskilful, who does not know how to mark them out . . . [88]

Everything indicates that the Pierrepont picture was commissioned to commemorate a recent creation and one wonders what prompted the new design. At the close of London and Wise's *The Retir'd Gard'ner* they print the plan of another garden (220), one which they laid out at Nottingham shortly before the publication of the book and it is tempting suggest some connexion between the two. Pierrepont House had in fact been eclipsed. That other garden was for Marshal Tallard who had surrendered to Marlborough after the battle of

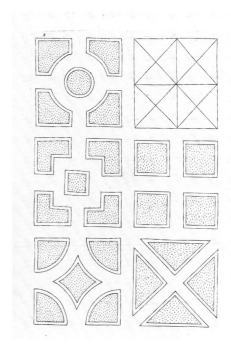

219. Patterns for beds of the type seen at Pierrepont House, from Leonard Meager, *The English Gardener*, 1670

220. Plan of Marshal Tallard's garden at Nottingham designed by Henry Wise. Engraving from George London and Henry Wise, *The Retir'd Gard'ner*, 1706

Blenheim in 1704. He spent his exile in England at Newdigate House in Nottingham, within walking distance of the Pierrepont mansion. There he laid out, in a space which apparently only measured 150 feet in length by 140 in width, an extremely complex garden, cramming into the space three parterres, raised terraces, flower borders, a fountain and a banqueting house.[89]

Marshal Tallard's garden was the acme of French sophistication – the genius of Le Nôtre as it were reduced to the size of a pocket-handkerchief. Its show-piece was a parterre of *gazon coupé* delineating a baroque swirl emphasised by its contours being set against red brick-dust or sand, black coal-dust, yellow sand and 'Spar that comes from the Lead-Mines, or Cockle-shell beaten very fine'. It was what that codifier of the French formal garden, Dézallier d'Argenville (1709) categorises as a 'Parterre de compartiment' and in comparison with the Pierrepont House garden it is almost aggressively francophile with what look like two sunbursts for *le roi soleil* incorporated into the design.

The rest of the garden, however, is far more compatible with what we know of George London and Henry Wise's garden style. Near the house there is a small *Parterre à l'Angloise*, turf cut into a pattern with vertical topiary accents and a fountain at the centre but no flower border. It is close to 'The Form a Parterre only of green Turf' in *The Retir'd Gard'ner* (221). That format is not recommended for use in small gardens except 'in a small Court before a House, or upon a Terrass on purpose to render the House more agreeable', which fits the bill here. The design is virtually a miniaturized version of the vast grass parterre that they laid out at Longleat in the 1680s.

Finally there was the third parterre in Tallard's garden: 'Four Quarters with Verges of Grass, Borders for Pyramids and Flowers, Verges of Grass within, and white Lines of Spar; then the four Grass Quarters, Gravel Walks, and an oval Centre of a Grass Verge and Border.' This is another *Parterre à l'Angloise* and repeats in miniature those that London and Wise had designed for the Maestricht Garden at Windsor Castle. By the time Daniel Defoe visited Nottingham on his tour in 1724 the Pierrepont Garden was not referred to among his listing of the town's 'beauties', unlike Marshal Tallard's 'small, but beautiful parterre', although that comes with a sting in its tail for 'it does not gain by English keeping'.[90] But by then its creator had long since returned to his native country.

The last parterre bears a striking resemblance to the only other known painting of a town garden from the same period. It represents the garden of a house in a street called Dogpole, Shrewsbury, that still stands today (222).[91] The fact that a garden of such sophistication should be laid out there must be considered in the context of the town itself as described by Celia Fiennes on her visit in 1698: 'there are abundance of people of quality lives in Shrewsbury more than in any other town except Nottingham...'[92] Add to that the words of Defoe a generation on: 'This is indeed a beautiful, large, pleasant, populous, and rich town; full of gentry and yet full of trade too; for here too is great manufacture...which enriches all the country round it.'[93] Furthermore, Shrewsbury was the setting for George Farquhar's *The Recruiting Officer*. Dogpole included the town houses of Francis, Lord Newport, created Earl of Bradford in 1694, and of the Rocke family who lived in what is known as the Old House, seen to the right of the house in our picture with a garden of old-fashioned grass plats. The house with the grand garden belonged at this period to a prosperous merchant family, the Peeles.[94] It all matches Celia Fiennes's comment: 'there are many large old houses that are convenient and stately.'[95]

But what of the garden? That is in two parts. A smaller walled garden next to the house and the street is of minor importance, filled with espaliered fruit trees and with one notable topiary feature. The picture sets out to record the main garden, a large brick rectangle with summer houses in the corners – a *parterre à l'Angloise*. There are espaliered fruit trees along the west wall that includes the back of the house up which climbers scramble. Close to the house there is a cistern for watering the garden and supplying the house. A gate flanked by topiary cakestands gives access to the garden from the yard beyond. On the north and south walls there are more fruit trees alternating with an evergreen, perhaps pyracantha, clipped flat against the wall to form a pyramid, but with one branch allowed to grow above it to form a ball. As in the case of Pierrepont House there are narrow beds and also there is pattern planting, this time quite sparse and made up of low-growing white and deep pink flowers (which might be hyacinths) within a tiny box edging. At the centre of the wall opposite the house there is a sundial with a gnomon on

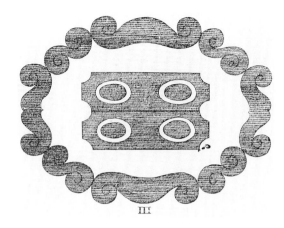

221. Diagram of a turf parterre in London and Wise's *The Retir'd Gard'ner*, 1706

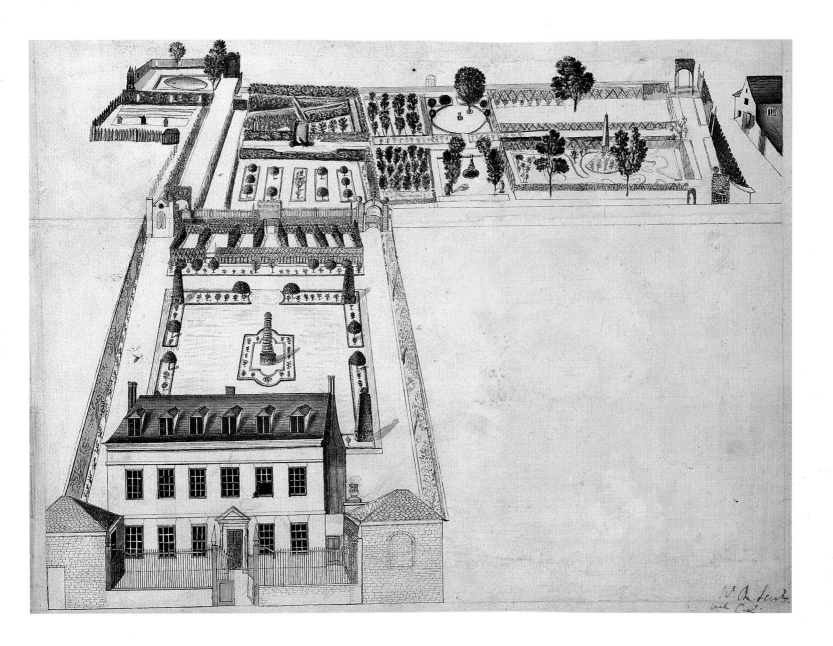

every face and below that there must have been some kind of eyecatcher. The sundial is flanked by a parade of classical busts alternating with glazed containers filled with evergreens. A gardener is busy rolling the broad gravel walk that encompasses the *parterre à l'Angloise*. The spandrels are of green turf punctuated with mopheaded evergreens, perhaps hollies, and clipped yew cones, then a band of brick dust or red sand and finally the outer flower border or *plate-bande* held in by a very low box hedge and with yew cones symmetrically arranged, marking the corners. The central grass oval is outlined with clipped yews and filled with complicated cut-work using various coloured materials and also with two circular flowerbeds. The costume indicates a date around 1710.

The really opulent feature of this garden is the lead figure of *Mercury* after – a long way after – Giambologna. That, together with *Samson slaying the Philistine*, were the most popular of the models available from his sculpture. The figure would have been painted a shade of white to resemble stone or marble. Such a piece presupposes a London source, for their mass manufacture

223. Charles Lewis, *Dr Charles Greville's Garden in Gloucester*, 1750s, the garden immediately at the back of the house is likely to be *c.* 1700. Collection of Mrs Paul Mellon, Oak Spring Garden Library, Upperville, Virginia

222. Artist unknown, *Town Garden in Dogpole, Shrewsbury*, *c.* 1710. Shrewsbury Civic Society

224. George Lambert, *The garden of 10 Downing Street, London,* 1736–40, with a view to the canal in St James's Park. Museum of London

was centred almost entirely on the Hyde Park area of London.[96] By the close of the first decade of the eighteenth century the workshops of both Jan van Nost and Andries Carpentière were in full operation supplying an increasing market for garden sculpture. All these elements contribute to what, in provincial terms, must have been an astonishing garden. It makes no gesture, apart from a few espaliered fruit trees, to produce, but deliberately sets out to be a place of display and public parade fully caught in the elegant figures who stroll in it. Such a picture sums up the urban renaissance and its creation of a distinct 'polite' culture in horticultural terms.

The urban story continues with two gardens that existed in Gloucester in the middle of the eighteenth century. In both cases the new gardens were grafted onto earlier ones. John Hyett, a Gloucestershire squire, may have acquired Marybone House on his marriage in 1744 and gone on to erect the quite extraordinary chinoiserie pagoda garden, but it was an addition to a series of older enclosed gardens that were left untouched.[97] These included a *gazon coupé* parterre that must be far earlier in date. At Dr Charles Grevile's 'knick-knackery' garden at 2 Barton Street (94)[98] a quite bizarre series of gardens were added in the 1750s to a house that was described as 'lately erected' in 1700. It would be difficult to argue that the parterre we see directly behind the house with its *plate-bande* and obelisk yews was not laid out at the time of its building. The yews would have taken years to grow to such a height and density. It is a timely reminder that gardens linger on.

George Lambert's painting of the garden of 10 Downing Street, datable to between 1736 and 1740, takes the story of town gardens into the middle of the eighteenth century (96).[99] It is an example of the Dutch practice of planting in which flowers, especially in the case of a narrow border, were arranged in a single row in a repeat pattern. Here Canterbury bells and lilies alternate with smaller flowers in a rhythmic pattern interspersed, no longer with baroque cones of clipped box or yew, but with shrubs left to grow loose and left seemingly unclipped. This is a concession to the new style of gardening marked by the demise of formality in the years after 1740. However, town gardens throughout the eighteenth century remained resolutely, one might add inevitably, formal, ensuring a continuity of that tradition until its rediscovery after 1800. This remained true during those decades when, on their country estates, the aristocracy and gentry progressively obliterated any traces of the great formal gardens of late Stuart England.

IV

EVERY PROSPECT PLEASES

THE GARDEN PANORAMA

The Family of Henry VIII has already served as a point of departure more than once in this book. In the context of the emergence of sets of pictures depicting a single garden, it is an almost unique precursor of developments in the eighteenth century. Within this single canvas we are given two different views of the same garden (4–6). These twin glimpses represent the seed of a pictorial idea that only germinated at the close of the 1720s. This development depended on the spread of a totally revolutionary concept of what constituted a garden, in which the garden was recast as a succession of carefully composed pictures. This transformation was part of the aesthetic of the revolutionary landscape style that gained supremacy during the first half of the eighteenth century. Garden panoramas, sets of paintings, watercolours and prints present a garden as a series of views, in short as pictures. Some series went on to be engraved, telling likely visitors what to look for when they came. And occasionally what to think, for a great garden like Lord Cobham's Stowe was also a polemic for the opposition, rich in tableaux celebrating ancient liberties seemingly betrayed by the rule of Sir Robert Walpole.

These pictures embody a dramatic change in perception: for the first time we are invited to move through a garden on foot and not, as in *Britannia Illustrata*, to look down on it from an imaginary viewpoint. *Britannia Illustrata* appeared in 1707 and the earliest of the garden sequences date from the late 1720s, pinpointing the shift in observation, and prompting some of the most mesmerising images in the whole history of gardening in England. Some were the work of competent artists like Jacques Rigaud or Balthasar Nebot, others, the work of men like Thomas Robins the Elder, embodying a naivety that still enchants.

Although studies of this or that group of pictures already exist no one has gathered this scattered material together to consider the phenomenon as a whole.[1] Nor has much attention been paid to its iconographical origin, which, though not entirely devoid of indigenous forebears, has its roots on the mainland of Europe.

WILTON GARDEN

The garden at Wilton has been referred to more than once already but it is now time to consider it more fully in the light of a unique document that records its appearance in the first multiple panorama of an English garden ever made.[2] It was published during the 1640s by one Thomas Rowlett,[3] and it consisted of a series of twenty-six etchings (228, 230, 231, 233–6) whose contents were

225. Vista to the lake and pavilion at Claremont. Detail from plate 300

226. Bird's-eye view of the Palatine garden at Heidelberg, from Salomon de Caus, *Hortus Palatinus*, 1620

heralded in the first plate, which bears the title *Wilton Garden* in capitals. That was followed by two plates of text, in English and in French, the latter presupposing a market beyond England, and by two folding plates, one that we have already discussed in the previous chapter, the bird's-eye panoramic view of the whole garden, the other its groundplan. Twenty plates follow which depict various parts or elements of the garden section by section, including particular items like a statue or an arcade or the groundplans of features such as a grotto or a parterre.

Nothing like this publication had ever been seen in England before. *Wilton Garden* stands as a unique and deeply intriguing, one might say almost mysterious, document. Wilton was among the most famous of all Caroline gardens, one categorised by John Evelyn in 1654 as 'heretofore esteem'd the noblest in all *England*'.[4] Its publication during a period that saw the defeat of the royalist cause at Naseby in 1645 and the terrible events leading up to the king's execution four years later is remarkable. In 1654 the plates, which had been acquired by Peter Stent, were re-issued with plate 20, the etching of the cast of the antique statue known as the Borghese Warrior, turned into a new title-plate by adding the words 'A Colecktione of Fountaines, Gardens and Statues' and the date.[5] The text was dropped altogether as were the two folding plates giving a far more compact publication, for the twenty remaining were all the same size. Stent sold the bird's-eye view separately and his 1654 catalogue listed 'Twenty plats of Wilton's Garden.'

Wilton was laid out between 1632 and 1635 for Philip Herbert, 4th Earl of Pembroke. The earl is usually billed as a somewhat rough diamond but in fact he shared many of the cultivated tastes of his family. At the time of the garden's creation Pembroke was a man of huge financial means, thanks to the offices he held as Lord Chamberlain and as Lord Warden of the Stanneries. In 1630 he married a great heiress, Anne Clifford, Baroness Clifford in her own right, who brought with her the revenues of her vast estates in the north of England. She was also highly educated, Samuel Daniel the poet having been her tutor.

According to John Aubrey both the rebuilding of the house and the creation of the new garden at Wilton owed their impulse to Charles I. As was usual the garden went ahead of the house, work on which was not started until 1636, by which time the financial resources of the earl had radically contracted, so that the garden was laid out for a house that was to have been twice the size and which he could no longer afford. By 1636 not only had his marriage to Anne Clifford broken down, but also the large dowry which he had received for the marriage of his eldest son, who died in 1635, had to be returned. The result was the new house occupied only half the width assigned to it.

Aubrey further records that both house and garden were 'all *al italiano*'. Inigo Jones we know was the driving force behind both, chosing as his amanuensis the Huguenot Isaac de Caus. De Caus was, like Jones, something of a polymath, being also an architect, an expert in hydraulics and garden design and, on the evidence of these prints, able to turn his hand to the art of etching. De Caus was the brother of Salomon de Caus, who had worked for Anne of Denmark and Henry Prince of Wales on similar garden projects but who had left the country in 1613 for the employ of James I's daughter, Elizabeth, and her husband, the Elector Palatine. Isaac had been in England since the middle of the 1620s. The garden he laid out for Pembroke, under Jones's supervision, was basically Venetian, a rectangular enclosed space with a broad central path linking the centre of a vast classical villa at one end with a garden grotto at the other. Into this composition de Caus poured elements derived from a variety of sources: parterres in the manner of the French Mollet dynasty, old-fashioned *berceaux,* statuary *à l'antique*, fountains and water effects which looked backed for their inspiration to the great Medici garden of Pratolino. Above all there were a number of features lifted, with but the slightest modifications, from the greatest garden created in the second decade of the seventeenth century, the *Hortus Palatinus* in Heidelberg laid out in the years before 1619 by Isaac's brother Salomon for the Elector Palatine.

The reference to the *Hortus Palatinus* in fact provides a vital clue, for it was the subject of the lavish publication in 1620 that was the prototype for *Wilton Garden*. The *Hortus Palatinus* recorded a garden still in making, indeed one whose completion was rudely interrupted by the outbreak of the Thirty Years War.[6] The etchings record much that was never built raising the intriguing question of whether the same can be said of the etchings of *Wilton Garden*? The publication of the *Hortus Palatinus*, which set out to record a garden that, in the words of its creator, was 'ornamented with all the rarities one can make', was part of Palatine propaganda. It postulated a 'Reformation of the World' by taming the material world and unleashing the potential of its occult forces by means of deploying harmonic proportion in relation to the structure of the cosmos.[7] In the light of this information one must consider whether *Wilton Garden* did have a message.

The *Hortus Palatinus* was undoubtedly the blueprint for *Wilton Garden*. It is made up in exactly the same way, opening with a short text, then folding plates giving a bird's-eye view (226) and the groundplan followed by ones depicting the garden section by section with both views and plans (227). Its

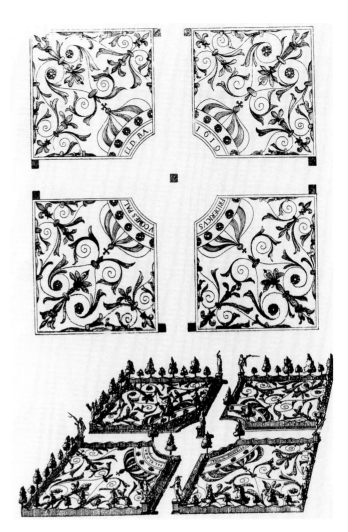

227. Plan and bird's-eye view of the *parterre de broderie* at Heidelberg from Salomon de Caus, *Hortus Palatinus*, 1620

228. Bird's-eye view of the garden at Wilton from Isaac de Caus, *Wilton Garden*, c. 1645–6

forebear must be have been du Cerceau's *Les Plus Excellents Bastiments de France* which gave not only bird's-eye views of this or that château but also the groundplan and occasionally an elevation. The *Hortus Palatinus* applies this treatment to a garden alone multiplying depictions of its features.

The etchings of *Wilton Garden* are accepted as being by de Caus himself and Thomas Rowlett would have commissioned them.[8] In 1644 de Caus published his *Nouvelle Invention de lever l'eau* with a London imprint. It was derived from his brother's earlier publication, *Les Raisons des Forces Mouvantes* (1615). Pembroke bestowed both a pension and a lodging on de Caus at Wilton but it is difficult not to believe that that arrangement was dislocated by the Civil War in which Pembroke took the side of Parliament. At some unknown date de Caus returned to France where he died in Paris on 22 February 1648 and was buried in the Protestant cemetery of Charenton.[9]

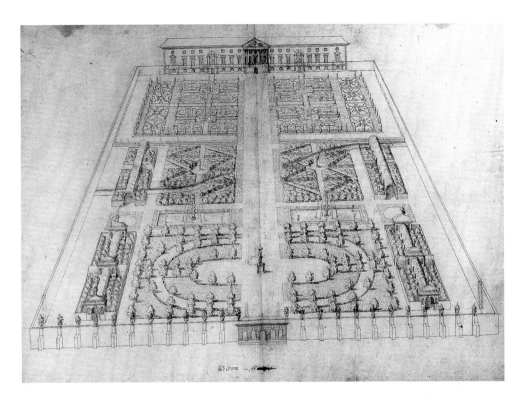

229. Isaac de Caus, *View of the garden at Wilton,* with the great classical villa as originally envisaged, *c.* 1635? Worcester College, Oxford

Although de Caus was probably in London in 1644 for his book, the evidence suggests that he had left England by 1647. In that year a fire at Wilton devastated de Caus's building. The earl turned to Inigo Jones and it was John Webb who supervised the rebuilding, indicating that de Caus was no longer in the country. All this evidence suggest that *Wilton Garden* was published in 1645–6. Rowlett did not set himself up as a publisher until 1645; he continued until 1649, during which period he published a remarkable range of prints, in the main etchings, aimed at a connoisseur aesthete audience.

Wilton Garden cannot have been put together without the consent of the earl. Indeed the opening bird's-eye view (228) is billed as the *Hortus Pembrochianus* with an inscription listing his titles and offices. Unexpectedly, the view is from the house. A drawing by de Caus exists showing the garden with the postulated huge classical villa beyond (229),[10] but a decision must have been taken not to include the south front as it was executed. Instead we are presented with the reverse viewpoint framed within a dramatic staffage of rocky promontories, cliffs, from which twisted and gnarled trees soar upwards and from which we gaze down on what could be a design for a backshutter for a Caroline masque. There is other evidence that suggest that the masque allusion is more deliberate than at first it seems. To one side we discern cavaliers gesturing in astonishment at this vision of paradise, while on the other a horse and rider rear upwards in wonder at the spectacle laid out below. In this way de Caus heightens and dramatises that fundamental premise of the Renaissance garden, the contrast between untamed and tamed nature, of nature as she is found and nature as she has been reformed to accord with the divine, cosmic harmonies through the imposition of geometry, number and proportion. This is the renaissance topos of *representatio*, where visible expression is given to the idea of the patron dispensing power and civilising largesse – the benign image of Eden restored. But it is a closed world for in the garden we see no gardeners but only cavaliers and their ladies.

230. Grand Plan from Isaac de Caus, *Wilton Garden*, *c.*1645–6

231. Flowerbed ground plans from *Wilton Garden*

232. Parterre design by André Mollet from Claude Mollet, *Théâtre des plans et jardinages*, 1652

233. Bird's-eye view of one of the two Wildernesses in *Wilton Garden*

After this panorama comes a plan with dotted lines to indicate the course of the pipes that fed the fountains and other water features (230). It also truthfully records, as does the bird's-eye view, the river Nadder which in fact disrupts the garden's symmetry by cutting right through the middle of it. The next plate carries the explanatory text. This describes some but by no means all of what follows, beginning with fact that the garden is a thousand feet in length and divided into three rectangular areas. In the first there are four *parterres de broderie* flanked by four beds for flowers encompassed by a raised terrace. Views and plans of these are included, although the text does not identify the statuary whose attributes tell us that they must be Susanna, Cleopatra, Venus and Diana. These are amongst the earliest *parterre de broderie* plans to be published in Europe and their relationship to the work of the Mollet family is patent. One of the designs for the flanking 'Platts of fflowers' is virtually copied from one by the young André Mollet included in his father's book *Théâtre des plans et jardinages* (231, 232).[11] As that was not published until 1652 it is evidence that, as we have already seen in the case of the Duke of Cisterna's flower garden (148), such plans travelled on their own. In this section of the garden the plan of each parterre matches those in the overall view but that is not true in the case of the flanking 'Platts of fflowers' where one pattern is repeated whereas in the separate plan there are two different ones. These were in a way knots filled with flowers in the manner of those in the portrait of Lady Holles (124). They did not constitute a flower garden.

Moving on two 'Groves or woods' focus on statues of Flora and Bacchus who are identified (233). However, the river is omitted in the separate prints. On the outer side of these groves were two three-hundred-foot long arbours of the *Hortorum Formae* type, a feature that is repeated in the last section of the garden. Beyond the groves come two ponds with rustic columns topped by an earl's coronet which water 'causeth the moueing and turning of two Crownes att the top of the same...' (234) Then follows the final part of the garden, parts of which are recorded separately, the cast of the Borghese warrior which was at its centre and the great 'Portico of stone cutt and adorned with Pilasters and Niches' with flights of steps, 'whereof instead of Ballasters are Sea Monsters

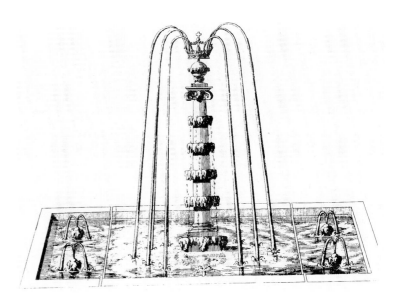

234. A coronet fountain in *Wilton Garden*

235. Unlocated amphitheatre in *Wilton Garden*

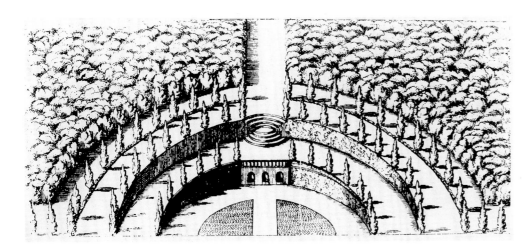

236. Unlocated water parterre in *Wilton Garden*

casting water from one to the other', leading to a terrace which ran the whole width of the garden. There is a groundplan of the portico and two views of the inside of the grotto.

We are, however, left with three plates whose contents cannot be located on the bird's-eye view. One is for an amphitheatre (235) which might have been a continuation of the garden beyond the portico grotto up the hill. There is also a water parterre (236) that emulated the one in the *Hortus Palatinus* but there is no clue as to its siting. One of its sculptures, Venus with a dolphin, still survives indicating that the feature seems likely to have existed somewhere. In addition there are elevations of two quite elaborate arcades, one with twisted Solomonic columns derived from Heidelberg, but again we have no notion as to their location, if indeed they were ever erected. Even more puzzling is the absence of any etching of the grotto's parkside façade which still exists today.

What is the significance of this puzzling publication? In the 1630s the garden at Wilton was one of the supreme expressions of the King's peace, a manifestation of the garden visions seen at the climax of so many of the masques. There they spoke emblematically to the audience of the blessings showered upon the nation by the rule of the Stuart dynasty. Could this possibly be its message still in 1645–6? It seems more than likely bearing in mind that Rowlett the publisher was a royalist and that those who worked for him were associated with the royalist cause, men like William Dobson, painter to the court at Oxford during the Civil War, and the engraver William Faithorne who was aided by Rowlett when he was imprisoned after his capture at the siege of Basing House in 1645.[12] In 1649 Rowlett published the etchings of another royalist, John Evelyn, one set of which was provocatively dedicated to Lady Isabella Thynne, daughter of Henry, Earl of Holland whose head fell on the scaffold shortly after that of the king. Pembroke may have fought for Parliament but when his garden was laid out it acknowledged Charles I who 'did love Wilton above all places, and came thither every summer.' There is something, therefore, deeply poignant and brave about this publication issued during the period following the decisive defeat of the king at Naseby. In the months that followed the remaining royalist detachments were decimated and royalist fortresses stormed or reduced by famine. At a dark hour came this symbol of all that the years of Personal Rule had stood

for. It would have been perused and acquired by the very people who had been present at Whitehall for the court masques. In this context *Wilton Garden* emerges not just as a document in the history of garden design but also as a tremendous and brave testament by the vanquished. No wonder men like John Evelyn and Sir Thomas Hanmer retreated to their estates to garden.

Sometime about 1700 an unknown artist, identified by some as Leonard Knyff, recorded the garden at Wilton as it was at that date (237).[13] It is the one picture in England that anticipates the sequences of garden paintings of the 1720s. Its top half is filled with a bird's-eye view of the garden; the lower half records six vignettes of its various features: the south front of the house as it was finally built; a cascade that came after the 1630s; the stables; the middle room of the grotto; the portico of the grotto; and, finally, the grotto façade. By then the main garden had been altered, the *parterres de broderie* and the *berceaux* swept away in favour of simple grass plats and a fountain, but much was still there. That was to vanish in the 1730s when the 9th Earl, aided by his amanuensis Roger Morris, designed the palladian bridge we see today replacing what was left of the de Caus garden.

237. Leonard Knyff, *Topographical View of Wilton*, c.1700, collection of the Earl of Pembroke, and the Trustees of the Wilton House Trust

The painting was undoubtedly influenced by *Wilton Garden* in presenting both an overall view and then separate sections. However, the idea of such a composition in fact goes more directly back to the emergence of this formula in the Netherlands, out of an indigenous cartographic tradition.

THE CONTINENTAL BACKGROUND TO THE GARDEN PANORAMA

Wilton Garden engendered no immediate successors. When the earliest panoramas of English gardens emerged at the close of the 1720s their source was quite different, looking first to France and latterly to the Low Countries.[14] In both countries the notion of recording a garden in a series of engraved views, if not paintings, had emerged as an established genre decades before. The Netherlands was to play the more prominent part, hardly surprisingly in view of the fact that between 1688 and 1702 they and the British shared sovereigns in the figures of William III and Mary II. It is more surprising that it took so long for this new way of presenting a garden to be taken up in England.

Although Stefano della Bella had executed a major series of six etchings depicting the gardens of the famous Medici villa at Pratolino in the 1650s (238), an act fully in accord with the long tradition of prints celebrating the aesthetic taste of the grandducal dynasty, its successors were to come from North of the Alps.[15] Nonetheless, these depictions of Pratolino were influential, for they were no longer bird's-eye but, rather, a series of views at the level experienced by the visitor on foot and indeed they include people sitting or strolling in the garden. They are also intensely atmospheric, catching this greatest of all mannerist gardens in a state of romantic and imminent dissolution.

By the 1660s multiple views of a single garden began to be issued in France. In the main these appeared under the auspices of Israel Silvestre, who was hugely influenced by della Bella. They had worked together in the studio of Silvestre's uncle, Israel Henreit, the publisher, before he went to Italy in the 1640s.[16] Silvestre's best work dated from after his return but before his appointment as official draughtsman to Louis XIV. To that period belong twenty-two engravings of Liancourt (1654), nineteen of Cardinal Richelieu's Rueil (1661) (239) and fourteen of Vaux-le-Vicomte (*c.* 1665). Silvestre continued to pour out records of the great French gardens, often doing only the drawing and leaving others to engrave, making use of a whole team of artists including Jean Marot, Jean Le Pautre and members of the Perelle family. French prints dominated the market in England after 1660, spreading the French garden style and, although after that date there was no shortage of native printmakers, there was no English equivalent.[17]

These engravings were part of the propaganda machine of Louis XIV proclaiming to the whole of Europe the superiority of French culture and the grandeur of France. Sometimes such engravings would be assembled to form a single publication, like those recording the great fêtes in the gardens of Versailles in 1664 in tribute to the king's mistress, Louise de la Vallière, *Les Plaisirs de l'Isle enchantée* published in 1673,

238. Stefano della Bella, *Pratolino. The Appenino of Giambiologna*, 1650s

239. Israel Silvestre, *Rueil, the Grande Cascade*, 1661

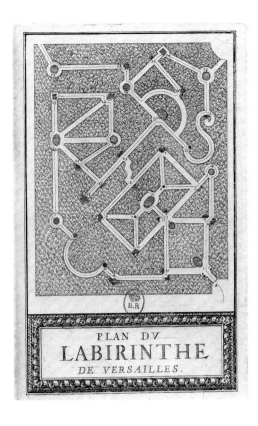

240. Plan of the labyrinth, with the route marked, from Charles Perrault, *Le Labyrinth de Versailles*, Paris 1677. Bibliothèque nationale de France, Paris

241. Fountain illustrating the fable of the cockerel and the fox. Charles Perrault, *Le Labyrinth de Versailles*, Paris, 1677. Bibliothèque nationale de France, Paris

242. Jean Cotelle, *Bosquet of the Water Theatre, Versailles*, 1693, Châteaux de Versailles et de Trianon

or the festivals staged in 1668 but only published in eleven years later, *Cabinet du Roi: Relation de la Faste de Versailles*. Both showed the gardens used as a setting for social spectacle and intercourse of the most exclusive kind.

But probably more important than these for the evolution of the garden panorama was a slim volume by Charles Perrault devoted to the single part of the garden for which he had drawn up the iconography, *Le Labyrinthe de Versailles* (1677). That was based on La Fontaine's translation of Aesop's *Fables* and it opens with a numbered plan of the labyrinth (240), which was one of love, and goes on to lead the reader to its thirty-nine fountain-statues, each of which is illustrated (241). Although the views are devoid of human beings, glimpses of winding paths receding into the distance suggest movement from one place to another. In terms of influence within in England these French engravings must have been very familiar, far more so than the series of twenty paintings of the gardens of Versailles by Jean Cotelle (242) which anticipate their English painted counterparts. These were commissioned in 1688 and went on into the nineties, forming part of the decoration of the gallery in the Grand Trianon. Each is an exact topographical rendering of a particular part of the palace gardens, but each scene is populated by the inhabitants of Olympus. However, the Olympians never disported themselves in a parallel series of paintings of William III's Hampton Court.

The genre was already established in France by the 1660s,

243. C. Huygens, *Vitaulium Hofwijck
Hofstede van den Heere van Zuylichem
onder Voorburg*, The Hague 1653, Haags
Gemeentearchief

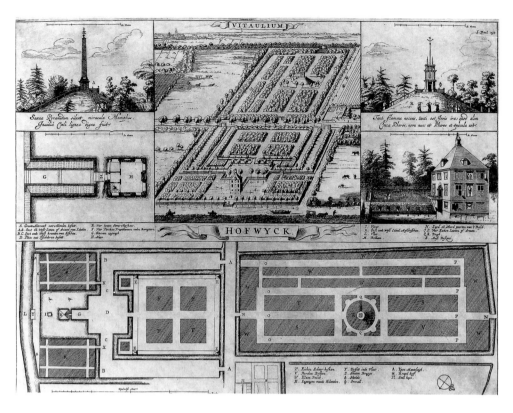

243. C. Huygens, *Vitaulium Hofwijck
Hofstede van den Heere van Zuylichem
onder Voorburg*, The Hague 1653, Haags
Gemeentearchief

and the English were remarkably slow to respond to it. This absence is the more pointed in light of the long sequence of panoramic views of the gardens of the King-Stadholder and his circle in the Netherlands. These poured from the presses in the 1690s as a counterblast to Louis XIV's propaganda machine.[18] In the Netherlands prototypes that were eventually to be utilised in England in the 1720s originated. There the impetus to move beyond the single view of a country house and its domain in favour of a series of different views of the surrounding gardens stemmed from the role of the Dutch country house and its garden as an ideal, particularly in the aftermath of the Treaty of Westphalia in 1648.[19] For the fiercely Protestant Dutch the garden was seen both through Christian eyes as the medieval Book of Nature rewritten in terms of the wonders of God's creation and through humanist ones as the world of Virgil's *Georgics* and the *Eclogues* recreated. The parallel with English attitudes in the seventeenth century was close, but until the eighteenth century England was never to produce as distinct a genre as the Dutch garden poem, a form in which the house hardly figured.

The diplomat and scholar, Constantine Huygens, friend of John Donne and Sir Henry Wotton, published in 1653 a seminal poem about his own country house, Hofwyck.[20] Huygens used a stroll through his estate as metaphor to describe a progress charged with emblematic meaning, more in a practical Baconian sense than in the old Renaissance one. His garden is suffused with deeply personal resonances. The published poem was illustrated with a single engraving (243) which presented to the reader a multiple image, a bird's-eye view of the house, a groundplan of the garden and vignettes of parts of the garden. For the first time the text of a garden poem is connected with a series of engraved views. This single engraving marries two distinct traditions: cartography in the shape of the plans and views that occur in sixteenth-century maps, and the purely painterly one.

244. Cornelis Elandts, *De Werve*, 1666. Voorburg, Westelijk Wegenbow Centrum

245. Fountain at Guntersheim based on Perrault's *Le Coq et le Renard*, engraving from the series by W. Suidde, *c.* 1690, Het Utrechts Archief

We can explore the development of this innovation in a map by Cornelis Elandts of a house called De Werve, near Voorburg dated 1661 (244).[21] Huygens's Hofwyck was the adjoining property and he is likely to have been a major influence on the making of the De Werve garden with its references to classical antiquity and Roman agricultural life. The Hofwyck engraving may well have exerted some influence on the decision to insert at the bottom of the estate plan a series of cartouches. These contained not only views of the house, but also ones of the smart new French-style parterre and the elaborate water garden peopled by classical marine deities. In the 1660s the garden as an individual landscape in its own right sprang out of such a diagrammatic configuration.

That new tradition led to the first series of Dutch garden views *c.* 1690, those by De Lespine and W. Swidde of Guntersheim.[22] These precede the long series that records the country estates of members of the Stadholder's court. The Guntersheim views stem directly out of the Hofwyck tradition but they also show a response to France, for the owner, Magdalena Poulle, the Lady of Guntersheim, built a fountain that was directly based on one in Perrault's *Labyrinthe de Versailles* (245). As a preface to the major sets of garden panoramas we have a series which fuses both traditions, reminding us that the prints of Silvestre, Perelle and the others were eagerly sought after in the Netherlands where they exerted a great influence on garden style.

But the major riposte to Louis XIV's formidable series was

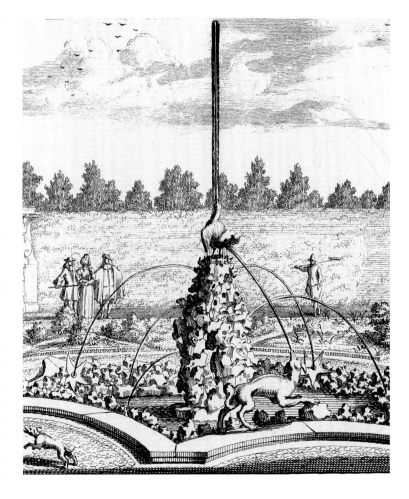

246. A series of engravings of Zorgvliet by J. vande Avelen, Johannes Covens and Nicolaas Visscher, in a late seventeenth-century mounting as a screen, collection Catshuis, The Hague

to follow.[23] Suddenly in the late 1690s virtually all the major gardens became the subject of a series of prints: Dieren, Zorgvliet, Clingendael, Roosendael, Heemstede and, above all, Het Loo. The summation of this came in 1702 with the publication by the publisher and engraver Peter Schenck of *Paradisus Oculorum, sive Conspectus elegantissimum centum*. This consisted of a series of sixteen engravings each of gardens including Het Loo, De Voorst, Duinvel, Roosendael, besides a number of Swedish estates. Then there were the separate series often published in the form of small books like the one on Heemstede with prints by Isaac de Moucheron in 1699. Zorgvliet, the incredible garden laid out by William III's confidant and Lord Chamberlain, Hans Willem Bentinck, Earl of Portland, was the subject of four large engravings and forty smaller etchings by Janne van de Avelen. The smaller etchings were to be mounted as a border to the bird's-eye view and the result hung as wall decoration (246).[24]

The coverage of the royal palace of Het Loo eclipsed them all. The greatest series was by Romeyn de Hooghe and consisted of a large bird's-eye view with thirteen small etchings surrounding it. Others sets depicting Het Loo were by Gerard Valk (1695), Justus Danckerts (*c.* 1698), Carel Allard (1699) and Peter Schenk (1702). Those by Allard appeared in an English publication by the king's physician, Walter Harris, *A Description of the King's Royal Palace and Gardens at Loo...* (247).[25] No doubt many of the others must have been known in England, particularly since between 1689 and 1698 the country was at war with France and the import of French prints came under embargo.

One other source perhaps contributed to the emergence of the panorama and

247. One of a series of eight etchings of Het Loo, by C. Allard, 1699

that is theatre. The seventeenth century saw the triumph of the illusionistic stage and a never ending flow of publications of stage sets, many of which were gardens.[26] Simultaneously the garden, working from the same illusionistic principles, became more and more like a theatre, presenting the visitor with a series of scenes which depended on the manipulation of light and single point perspective. Indeed looking from an engraving of a peopled garden to one of a stage set filled with costumed actors one realises the fragility of the borderline. Innumerable books were published recording the stunning stage visions conjured by masters of the baroque theatre such as Torelli, particularly for the new genre of opera. Significantly the first great series of paintings of a garden in England was commissioned by a man who not only was familiar with Italian operatic spectacle but was also a major patron of the Italian opera in England, Richard Boyle, 3rd Earl of Burlington. Nor should it be forgotten that he had in his collection Inigo Jones's designs for the court masques which included the garden scenes.

The English Garden Panorama

Seeing a garden as a series of pictures was not commonplace in England until after 1750. Although much earlier Alexander Pope is recorded as having said that 'all gardening is a landscape painting, just like a landscape hung up',[27] this notion did not gain common currency until the third quarter of the eighteenth century. By then the concept of looking at gardens as a sequence of pictures had developed to such an extent that Horace Walpole in *The History of the Modern Taste in Gardening* (1771) could write of them as 'a succession of pictures'.[28] This pictorialism became general in the 1750s and by the heydey of 'Capability' Brown it became standard to discuss gardening in terms of painting, and then to progress from a discussion of the great landscape painters to one on the great garden designers, as though they were two aspects of the same aesthetic.

The earliest and most important paintings and engravings of gardens belong

248. William Kent, *Rousham: The Vale of Venus*, c. 1737–41. C. Cottrell-Dormer, Rousham

to the period running from about 1730 to 1750 when the old garden style, which depended on the exercise of geometry and mathematics as reflections of the structure of the cosmos, was replaced by one that worked solely in pictorial terms. The transition was made by William Kent, who worked without 'either level or line' and whose garden designs are in fact pictures.[29] They use pen, ink and wash to present to a patron the effect of light and shadow on a garden, even showing the mystery of moonlight (248). These sketches are concerned with recording the effect of reflections in water, with catching only partial glimpses of a building through trees, with sophisticated asymmetrical orchestrations of perspective, with emphasising how a garden was a space through which people moved on foot, horseback, in a coach or boat. Their reference is to painting, to the landscapes of Claude, for instance, which evoke Ancient Arcady. Although this was well underway in the 1730s, it remained an avant-garde approach until the middle of the century. Once the notion caught on that a garden was a series of pictures, the step to recording them in that way was an obvious one.

More and more garden historians now recognise that the period before Brown, which witnessed the dissolution of the old formal style, was one of extraordinary innovation of a kind which makes the landscape design of the second half of the century seem positively dull by comparison. Firstly Charles Bridgeman and then William Kent dissolved the style of London and Wise as serpentine walks proliferated, ha-has replaced walls, ponds and streams took the place of formal fountains, vistas and views bringing in the country around became the norm and garden architecture and sculpture sprang up with the aim of provoking an associational response in the mind of the visitor. There is no sameness about these gardens as there is about those before 1700 and after 1750. They are idiosyncratic and original, the garden used as a vehicle for a whole raft of moral, political and personal allegory and emblem conjuring up loyalties, memories, affiliations and bewailing the loss of friends.

During this period the garden panorama emerges, charting exactly the visual

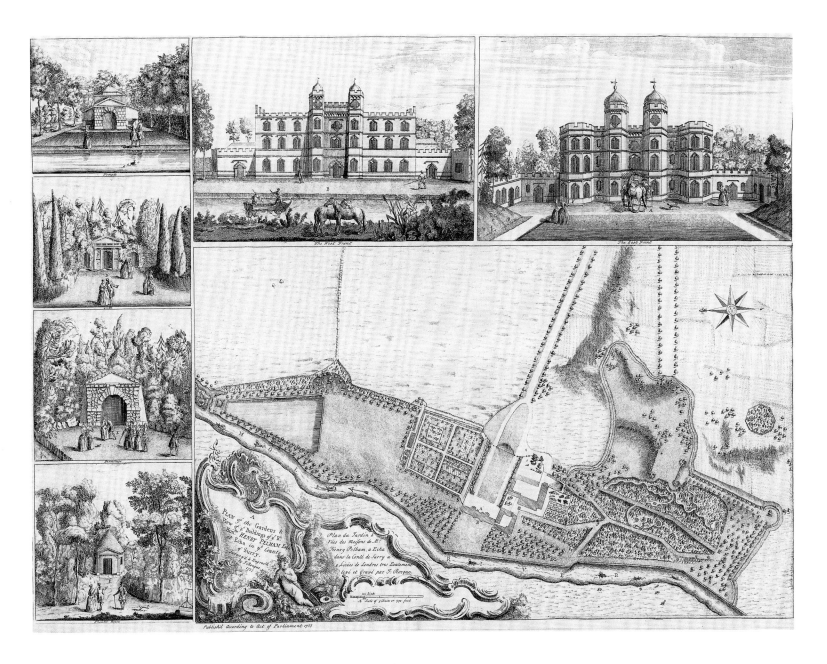

249. J. Rocque, Plan and views of Esher, 1737, British Library, London

journey from the old cartographic and topographical traditions to one that unashamedly records a garden as a picture. That transition is vividly caught in the work of the cartographer John Rocque who, between 1734 and 1740, was to produce a number of large garden plans in a quite idiosyncratic manner surrounded by inset views of architecture or other garden features.[30] Coming directly out of the Netherlandish tradition these prints break up each garden into a series of isolated visual experiences that in essence are pictures. He established his format in 1734 with *An Exact Plan of the Royal Palace Gardens and Park at Richmond* and went on to issue a whole series covering major gardens of the period including Chiswick (1736), Esher (1737) (249), Claremont (1738 and 1750), Wrest (1735 and 1737) and Wilton (1746). Ten of his surveys were included in Rocque and Badeslade's *Vitruvius Brittanicus Volume the Fourth* (1739). This established a market for such prints sold by subscription.

However, the old tradition of painting estate portraits did not wither. That continued and in many cases provides important information on gardens long since

250. John Harris the Younger, one of four bird's-eye panoramas of Dunham Massey Hall, Cheshire, 1751, recording the grounds as reordered by the 2nd Earl of Warrington in the 1730s. The National Trust

251. Jo. Lange (Langs?), *Castle Hill, Devon: prospect from the hill above the house toward the north*, 1741, one of a pair of paintings, showing the gardens laid out by Hugh Fortescue, 1st Earl of Clinton in the 1730s. Destroyed

gone. It is typified by the work of John Harris the Younger in his four breath-taking aerial views of Dunham Massey Hall, Cheshire, dated 1751 (250), or the mysterious 'Jo: Lange' (Langs?), whose two views of Castle Hill, Devon, dated 1741 provide a record of an astonishing formal garden laid out about 1730 (251).[31] But that was a very different thing from commissioning a series of images whose overwhelming focus was the garden around the great house. They could take the onlooker on a tour of its beauties, focusing the eye on a single feature or vista as it would have been encountered, and sometimes going on to people these domains with polite society and gardeners at work. The emphasis of such pictures was on the key criterion of the new garden style: variety.

These sets of pictures were a quite new departure whose credentials were established in the 1730s and 1740s in a series of commissions that established the genre. The earliest set was of Lord Burlington's villa at Chiswick, on the outskirts of London, executed between about 1729 and 1732. At about the same time the Duke of Kent commissioned views of Wrest Park, Bedfordshire, which survive in watercolour sketches but which never proceeded to be paintings. In 1733–4, under the aegis of Charles Bridgeman, Lord Cobham's garden at Stowe, in Buckinghamshire, was recorded by Jacques Rigaud with engraving in mind. Also in 1734 Lord Pembroke commissioned from George Lambert a set of four views of the surroundings of his villa on the Thames at Blackheath. Finally come Balthasar Nebot's seven canvases of the gardens at Hartwell House, Buckinghamshire, dated 1738, and the anonymous views of Claremont, Surrey, arguably dating from the 1740s but almost certainly later. By the time that these were painted garden visiting had become a popular pastime and sets of engravings were being issued for tourists.

AN ENIGMATIC ARCADIA: CHISWICK HOUSE

The garden of Chiswick House, Middlesex, has the distinction of being visually recorded more than any other eighteenth century garden. It was also the first English garden ever to be the subject of a complete series of paintings by the artist Pieter Andreas Rysbrack executed around the year 1730. Three years later the French topographical artist, Jacques Rigaud, executed a second series of views, this time in grisaille watercolour clearly with engraving in mind, although this never happened. In 1735 engravings after some of the Rysbrack canvases were issued and in 1736 John Rocque produced one of his garden plans which included vignettes of most of the important structures within the Chiswick garden (252). Six years later George Lambert, the landscape painter, was commissioned to paint two more views and, finally, in 1753 came a series of six engraved prospects by John Donowell. Reprints of all these engravings continued to be issued until early into the next century, testimony both to the garden's fame and to the public's intense interest in it. We are confronted with an unprecedented glut of visual information about one of the most famous gardens of the age.

Partly as a consequence of that, few other eighteenth-century gardens have attracted such a torrent of scholarship as this creation by Richard Boyle, 3rd Earl of Burlington and 4th Earl of Cork.[32] And yet it would be true to say that the exact motive behind the garden and its meaning, if indeed it had one and it is difficult to accept that it did not, remains opaque. The reason for this can be laid at the door of its mysterious and taciturn creator, whom modern research has suggested but not wholly proved to be a crypto-Jacobite, a kind of double

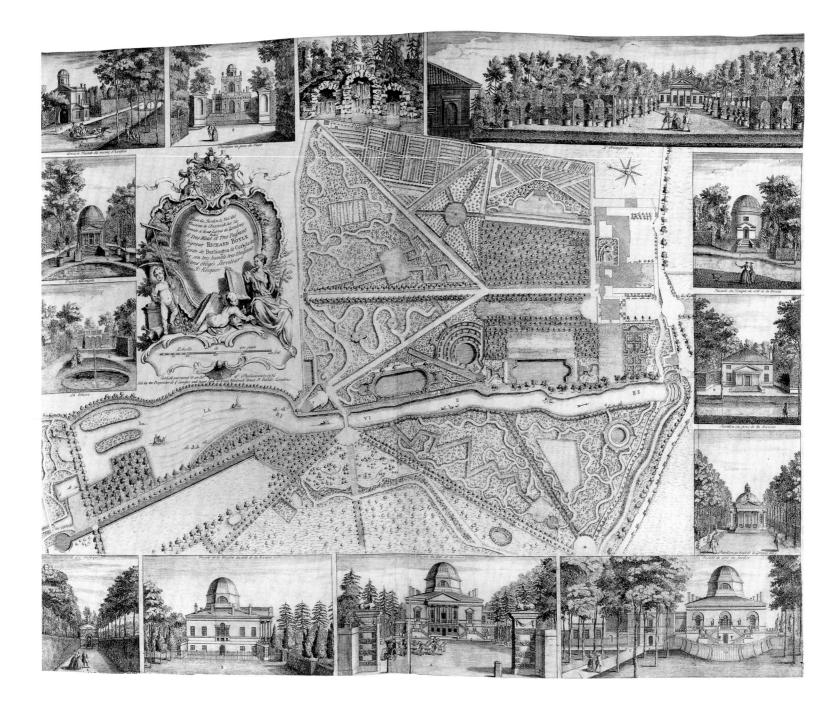

252. John Rocque, Plan and views of
Chiswick House, Middlesex, 1736

agent. On the surface he was taken to be a pillar of the new Whig establishment
ushered in by the Hanoverians, but, beneath that he had an alter ego as 'Mr
Buck', one of those who acknowledged the legitimacy of the king over the
water, James III.[33] As this has come to light, the famous villa at Chiswick (built
in a style which posterity has firmly associated with the Whigs) is adumbrated
to be something very different, a shrine to the exiled Stuart dynasty.

This knowledge must have implications for the reading of the garden, which
continues to defy any attempt to interpret its plot. If the subtext of the earl's promotion of an architectural style based on Inigo Jones's interpretation of Ancient
Roman architecture was, as advanced by some scholars, a hoped-for restoration
of the Stuarts, his horticultural vision should equally harbour such thoughts.
Chiswick was laid out during the very years when the return of the Stuarts was

still a real possibility. Indeed it was not until the defeat of the young Pretender in 1745 that hopes were finally dashed. However, there is in fact nothing in the garden that one could construe as an allusion to the exiled dynasty.

Scholars have already noted resemblances between one of William Kent's designs for Chiswick in the thirties and one of Inigo Jones's masque designs which Burlington purchased in 1723.[34] There are other designs which evoke the ambience of Chiswick with its classical temples nestling at the end of vistas or within groves. But those designs reflect Jones's own ambition to introduce into England the full fruits of Italian Renaissance garden design in the form of compartments, vistas, parterres, symmetry and grottoes. His set design based on the great parterre at Nancy and the garden of the princely villa at the close of *Coelum Britannicum* actually promote what Burlington and proponents of the landscape revolution set out to banish. The revival of Caroline architectural style was not matched by a similar return to its horticultural aspirations.

Burlington was educated at the hands of those in the forefront of the new ideals of the gentleman as connoisseur of the arts. When he first went to Italy in 1714 his interests were listed as 'Painting and gardening', but in fact his chief enthusiasm was for music and above all opera. And no one could deny that the garden created at Chiswick in the 1720s and 1730s was theatrical. Burlington was to be a major patron of the Italian opera and of Handel. It cannot therefore be a coincidence that the artist chosen to paint the first set of garden views was in fact also one who designed and painted sets for the theatre. On that first visit to Italy we know that Burlington visited the gardens of the villa Borghese in Rome and those of Mondragone and Aldobrandini at Frascati. But that is all that is certain. There is not a shred of evidence to support a tour of the major Italian gardens or of importing what he saw as a garden revolution.

Burlington's second visit to Italy in 1719 was not garden oriented but architectural, a desire to launch a revolution based on the works of Palladio and Inigo Jones. And both visits anyway were so eccentric in their choice of places and duration of stay that their subject at heart may well have been Jacobite intrigue. Be that as it may, by the middle of the 1720s the garden at Chiswick had come to be regarded as presaging a new style. 'The whole Continuance of the gardens', wrote John Macky in his *Journey* in 1724, 'is the Effect of his Lordship's own Genius, and singular fine Taste.'[35]

For all the outpouring of material it is surprising how little is actually known about the genesis of the Chiswick garden. Burlington, who had extensive estates in Yorkshire with a house at Londesborough and a palatial residence in Piccadilly, inherited a Jacobean mansion at Chiswick whose gardens are recorded in *Britannia Illustrata* (253). These are typically late Stuart and of no great distinction, although one of the existing avenues, that on an axis with the west side of the house, was to be Burlington's point of departure, when in 1716 he commissioned the architect James Gibbs to design the Domed Building at its far end. In this the Earl was adding a magnificent pavilion at the close of an existing feature, much in the same way as happened at Wrest Park with its canal. Gibbs usually worked with Charles Bridgeman but no one has been able to prove that Bridgeman had a hand in the initial alterations at Chiswick.

A second avenue, to the left of this central one, branching towards the boundary brook was planted by 1717, the date of Burlington's own first architectural essay, the Bagnio, which formed its climax. Whether the right hand avenue was also planted at this time or not to form a *patte d'oie* is unknown.

253. The house and garden at Chiswick as
inherited by Lord Burlington, from J. Kip,
Nouveau Théâtre de la Grande Bretagne,
London 1716, New Haven, Yale Center for
British Art, Paul Mellon Collection

254. Map of the Chiswick estate with
Rysbrack's viewpoints marked

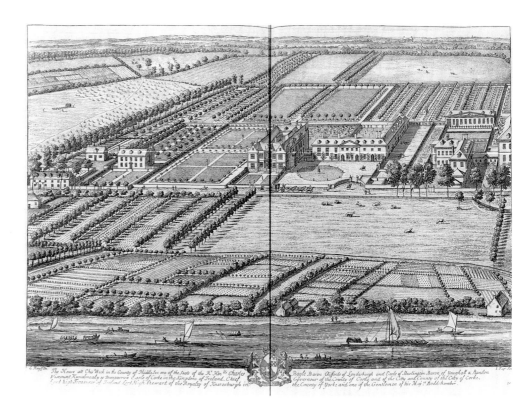

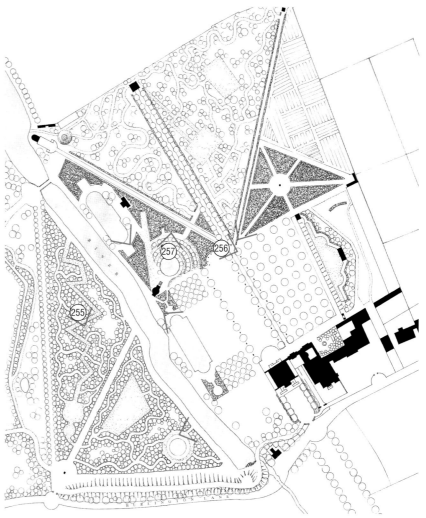

255. Peter Andreas Rysbrack, *View from across the new gardens toward the Bagnio, c.* 1728–32. Present whereabouts unknown

John Harris argues that it came after Burlington's second visit to Italy after which the Earl designed the Rustic Arch which formed its eye-catcher.

Everything indicates the pragmatic and the piecemeal. Thus far it was Burlington's own buildings that were revolutionary and not the garden, for this kind of formal *patte d'oie* went back to Hampton Court in the 1660s. Then, in 1721 when Burlington married the heiress, Dorothy Savile, the garden seems to enter a new phase. Between that date and 1728 there ensues a period of intense activity. The villa was to go up from 1725 while in the garden two geometric basins were dug by the canal, one with the Temple by the Water and the other bounded by topiary exedras. Between them was sandwiched the Orange Tree Garden presided over by its elegant temple and obelisk sited in the middle of a small circular pool. The design for the temple was published in 1727.

Then, in 1726–7, land was acquired on the other side of the Bollo brook, precipitating a wholesale revision of what had been done so far. The brook itself was enlarged to provide the illusion of a river while both Bagnio and Orange Tree Temple had to be supplied with reverses worthy of acting as the focal points of the vistas laid out on the new land. It was on the occasion of the completion of these and the planting of the newly acquired land that Peter Andreas Rysbrack was commissioned to paint a set of eight views (255–7).[36]

Although the suggestion has been made that Burlington was inspired to do this by a set of prints of the Chinese imperial gardens in his possession[37] there seems little point in looking beyond the ample precedent set by Dutch and French engravings. Burlington chose a minor painter, one who would do precisely what he was told. Vertue, writing in 1730, records that Rysbrack 'paints dead fowls Landskips & other things. in a very good & masterly tast he has much improvd his manner of painting, with spirit free pencilling. different from a heavy labour'd manner, as he used in Flanders.'[38] Rysbrack, whose brother John Michael the sculptor also worked at Chiswick, was Antwerp born and bred, arriving in England around 1720 to take his place in a circle of immigrant painters that included Peter Tillemans.

When exactly were these pictures painted? Linda Cabe has argued that the commission went in two phases, the first the two larger panoramic canvases (255), which, joined together, give the whole sweep of the Chiswick garden as

256. Peter Andreas Rysbrack, *Chiswick: vistas to the statue of Cain and Abel, the Bagnio and the Domed Building, c.* 1728–32. Devonshire Collection, Chatsworth. By permission of the Duke of Devonshire and the Chatsworth Settlement Trustees

257. Peter Andreas Rysbrack, *Chiswick. View of the Orange Tree Garden, c.* 1728–32. Devonshire Collection, Chatsworth. By permission of the Duke of Devonshire and the Chatsworth Settlement Trustees

seen from the opposite bank of the canal, followed five or six years later by the other closer-focus canvases. The two larger panoramas have to be after 1726–7 when the land was acquired and, judging by the young planting, cannot be earlier than about 1728. It would logical conclude that the whole series must have been complete by 1733–4 when Rigaud began work on a second set. And we must also take into account the payment of £40 on 25 September 1732 to 'P: and: Rysbrack'.[39] I see no reason for a gap of five or six years in the commission which it is reasonable to conclude was executed as a whole between 1728 and 1732.

The views record the garden before it was naturalised at the hand of William Kent in the 1730s. In terms of England they represent a new departure, a set of pictures commemorating an aristocratic garden, one which focuses on its individual features, in particular architectural ones. The pictures are notable for the absence of either the owner or his wife, peopled instead by working gardeners and a sprinkling of elegant company making the point that gardens were one of the arenas for polite society. Although these figures are anonymous they record a reality, for Burlington was one of the first to open his garden for a fee to members of the polite classes. Such a series assumes that they were painted to hang in a particular place, probably Burlington House, but we have no way of knowing and no sooner had Rysbrack finished them than the Burlingtons moved virtually permanently to Chiswick, abandoning London. There is a further complication in that two sets of these views seem once to have existed and they included variants. The second set, which was sold in this century, was in the possession of Burlington's sister who had married into an old Catholic recusant family, the Bedingfields of Oxburgh Hall. The set which today survives at Chatsworth is made up of pictures from both sources while others are scattered elsewhere or have not surfaced since their sale.

What they cover, or rather do not cover, of the garden is revealing. They open with the two largest which together provide a wide-angle lens view of it in its entirety. Two more provide a 180-degree coverage of the vistas from the modest *patte d'oie*: the statue of Cain and Abel, the Bagnio, the Domed Building and the Rustic Arch, the Doric Column topped by Venus and the Deer House (256). There are separate pictures of the Orange Tree Garden and of the two water basin gardens by the canal (257) as well as one of the less formal water gardens close to the Bagnio. None of the pictures is able to conceal the flatness of the site or that this was an inward looking garden devoid of prospects towards borrowed landscape. Virtually every canvas records formality, although it is of a kind which is asymmetrical in itself for there is no axis relating to either house or villa. Some areas, those to the north and north-east, are not covered at all. In terms of innovation it is the architecture which forms the news, although the mixture of regular and irregular planting on the opposite bank must surely have been in response to Robert Castell's *The Villas of the Ancients Illustrated* which was dedicated to Burlington and published in 1728, at the very time when the garden was planted. In this the Earl would have read of Pliny's villa with its contrasting regular and irregular areas. What the pictures do capture, and they must have been painted under Burlington's direction, is the fulfilment of the quest for variety. Indeed Chiswick fully lived up to Alexander Pope's injunction in his famous *Epistle to Lord Burlington* published in 1732:

258. Jacques Rigaud, *Chiswick. View of the Temple by the Water,* 1733–4. Devonshire Collection, Chatsworth, by permission of the Duke of Devonshire and the Chatsworth Settlement Trustees

To build, to plant, whatever you intend,
To rear the Column, or the Arch to bend,
To swell the Terras, or to sink the Grot;
In all, let Nature never be forgot.
But treat the Goddess like a modest fair,
Nor over-dress, nor leave her wholly bear;
Let not each beauty ev'ry where be spied,
Where half the skill is decently to hide.
He gains all points, who pleasingly confounds,
Surprizes, varies, and conceals the Bounds.
                    (ll. 47–56)

Rysbrack's approach to the garden is topographical and exact. There is no attempt to rearrange what he sees to make a better picture. This is the painter as camera and not artist. Nothing else could explain aberrant compositional features like the *allées* that slide off the edge of the canvas.

Jacques Rigaud's eight drawings of Chiswick (258, 2559) follow hard on the heels of the Rysbracks and one wonders why.[40] There must have been a reason. Do they indicate dissatisfaction with Rysbrack's work? That could be the answer, for their intent must have been, as was the case with the parallel series of Stowe to engrave. Rigaud undoubtedly bestows on Chiswick a high glamour and grandeur totally missing from Rysbrack's somewhat pedestrian and matter-of-fact records. The Rigaud commission, however, ended in disaster for artist and patron fell out. It was Charles Bridgeman who invited Rigaud to England

in 1733 to execute views of gardens for the purposes of issuing engravings. Rigaud ran a highly successful business in Paris in the rue Saint Jacques issuing engravings of the palaces, châteaux and gardens of Louis XV's France. Vertue provides us with an account of the fall-out with Lord Burlington:

> (Mons. Rigaud) who agreed to draw each drawing for 12 guineas. some being larger than others, when they were done insisted on it by agreement to have 24 guineas, some being larger than others, such my Ld proued to be a falesety, and did pay only his agreement, and sent him away like a lying ras[ca]l.[41]

These drawings can be firmly dated to the years 1733 to 1734 and consist of three larger panoramic views and five smaller closer focus ones. They largely repeat the viewpoints of Rysbrack, indicating that their purpose was to replace his vision with the public through engraving. Three, however, give us new viewpoints and information, one provides the only record of the grove of trees at the back of the house, a second a view of the front of the Burlington Lane Gate approach and a third the *rond point* on the opposite bank with the Obelisk and vistas along three alleys. Far more sophisticated than Rysbrack, Rigaud's response to Chiswick is to wave a wand over it, widening its narrow allées, inserting buildings which were never to be built (no doubt under Burlington's direction) adding foreground space to create stages in which a teeming mass of elegant company could disport themselves. All this animation and hustle in fact embodies the superimposition onto the English garden of something typical of

259. Jacques Rigaud, *Chiswick. View from the front of the Burlington Lane Gate at the rond-point with obelisk, looking along three alleys,* 1733. Devonshire Collection, Chatsworth, by permission of the Duke of Devonshire and the Chatsworth Settlement Trustees

260. John Donowell, *Chiswick: View from the back of the villa towards the exedra*, one of a set of six views, 1753, Museum of London

A View of the Garden of the Earl of BURLINGTON, at CHISWICK, taken from the Top of the Flight of Steps leading to y Grand Gallery in y Back Front.

Veüe du Jardin du Comte de BURLINGTON, a CHISWICK, prise du haut du Perron qui conduit a la Grande Gallerie.

Printed for John Bowles N°13 in Cornhill, Carington Bowles N°69 in S.t Pauls Churchyard, Rob.t Sayer at the Golden Buck in Fleet Street London.

the French tradition. The French used their gardens for socialising and theatre. The English, in sharp contrast, utilised their gardens not only for physical but also for intellectual exercise. Meditation in the garden was a common practice in the eighteenth century and indeed the new garden style reanimated it.

The Rigaud series also needs to be placed in the context of what was happening to Burlington himself. In 1733 he went into opposition over the Excise Bill and in May of the same year he resigned his offices at court. With that he moved his focus of residence from Burlington House to Chiswick, precipitating not only the construction of a link building between the old Jacobean house and the new villa but a new phase of garden alterations under the aegis of his protégé William Kent. How do these major events in his life relate to the Rigaud commission? Was the hoped-for publication of a series of engravings after them seen as in some way a political as well as an aesthetic statement? Burlington may not have preceded with a series of engravings after Rigaud but in 1734 some of the Rysbrack pictures were engraved by Claude du Bosc. The very act of engraving took his viewpoint out to a wider public.

More or less simultaneously with the Rigaud commission Kent was to set about naturalising the garden. In 1733 he swept away part of the grove, of which Rigaud provides the only record, to lay out an expanse of lawn ending with an exedra of clipped yew that framed classical statuary said to have come from Hadrian's villa at Tivoli. Attempts to impose some kind of iconography on this new development are dubious but it certainly gave Chiswick a Plinian hippodrome. The brook, already widened earlier to provide the illusion of a river, was now naturalised further and trees here and there were thinned to provide glimpses and prospects. Endless projects for a cascade and an orangery rambled on, both being eventually erected. Rocque's plan, published in 1736, for instance, contains designs for both that were never built (252)

In 1742 Burlington commissioned George Lambert to paint two more views, which add little to our knowledge of the garden, beyond giving us a glimpse of the handsome stone urns which lined the hippodrome leading to the classical exedra on the garden façade of the villa.[42] The writer of the Appendix to the edition of Defoe's *Tour* issued in that year wrote of the garden in terms of a major national monument: 'there is more Variety in this garden, than can be found in any other of the same Size in *England*, or perhaps in *Europe*.'

Burlington died in 1753, the year in which six engraved views (260) of the gardens by John Donowell were issued, or at least that can be taken as the likely date for only one of them carries the year.[43] Donowell was a second-rate architect but an accurate topographical draftsman who records the reality of Chiswick as it must have looked in the years immediately before. It includes the pathetic wooden bridge over the Bollo brook near the Bagnio, indicating that a stone one never came, and records the cascade as it was finally erected. Donowell apparently parted with his interest in the prints to book and print sellers, who marketed them either singly or in sets. The captions beneath were in both French and English establishing that they were seen as having an international market. By then Chiswick had become just one more garden among many in the garden engraving boom of the 1750s.

WHIG FORMALITY: WREST PARK

Horace Walpole's essay *The History of the Modern Taste in Gardening* was written during the 1750s and 1760s. It is a fiercely patriotic and doctrinaire version of the emergence of the landscape style: 'imitation of Nature in gardens, or rather laying out Ground, still called Gardening for want of a specific term to distinguish an Art totally new, is Original and indisputably English!'[44] By then he had made a simplistic equation between his perception of the French formal style and the rigours of absolutist rule and another one between the naturalistic asymmetrical landscape style and English constitutional government. He saw this as the consequence of Britain being 'an Empire of Freemen, an Empire formed by Trade, not by a military conquering Spirit, maintained by the valour of independent Property...'[45] In this scenario William Kent is inevitably cast as the hero who leapt over the fence and saw all nature as a garden, to be swiftly followed by 'Capability' Brown.

Such a simplistic view of developments in garden style was in fact far from the truth. Even within Le Nôtre's exact submission of nature to regularity there remained room for irregular wild parts in a garden. Indeed it has recently been argued that Le Nôtre anticipated the work of Bridgeman and Kent.[46] Nor is it altogether true to regard the landscape movement as an inevitable triumphant progression. Formal gardens looking both to France and to the Netherlands continued to be made in the first half of the century. Nor were all elements of formality to be swept away with the advent of the park. Tucked away within even the most seemingly naturalistic of domains would lurk a formal flower garden.

It is in this context that the series of views by Pieter Tillemans (261, 262) of the magnificent garden at Wrest Park, Bedfordshire, laid out by Henry Grey, 12th Earl and 1st Duke of Kent are so enlightening. In the first instance it disproves Walpole's political equation, for the Duke was both strongly Protestant and a Whig, a man who had been one of the group instrumental in inviting William III to Britain. He, if anyone, certainly belonged to the 'Empire of

261. Pieter Tillemans, *The South Garden at Wrest Park: The Seat in the Duchess's Square*, c.1729–30, Bedfordshire and Luton Archives and Record Service

262. Pieter Tillemans, *The South Garden at Wrest Park: The Pavilion and Obelisk canal*, *c.* 1729–30, Bedfordshire and Luton Archives and Record Service

263. John Rocque, *Plan and views of Wrest Park*, 1735. English Heritage. Marked with Tillemans's viewpoints

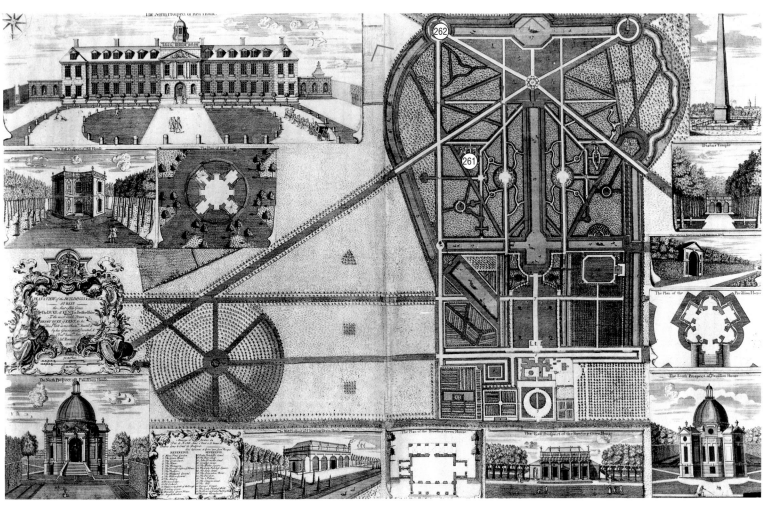

264. Artist unknown, *Bird's-eye view of the gardens at Wrest Park, seen from the park*, c. 1721–2, Bedfordshire and Luton Archives and Record Service

Freemen'. Although written down by his contemporaries, he remained at the heart of court and public affairs through two reigns. He was Lord Chamberlain to Queen Anne, who created him a Marquess in 1706 and, four years later, on his dismissal from office, a Duke. With the accession of the House of Hanover he was to occupy a succession of posts including Gentleman of the Bedchamber, Lord Steward and Lord Privy Seal as well as being made a Knight of the Garter. Both his own second marriage and that of his eldest son forged alliances with other great Whig dynasties. But his garden, one of the most splendid of the period, so splendid in fact that John Rocque was to record it twice in 1735 and 1739 (263), looked in its design to Versailles and continental courts. This is a garden to remind us that the formal style continued to be conducive, as it had been under William and Mary and Anne, to a celebration of British liberties.

265. Pieter Tillemans, *A view of the garden and house at Upper Winchendon, Buckinghamshire*, late 1720s, New Haven, Yale Center for British Art, Paul Mellon Collection

266. The garden at Wrest Park before the alterations and additions of the 1st Duke of Kent, from Jan Kip, *Nouveau Théâtre de la Grande Bretagne*, London, 1716, New Haven, Yale Center for British Art, Paul Mellon Collection

Wrest had a statue of William III, whose exact location is unknown, erected to his 'glorious and immortell memory', which still survives.

The watercolours form a confusing body of pictorial evidence, for the garden was in fact depicted twice, on the first occasion in two bird's-eye panoramic views (264), which can dated to 1721–2 and on the second in nine sketches from around 1729–30. Although Robert Raines accepts both series as the work of Pieter Tillemans, modern scholarship rejects the first.[47]

We have already encountered Tillemans in connexion with the portrait of the children of his great patron, Dr Cox Macro (71). Antwerp born and trained, he was the type of painter who could turn his skills in virtually any direction capable of engendering income: Italianate landscapes, still life, copies of old masters,

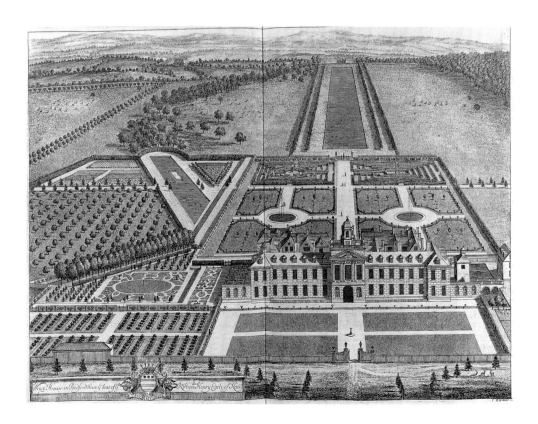

decorative schemes, country house views as well as scenery for the theatre. At a pinch he would even take on portraits, although the figures in some of his paintings are often by another hand. One of his projects, which petered out, was to make some five-hundred drawings for a history of Northamptonshire.

The suite of nine drawings of Wrest are typical of Tillemans's working method in preparation for an oil painting. This can be demonstrated in the case of a view of another garden in the grand formal manner, Winchendon House, Buckinghamshire (265) executed at about the same time where both drawing and finished painting survive.[48] One finished painting by Tillemans of Wrest certainly existed for it is recorded by Horace Walpole in what had been the Duke's London house: 'A View of Wrest by Tillemans'. Whether that picture was of both house and gardens we have no means of knowing. Inventories of Wrest in the Duke's period include pictures of the gardens, although no painter's name is given. In the Duke's dressing room besides 'Two draughts [i.e. plans] of the Gardens' there was 'A Picture of Rest Gardens' and in his bedroom 'A Picture, A View of Rest House and Gardens'.[49]

If this is evidence of nothing else it establishes that the Duke of Kent was obsessed by his gardens, an obsession matched by his dynastic megalomania,[50] which was intensified by family tragedy, for his second son died in 1717, his heir in 1723 and his first wife in 1728. Only two months before his own death he had been created Marquess Grey with the provision that the title could pass to his granddaughter. This is vividly reflected in the iconography of the garden, which includes monuments to members of his family and even to himself besides making ample use of the Grey heraldic wyvern. All of this must have contributed to his desire for a series of garden pictures that must have been commissioned in the wake of his second marriage to the daughter of the Whig Earl of Portland.

Kent inherited Wrest from his father in 1702. The 11th Earl had laid out the garden recorded in Kip's *Britannia Illustrata* (266). It was absolutely symmetrical and stretched southwards with two mirror-image parterres centred on fountains and two mazes of different design, the whole terminated by a pair of iron gates flanked by gatepiers topped by the Grey wyvern. Beyond stretched a long canal exactly on the lines of that created for Charles II at Hampton Court and in St James's Park in the 1660s. Bordering this garden to the east there was a terrace looking over a second canal stretching south-east.

Kent was to commission architectural projects from Giacomo Leoni, Nicholas Hawksmoor, James Gibbs, Thomas Archer, William Kent and, deeply indicative of his stylistic leanings, from that master of the flamboyant baroque, Filippo Juvarra. Most were for a new house that never materialised, Kent's fortunes having been severely dented by the South Sea Bubble. The history of the gardens vividly catches his restless desire for change. The two bird's-eye panoramas from 1721–2 record the transformation achieved during the first twenty years. Of this the single most important commission was to Thomas Archer for the pavilion at the southernmost point of the canal. It was in place by 1711. Only the gardens of the baroque courts indulged in buildings comparable in scale. Indeed if it were not for the fact that we know the view to be of Wrest, on a first glance one would take it be the garden of a minor German court glancing towards Versailles.

By the time that these views were drawn the mazes had gone and also the divisions between one section of the garden and another, bringing it in line with

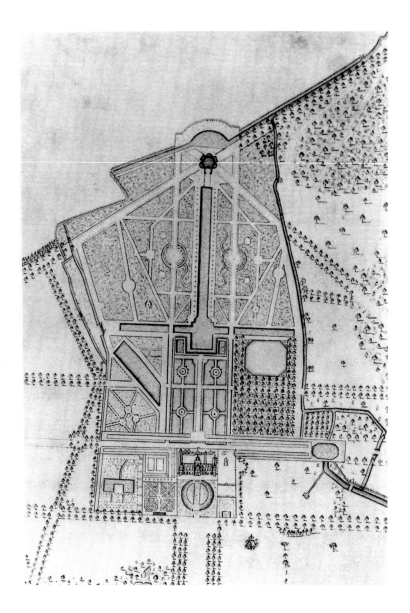

267. Anonymous estate map of Wrest Park, *c*.1719–21, collection of Lord Lucas

268. The Duke's Square and the Duchess's Square from J. Badeslade and John Rocque, *Wrest Park*, from *Vitruvius Britannicus Volume the Fourth*, London 1739, New Haven, Yale Centre for British Art, Paul Mellon Collection

the French manner. The iron gates and wyvern-topped piers had also vanished, providing a clear vista to the great pavilion. The canal itself had gained a cross axis directly inspired by Versailles. On either side of the canal the South Garden had been laid out as a mirror-image wilderness with vistas to the pavilion, straight walks as well as a few squiggly ones. The view north looks towards the back of the pavilion across a newly constructed geometric sheet of water. Around it walks proliferate, there is a planting of young trees and statues of rustics clutching garden implements. All of this matches an estate plan of *c*. 1719–21 (267).

These changes were carried out under the aegis of Thomas Ackers, a nephew of George London. Ackers was certainly in post at Wrest by 1708 and probably earlier. He, like his master, was closely associated with the court, being Groom Porter. That proximity may account for the absence of any box parterre, for Queen Anne hated the smell of box and had the vast parterre in the Fountain Court at Hampton Court ripped out.

The Tillemans watercolours are ten years later. By the time that they were made, 1729–30, Chiswick and Claremont, under the direction of Bridgeman and Kent, were being loosened-up. Both continued to have symmetrical and formal elements, but in neither was house and garden locked into a geometric grid. Surprisingly, at Wrest formality increases rather than decreases during precisely the same period. Rocque's 1735 plan records a garden where every formal ingredient has been reinforced, the South Garden having being extended with a new formal canal leading to ponds with monuments to both the Duke and Duchess. These act as focal points of a new grid of straight vistas. The additions fill out a garden that had irregularities at the perimeters, transforming it into one large rectangle that recalls even more sharply gardens such as Nymphenburg in Bavaria.

Tillemans's views only cover the South Garden. When we compare them with both those of Chiswick and Hartwell House we are struck by the total absence of any attempt to break out and embrace the world of nature beyond. The two remain sharply separated, even if ha-has have been introduced. Five of the views focus on different approaches to Archer's pavilion and therefore all look inward. The others record aspects of what were called the Duke's and the Duchess's Squares. These are both are also recorded in vignettes in the borders to Rocque's 1737 plan of Wrest (268). One view includes a couple ambling along a path indicating that if the paintings had been made they would have been peopled with the familiar elegant company. The duke seems to have been a person of whim and he may have decided suddenly not to proceed with the painted series. Equally Tillemans was a chronic asthmatic and his health was failing. Whatever the reason the drawings at least remain, providing a unique record of another kind of garden. After his death 'Capability' Brown was brought in to correct what Horace Walpole regarded with characteristic biased venom as an 'execrable' garden.[51]

'A Work to wonder at': Stowe

Jacques Rigaud's work for Lord Burlington had ended in disaster, precipitating the artist's return to France, leaving unfinished a series of no fewer than fifteen large engraved views of another famous garden, Stowe, Buckinghamshire (273–8). George Vertue, somewhat darkly, records the underhand activities of another French engraver, Bernard Baron, who 'managed it so as to get him [Rigaud] away and got the finishing part to himself.'[52] This is only one incident in what added up to a sorry saga, but it is one that resulted in the first suite of engravings recording an English garden as it would be experienced by a visitor. Furthermore, in aesthetic terms, the suite was to remain unmatched for the rest of the century.

In the case of Chiswick it could only ever have been Lord Burlington who commissioned the drawings. If evidence did not exist to prove the contrary one would assume that in the instance of Stowe it would have been its creator, Richard Temple, 1st Viscount Cobham, who must have commissioned them. But in fact it was not. Vertue provides a full account of the genesis and progress of this commission. The initiative came from Charles Bridgeman, who was instrumental in bringing Rigaud to England in about February 1733 'to be employd by him to make designs of Gardens Views &c. etc.'[53] Stowe is the only garden specifically mentioned, but the other gardens of which Rigaud views exist – Richmond and Claremont – were ones where Bridgeman had worked.

Vertue records later that year how Rigaud had begun to engrave the plates but in the autumn of 1734, presumably after his fall-out with Lord Burlington,

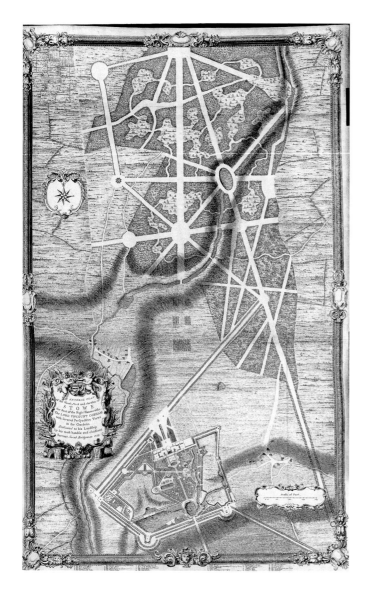

269. Stowe. General Plan. Unsigned engraving from *Views of Stowe*, 1739

270. Detail of the main area with vantage points of Rigaud's perspectives of 1733–4 superimposed.

he 'returnd to Paris leaving Mr. Bridgemans work not intirely finishd.'[54] It was at this point that Bernard Baron insinuated his way into the project, so much so that he was to add his name to all of the plates, when in fact all fifteen had originated in drawings by Rigaud and ten had already been engraved. Vertue lists the five for which Baron alone was responsible. What happened next was extraordinary, for a gap of five years occurs until they were actually published, by which time Bridgeman was dead, leaving them to appear under the aegis of his widow, Sarah, in 1739.

The delay may have been due to the fact that Bridgeman was unable to find enough subscribers to issue them.[55] In addition his garden style was rapidly being eclipsed at that very moment. William Kent was already working on the Elysian Fields at Stowe and it is noticeable that his work is only ever glimpsed from a distance in the engravings, a decision that must have been deliberate. These engraved views formed a hugely expensive project, costing Bridgeman some £1,400. When his widow did at last publish them, adding a groundplan of the garden and estate (269), they were sold for 4gns a set, but even then she must have had few takers. Lord Cobham took two. She was left with bulk of the stock and after her death in 1744 a consortium of booksellers bought them

271. The house and garden at Stowe, as they were before Lord Cobham's alterations of the 1720s. Anonymous drawing, *c.* 1680, pen and wash. © Crown copyright, NMR

up, repackaged them, adding a titlepage, and sold them at half the price. This is a sad end to a task which Vertue, himself an engraver, recognised Rigaud had 'most excellently performd. He being perfect Master of perspective finely disposes his groups of Trees, light and shade and figures in a masterly manner.'[56]

The fact that they were a novelty and that garden tourism had not as yet got underway must also have contributed to their failure. There was no precedent in England for such a series of engravings and Bridgeman was anticipating by two decades the surge of garden view publishing for the tourist market that happened after 1750. By the time that the prints were sold off in 1746 they were records of a garden already vastly altered, a record indeed of a garden style hopelessly old-fashioned, one created in the 1720s in the earliest stages of the break up of the old formality.

Rigaud records for posterity perhaps the greatest and most seminal garden of the whole century. Lord Cobham had developed it over twenty years, building on an inheritance that was a mansion completed in 1683 standing on the crest of a hill with commanding views over the Buckinghamshire countryside (271).[57] Ascent to the status of a viscount and a marriage to a great heiress precipitated what was to be a garden on a huge scale, one whose originality sprang from an awkward site whose very nature dictated an abandonment of symmetry. To that must be added the ideological input of Cobham and his circle, who were to transform Stowe into a series of tableaux expressing their political and ideological allegiances.

Bridgeman was in post by 1714, to be joined by Vanbrugh as architect two years later. He was succeeded in the 1720s by James Gibbs, and in the 1730s by William Kent. The garden we see in the Rigaud views was laid out between 1721 and 1730, and stemmed from Bridgeman's proposals to Lord Cobham in the former year (272). This scheme superimposed onto disparate elements a network of avenues and *rond points* that drew the garden together in a strikingly original manner.

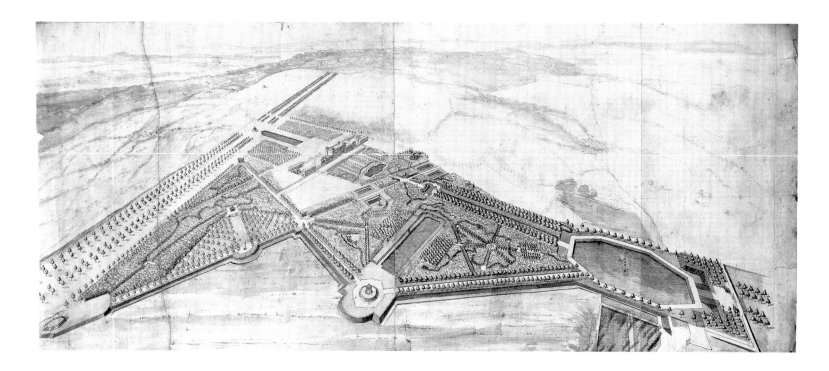

272. Stowe, bird's-eye view, 1719–20. Drawing attributed to Charles Bridgeman. Bodlian Library, University of Oxford, MS. Gough Drawings, a4.fol.46

This is what Rigaud so superbly records. His inaccuracies are few, the worst being the transformation of the straight canal opposite the south front of the house into a round pond, and the addition of wings that were never built to the house. There is little artistic licence beyond arranging trees, enhancing occasionally the grandeur of a building and a tendency to emphasise the formal aspects of the design, an unsurprising trait from a man whose major work had been *Les Maisons Royales de France*. And, as in the case of Chiswick, each scene is animated by people, many are portraits, in particular of Lord and Lady Cobham. One identifiable example included the famous Italian castrato, Senesino, singing in a musical group. He in fact is a replacement for the unidentified figure in the original drawing. All the drawings, bar one, have survived and are now in the Metropolitan Museum of Art, New York. In the original drawing Alexander Pope also appears but he was suppressed in the final engraving, probably on account of sensitivity over his hunched back. Rigaud was to repeat this formula in his series of drawings of Chiswick, where again he inserts Senesino and Pope. In doing this he was innovatory in introducing recognisable leaders of fashion and stars in the creative firmament amidst ordinary visitors to the garden. This peopling of garden views was to be taken up by mid-century English printmakers. They also were to follow these pioneering prints in captioning in both English and French, indicating sales possibilities on the continent.[58]

Rigaud takes the viewer on a tour of the gardens starting at the south front looking over the parterre first one way and then the other (273). From there we wander down the Abele Walk of poplars southwards, stopping to contemplate the large octagonal lake with its Guglio Fountain again from opposing viewpoints (274), the furthest looking back towards the south front of the house with the two entrance pavilions to the garden providing a frame. We then stroll on along the perimeter avenues westwards pausing at the head of the Eleven-Acre Lake (275) to catch a glimpse of the Rotunda in the middle distance, the architectural lynchpin of the garden. A short distance on affords a second

273. Jacques Rigaud, *Stowe.* *'View of the parterre from the Portico of the House'*, 1733–4, Metropolitan Museum of Art, New York (Harris Brisbane Dick Fund, 1942), 42.79(15)

274. Jacques Rigaud, *Stowe.* *'View of the great Bason, from the Entrance of the Great Walk to the House'*, 1733–4, Metropolitan Museum of Art (Harris Brisbane Dick Fund, 1942) 42,79(10)

275. Jacques Rigaud, *Stowe.* *'View of such parts as are seen from the Building at the Head of the Lake'*, 1733–4, Metropolitan Museum of Art (Harris Brisbane Dick Fund, 1942) 42.79(2)

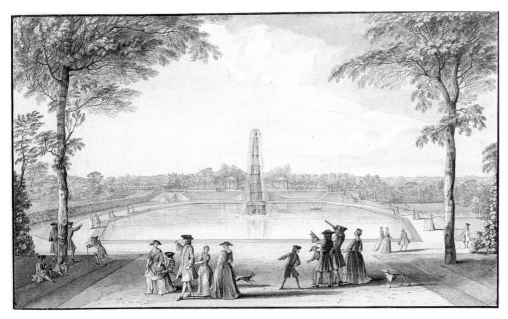

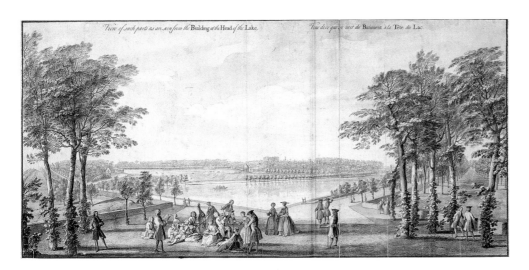

276. Jacques Rigaud, *Stowe. 'View from the Head of the Lake'*, 1733–4, Metropolitan Museum of Art (Harris Brisbane Dick Fund, 1942)

277. Jacques Rigaud, *Stowe. 'View from the Gibbs Building'*, 1733–4, Metropolitan Museum of Art (Harris Brisbane Dick Fund, 1942)

278. Jacques Rigaud, *Stowe. 'View from the foot of the Pyramid'*, 1733–4, Metropolitan Museum of Art (Harris Brisbane Dick Fund, 1942)

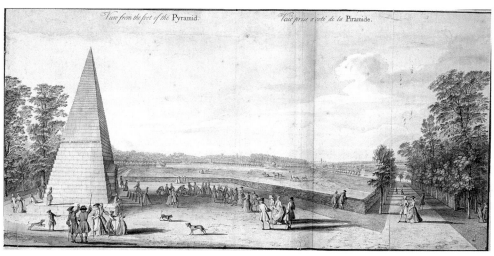

panorama across the Lake, this time towards the cascade with the Guglio Fountain beyond (276), the waters enlivened by a boating party unfurling a sail. Continuing along the edges there is a final glance across the Lake from James Gibbs's building, which contained statues of British Worthies admired by Cobham and his political associates (277).

And here, for the first time, the iconography of the garden unfolds, for this is a Whig garden celebrating the principles of the Constitution as epitomised in the 1688 Revolution settlement and the Hanoverian succession. The worthies whose busts were gathered here were Elizabeth I, Shakespeare, William III, Locke, John Hampden, Milton and Newton. To understand the garden Willis points out that the prints should be viewed hand-in-hand with reading a poem by Cobham's nephew, Gilbert West, on Stowe. It evokes the thoughts which visitors should have on coming across such a 'sacred Band/ Of Princes, Patriots, Bards, and Sages.'[59]

Vanbrugh's great pyramid is the next stopping point (278), after which the route turns eastwards back towards the house by way of the Great Cross Walk. Along that walk a space opens up and views in either direction are given away from and towards Vanbrugh's Brick Temple. Strolling north we come next to Bridgeman's master-stroke, the Rotunda raised on a mount, a circular temple dedicated for a time to Venus, which looks across the Queen's Theatre towards a column bearing a statue of Queen Caroline. Again there is a view the other way, back to the Rotunda and, in the distance right, to Vanbrugh's Pyramid. The peregrination is brought to its close going north with a vista southwards named after a gardener called Nelson, and views away and towards the north front of the mansion. In one we look down the steps leading from the house as a carriage disgorges its occupants and in the other we look across the round pond which should have been a canal from just by an equestrian statue of George I proclaiming loyalty to the new dynasty.

No other set of garden engravings was to eclipse these in terms of aesthetic achievement or sheer elegance and accuracy of record. Almost two decades passed before Stowe was to be recorded again. By then much had happened. Kent had created the Elysian Fields in the thirties as a political statement by Cobham, who, like Burlington, had gone into opposition over the Excise Bill in 1733. Up went the Temples of Ancient and Modern Virtue, the latter a ruin with a headless statue of their arch-enemy, Sir Robert Walpole, with, beyond, Gibbs's Gothic Temple, the summation of Cobham's hymn to Liberty, the Enlightenment and the British Constitution. When the new set of engravings appeared Stowe was well and truly on the tourist map. George Bickham's *The Beauties of Stowe* (1750) was billed as 'a necessary Pocket Companion for such as Visit those Gardens' and copies of it were available from an inn at the gate, in nearby Buckingham as well as from Bickham's own shop in London. The engravings, it goes on to say, could be purchased separately 'neatly framed and glazed for the Closet' in both a plain as well as a coloured state. Bickham later issued sixteen views in 1752 (279) for a guinea, a set which he then updated with six larger views. All of these capture the increasing naturalisation of the garden both at the hands of Kent and then 'Capability' Brown, who was head gardener there in the 1740s. Ha-has vanished, lakes

279. G. Bickham and J. B. Chatelain, *Stowe. A View from the Temple of Diana*, from Bickham, *Views of Stowe*, 1753

280. Plan of the garden at Hartwell House based on the research of Eric Throssell FRIBA, marking Nebot's viewpoints

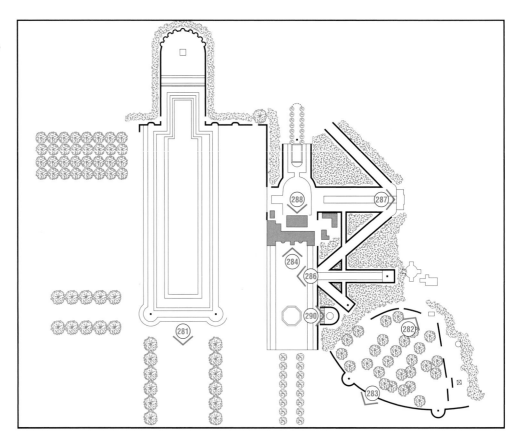

were irregularised and trees thinned into asymmetrical clumps.[60] In short we have arrived in the age of the garden tour and the souvenir guide book.

A MINOR WHIG PARADISE: HARTWELL HOUSE

Hartwell House lies just south of Aylesbury, Buckinghamshire. Its gardens were to be the subject of the most spectacular series of paintings, apart from Rysbrack's views of Chiswick, made in the eighteenth century (281–7).[61] Two bear the date 1738. They were commissioned by a minor aristocrat, Sir Thomas Lee, from a minor painter called Balthasar Nebot, a Spaniard whose studio was in Covent Garden. The ostensible purpose of the paintings was to mark the transformation of the garden at Hartwell during the previous decade and a half at the hand of the architect James Gibbs and, arguably, as I shall demonstrate, that of the landscape gardener Charles Bridgeman.

These pictures are remarkable for giving such a comprehensive a record of, compared with either Stowe or Claremont, a relatively small garden. Their panoramic nature sets them apart, the effect being that we are looking at some precursor of the panning shot of a film camera, moving from left to right in a wide arc taking in what it sees section by section in a way that the human eye could never do at a single glance. A reconstructed plan of the garden (280) (none exists from the period itself) makes clear the quite exceptional nature of the Hartwell series for they cover virtually every viewpoint from both directions. The only unrecorded vista is the one looking north from the pavilion at the head of the great canal. Two of the pictures provide particularly vivid evidence of this wide-angle lens approach. The smallest painting (281) covers in a

281. Balthasar Nebot, *Hartwell House. Axial view of the canal from the south, showing Gibbs's temple at the end of the canal, the house and topiary alleys on the west side*, Buckinghamshire County Museum, Aylesbury

282. Balthasar Nebot, *Hartwell House. North west area of the gardens with two bastions and men scything*, Buckinghamshire County Museum, Aylesbury

single sweep the canal, the temple, the quite extraordinary clipped evergreen exedra, the house, the topiary arcades overlooking the bowling green ending with the octagonal pond and the domed octagonal temple. The second is even more striking (283). This records the wilderness in a sequence which reads almost like incidents in a strip cartoon that runs from east to west, embracing a quite incredible sequence of visual experiences that the visitor could only have ever taken in one at a time. They include a statue of Hercules, a gap in the boscage giving a vista through to the great canal, next a glimpse of the column bearing a statue of William III, then the tower of the old parish church followed

283. Balthasar Nebot, *Hartwell House. In the wilderness behind the topiary alleys with various Gibbs buildings*, Buckinghamshire County Museum, Aylesbury

by a pillared pavilion in the Tuscan style, a small Gothic tower and, to the extreme right, a pyramid and, last of all, a statue of Marsyas.

This desire that everything be recorded can result in somewhat awkward compositions like those looking down the tall clipped allées (286). Sir Thomas Lee's brief must have been exact and that is perhaps why he chose a minor painter, otherwise known only for low-life subject matter and still lifes of fruit and fish.[62] The figures too are poles away from the elegant company of Rigaud's scenes. Instead there are portraits presumably of Lee, members of his family and friends, including a Garter Knight, gardeners and estate employees. The series must undoubtedly have been painted with some particular location in mind. The usual place to hang such pictures would have been in the family's London house but we have no way of knowing. It has been pointed out that the perspective of the smallest painting (281) suggests that it was designed to hang high, perhaps over a chimneypiece, with the remaining canvases disposed around the walls.

284. Balthasar Nebot, *Hartwell House, the bowling green and octagon pond from the north,* Buckinghamshire County Museum, Aylesbury

285. Detail of plate 284. The Garter Knight is probably Frederick, Prince of Wales, whose likely visit to Hartwell in 1737 occasioned the pictures.

Sir Thomas Lee came from a family that first rose to prominence in the fifteenth century.[63] Early in the seventeenth they married into the Hampdens, another prominent Buckinghamshire family, whose most notable member, John, famous for his protest over the imposition of Ship Money, was to be celebrated by Sir Thomas in the form of a bust in his garden. The first baronet, another Sir Thomas, was a distinguished parliamentarian, owing patronage to Lord Wharton and sitting as MP both for Aylesbury and the county for over thirty years following the Restoration. His successors were to maintain the Wharton link, until 1725 when the Duke of Wharton declared for the titular James III and went into exile. The creator of the garden came into his estate aged fifteen in 1702 and was to sit later as MP for Chipping Wycombe and also for the county on and off from 1710 to 1741. The Lees were opposition Whigs, part of a connexion that in the middle 1730s found its centre in the Leicester House set around the Prince of Wales. Indeed Sir Thomas's son commissioned an equestrian statue of the Prince from John Cheere in 1757.[64]

That link raises intriguing questions as to the identity of the Knight of the Garter who appears in the picture of the Bowling Green (284–5). Whoever he is he is gesturing towards the vista whose culmination is the pillar with the statue of William III. Could this be Frederick, Prince of Wales? And, therefore, could one of the reasons behind the series be a desire to immortalise in one of the canvases a

286. Balthasar Nebot, *Hartwell House topiary arcades and allée to the William III Column*, Buckinghamshire County Museum, Aylesbury

royal visit? The dates would fit, for Frederick visited Stowe in 1737, and could he not also have visited Hartwell? None of the known aristocratic connexions of the Lees in the 1730s were Garter Knights. It is an hypothesis at least worth the making.[65]

In 1720 Sir Thomas had married a rich city heiress, Elizabeth Sandys, and it is difficult not to equate the making of such a spectacular garden with that marriage, although she was to die ten years later – a decade before the pictures were painted. Sir Thomas was a widower when he commissioned the series, for he never remarried. There is remarkably little documentation on the garden: a mention of a reservoir planned to supply a *jet d'eau* in 1723, a payment to Henry Cheere, the sculptor, in 1725 for the statue of William III and one in 1737 to an itinerant painter for 'a History Painting in the Octagon Building', the Temple of Love, looking towards the octagon pond.[66] And that is all. We have no certain evidence as to when Sir Thomas actually began work but it was certainly going on during the twenties and thirties and there is nothing to disprove the possibility that it in fact began as early 1720.

Everyone who has so far written about the Hartwell garden has worked from the premise that we are looking at the remodelling of an old Stuart topiary garden inspired by the nearby Wharton seat of Winchendon.[67] The only information about the earlier garden comes from Smyth's *Aedes Hartwellianae* (1851) where it is stated, with no source, that 'by about the year 1695, [the grounds] were squared out around the house, divided by walls and evergreen fences, with prim yews cut into architectural forms, and watered by canals as straight as a pikestaff.'[68] There is, however, no reason to believe this, for, if planting had begun in the early 1720s, the clipped palisades would easily have reached the height we see in fifteen years, allowance being made for the fact that the painter

287. Balthasar Nebot, *Hartwell House. Topiary alleys behind the wilderness and William III Column*, Buckinghamshire County Museum, Aylesbury

might have enhanced their finish. The very design of the green architecture indicates that it must have gone hand in hand with the built one in exactly the same way as the garden developed at Chiswick. Some older elements may have been incorporated but overall we are looking at a composition conceived simultaneously with the house.

The garden at Chiswick was to Hartwell in design what Stowe was to it in terms of iconography. Rysbrack, the painter of Chiswick, may well have been a member of the same group of Covent Garden painters as Nebot. The resemblance of one Chiswick picture to one in the Hartwell series (256, 286) has been pointed out, but the relationship surely goes beyond that. We know that Sir Thomas's uncle Sir George Lee was a frequent visitor to Lord Burlington's garden and it is difficult not to suppose that the *patte d'oie* with its terminal built structures at Chiswick, for example, was not the source of the similar but more modest arrangement at Hartwell. Chiswick and Hartwell both had obelisks and the Burlington Lane Gate at Chiswick closely resembles the one that closes a vista from the menagerie at Hartwell. The lack of a groundplan for Hartwell makes closer comparisons difficult. However, Hartwell clearly shares with Chiswick the balance between formal and informal. Compared with what was to happen in the 1750s both are essentially formal gardens. The groundplan of Chiswick shows an abundance of squiggly walks between the formal areas.[70] Without that plan and with only Rysbrack's pictures as evidence we would have no notion of just how many of these there were. Nebot's two pictures of the wilderness at Hartwell also give us no idea about the presence or otherwise of the ubiquitous squiggly walk which was such a feature of English gardens during the opening decades of the century. In all probability the Wilderness was indeed a squiggly area.

The architect James Gibbs was certainly responsible for the buildings, many of which still survive on site. Having disposed of the notion that these were inserted into a pre-existing evergreen setting we can suggest that surely we are looking at the norm, a garden by Charles Bridgeman with architectural features by Gibbs. There is nothing inherent that contradicts setting Hartwell into a long line of garden designs carried out by these two men through the 1720s and 1730s. Stowe, Bridgeman's greatest work, was after all nearby. In the formal canal or lake in front of the house at Hartwell we have one of Bridgeman's signatures, his habit of replacing parterres with lakes. Then there is his penchant for terminating every walk with a built feature, be it obelisk, temple or statue, and his delight in garden buildings in an amazing assortment of styles. At Hartwell we have ones in classical, rustic and gothick guise. Often those buildings are juxtaposed to a rural landscape or set into it.[71] The Hartwell pictures represent a definite statement of the interplay of the garden with the working landscape. Crops in the fields are firmly brought in as part of the composition, together with the unashamed presence of sheep and cattle and those who work the land. All of those elements, typical of Bridgeman's garden style, are here at Hartwell, so Nebot's paintings may preserve a precious panorama of a lost garden by Bridgeman at its height, recorded with a rare honesty.

With regard to its meaning much remains unknown, like the significance of the temple at the head of the lake or the obelisk behind the amazing topiary exedra (288). The exedra indeed is a feature without parallel as far as we know in any other contemporary garden. But the technique of training evergreens in such a manner, which is repeated in the other green arcades, is given in Dézallier d'Argenville (289). Hartwell belongs resolutely to a series of Whig gardens, and a poem by a Mr Merrick of Aylesbury unhesitatingly places Hartwell in the context of Stowe.[72] Indeed he compares himself to Gilbert West who had penned a poem on that famous garden:

'Tis Hartwell's pleasing shades inspire my lays
Of her fair Groves I wou'd attempt ye praise
Cou'd I with justice the description show
In numbers such as his who sung fam'd Stow.
(ll. 19–22)

Alas, Mr Merrick seems to have only been partly cognisant of the iconography of the garden whose praises he sings. His reference to Stowe is important, however, for both William III and John Hampden, whose full-length statue and bust form the culmination of two of the *allées* of the great *patte d'oie* at Hartwell appear also at Stowe. There they figure in the pantheon of Whig heroes, the Temple of British Worthies. Hampden had an added attraction for Lee, for he appears on the family tree through his great grandmother. Merrick in his poem at least gets the drift of the garden's general meaning as expressing a 'love of Liberty':

Your Bosom with the Patriot's passion glows
The sons of Fredom own with just applause
This noble ardour for the glorious Cause.
(ll. 103–6)

Much, however, remains unexplained. One might hazard a guess that the minute gothick tower is a lilliputian version of the summit of Stowe's political

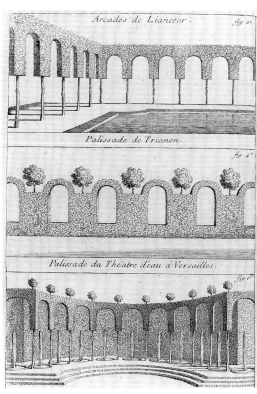

288. Balthasar Nebot, *Hartwell House. Topiary arcades framing a vista to the obelisk,* Buckinghamshire County Museum, Aylesbury

289. Palisades from Dézallier d'Argenville, *La Théorie et Pratique du jardinage...,* 1709. British Library, London

290. Balthasar Nebot, *Hartwell House. The Bowling green and octagon pond with Aylesbury church in the distance,* 1738, Buckinghamshire County Museum, Aylesbury

landscape, the Temple of Liberty, also in the Gothick style. But the meaning of statues of Jupiter and Juno by the canal, Hercules and Marsyas in the Wilderness, the Tuscan pavilion, the obelisk and the canal temple with its herms remains opaque.

The classical gods and goddesses at least establish that Lee's view of his domain was that of a Plinian villa transported to England. Gibbs was to have rebuilt the house but in fact his remodelling never got beyond the hall where this classical side to the Hartwell garden is developed in a relief over the fireplace of Horace crowned with flowers and standing on a terrace overlooking a landscape.[73] The allusion is to a passage in his Ode, *Ad Muntium Plancum* (I, vii) in which the poet refers to spring on his estate at Tivoli. The poet Merrick casts Hartwell in such a role, praising its features as those worthy of an antique villa, with its contrast of regular and irregular, its delight in variety of visual experience, its emphasis on the beauty of prospects across the surrounding landscape, and its concern to integrate into the scene the bounty of working farmland.

> A stately terrace the canal surrounds
> That yields a prospect o'er the neighb'ring grounds
> Whose fertile pastures with rich herbage rise
> And golden plenty thence salutes our eyes.
> (ll. 139–42)

The Hartwell pictures are a fascinating record of garden style at the crossroads as the formal loosened up integrating into it this new impulse for variety, for asymmetry and for evocative pictorial tableaux. Sir Thomas died in 1749 and his son was to call in 'Capability' Brown. W. H. Smyth in his *Aedes Hartwellianae* (1851) wrote: 'Brown was a great intermeddler at various seats in Buckinghamshire, but especially at Stowe and Hartwell',[74] but modern research has established it to be by a lesser improver, Richard Woods. Sir Thomas's Whig paradise was to prove an all too transitory one. By the close of the 1760s it had gone.

A Ducal Arcady: Claremont, Surrey

In terms of beguiling naivety nothing approaches the six canvases by an unknown painter of the garden of Thomas Pelham-Holles, 1st Duke of Newcastle at Claremont, Surrey (293, 299–300), apart from Thomas Robins's rococo reveries .[75] The Duke was conscious of other sets of such views for he employed Rigaud to execute two of Claremont, one of the house and the other of the bowling green (291) in 1733–4, although whether more were planned, along with engravings is unknown. Newcastle may have intended more, for the absence of the magnificent amphitheatre is inexplicable, but the Duke may have disliked the Frenchification of his domain, which had presented it as the equivalent of a painting by Watteau. The six somewhat primitive canvases form a stark contrast, notable for the absence of any human beings at all in the four strictly garden views, although the numerous seats dotted here and there bespeak their presence. Indeed the number of chairs depicted upturned onto the greensward has led John Harris to bestow upon this anonymous artist the name of the 'The Master of the Tumbled Chairs'.

By the time that these gardens were painted the Duke of Newcastle had been working on his garden for over four decades.[76] Chargate Farm had been pur-

291. Jacques Rigaud, *Claremont, view towards the Belvedere with Kent's pavilion right*, c. 1733–4. Victoria & Albert Museum, London

chased in 1708 by the architect Sir John Vanbrugh who built for himself a small house with stables and a walled garden. A recently discovered drawing indicates that the main spine of the garden running over the hill at the back with a belvedere at its summit was already in Vanbrugh's scheme when, in 1711, he sold it to the young Thomas Pelham-Holles who had just inherited a fortune and vast estates from the last Duke of Newcastle. His rise in the aristocratic ranks was rapid, being made Earl of Clare in 1714, renaming the estate Claremont, and a year later he was made Duke of Newcastle. With both wealth

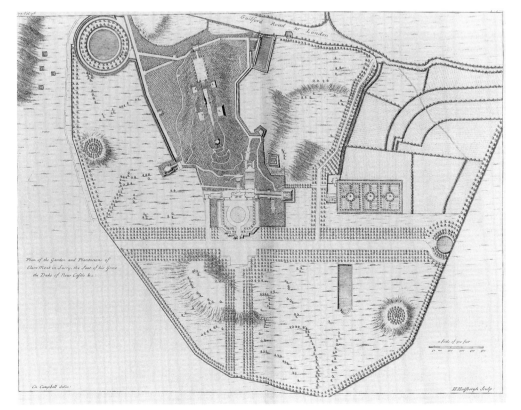

292. Plan of Claremont from Colen Campbell, *Vitruvius Britannicus*, volume the third, 1725

293 (overleaf). Artist unknown, *Claremont. View of the Amphitheatre and Lake*, c. 1760, Private collection

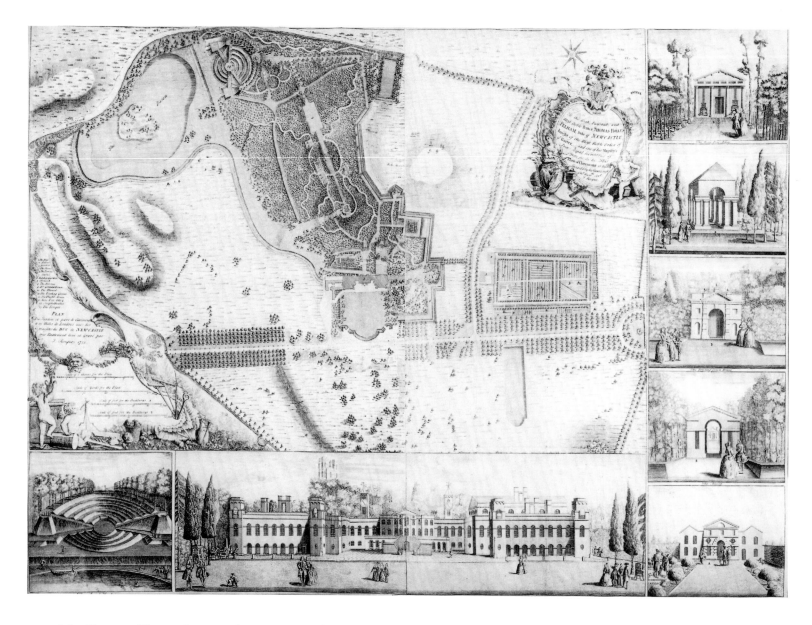

294. John Rocque, *Plan and views of Claremont*, 1737, British Library, London

and rank he set out to create a *mise-en-scène* appropriate to a man who was to be one of the greatest political fixers of the age.

Newcastle was connected by marriage to Sir Robert Walpole and hence became one of the mainstays of the long era of Whig dominance. He did not attract a good press from his contemporaries, Lord Chesterfield casting him as:

> good-natured, to a degree of weakness, even to tears, upon the slightest occasion. Exceedingly timorous, both personally and politically... His ruling, or rather his only, passion was the agitation, the bustle, and the hurry of business... Upon the whole, he was a compound of most human weaknesses, but untainted by any vice or crime...[77]

The motives for his interest in gardening remains unexplained but he was one of the leaders of the new style, initially employing Vanbrugh, and later Charles Bridgeman and William Kent.

Few other gardens are so fortunate in having a succession of engraved plans plotting their development within a period so graphically, the first comes in Colen Campbell's *Vitruvius Britannicus*, published in 1725 (292) followed by

two by John Rocque, one in 1737 and the second in 1750 (294, 297). The first forms a record of virtually the whole first phase of the garden. The estate as it was purchased comprised some fifty acres and Vanbrugh was employed at once to enlarge the house, with the addition of massive wings to the east and west. Behind the house to the north-west the land rose sharply, forming the mount of its name. On the summit of this Vanbrugh was to erect the first garden building, a belvedere, known as the White Tower. This was in a vaguely medieval style with four crenellated corner towers. Campbell, who provides us with the 1725 groundplan, writes that it afforded 'a most prodigious fine Prospect of the Thames and adjacent villas.'

That effectively ended Vanbrugh's contribution, for the garden was laid out in the decade and a half following 1710 by Bridgeman. As a consequence Claremont is one of the earliest instances of the dissolution of the old formal style. In this phase the approach to the house retained its full baroque panoply with a magnificent avenue from the south and a cross-axis one running east to west, each flanked by rows of trees, four deep. There formality ended and the garden became a personal elysium, wandering off from the mansion house to which it had no axial relationship whatsoever. The amount of land available for landscaping was doubled in 1716 when Newcastle acquired two neighbouring manors. In the plan we can see a bold avenue stretching down from the belvedere to a rectangular bowling green giving the garden a formal spine. Further on to the north-west a large circular pond was dug surrounded by a double avenue of trees. But the overall shape of the cultivated area was wildly asymmetrical, and retained by earth bulwarks which held in the wooded walks.

The 1725 plan must have been drawn and in the press immediately before Bridgeman set to work on the garden's most famous feature, the amphitheatre. That and the obelisk in the middle of the pond were in place by the following

295. *Claremont: View of the circular pond, obelisk and amphitheatre*, anonymous engraving, *c.* 1725. The National Trust

296. Stephen Switzer's proposal for a cascade, canal and fountain before the amphitheatre at Claremont. From his *An Introduction to a general System of hydrostatics and hydraulics*, London, 1727. British Library, London

297. John Rocque, *Plan of Claremont*, 1750. Marked with viewpoints of five of the pictures. British Library, London

298. William Kent, *Design for the planting around the Temple at Claremont with the Belvedere beyond*, late 1730s. British Museum, London

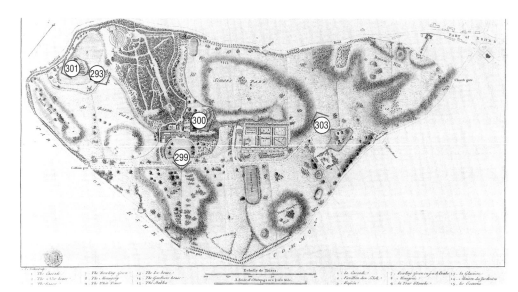

year, for the theatre is mentioned by Batty Langley in his *New Principles of Gardening* (1726) and by Stephen Switzer in *An Introduction to a General System of Hydrostatics and Hydraulics* (1727). Switzer indeed includes a plan (296) of the amphitheatre but amended to incorporate a cascade, canals and *jet d'eau*, which he thought far more appropriate than the round pond. Shortly afterwards an engraving was issued of this ensemble (295), which in fact follows Switzer in offering suggestions for its improvement. It is the earliest published record of a monument to the birth of the new garden style. In it we see features which bring the name of William Kent to mind, a temple at the summit of the amphitheatre recalling the one at Chiswick as does the porticoed temple glimpsed to the right, but there is no evidence that either ever existed.[78]

Vanbrugh died in 1726 and Bridgeman in 1738 but already by 1734 Kent was busy at Claremont. In the well-known letter from Sir Thomas Robinson to Lord Carlisle in the summer of that year he signals a

299. Artist unknown, *Claremont. Entrance front with the Belvedere seen in the background, c.* 1750. Private collection

300. Artist unknown, *Claremont. View of William Kent's Temple to the right and a vista to a lake and a pavilion, c.* 1750. Private collection

general alteration of some of the most considerable gardens in the Kingdom...after Mr Kent's notion, viz. to lay them out and work without level or line...The method of gardening is the more agreeable as, when finished, it has the appearance of beautiful nature...The celebrated gardens at Claremont, Chiswick and Stowe are now full of labourers to modernize expensive works finished in them since everyone's memory.[79]

In the case of Claremont we can add some surviving sketches by Kent (298) in which he sets his new architectural and sculptural features, a herm, a temple and a cascade into a painterly vision in which trees are dotted in clumps to provide dramatic chiaroscuro.[80]

In the 1738 plan by Rocque (294) the effect of Kent's loosening hand can be seen at work. The earthen bulwarks are gone, in favour of a grassy ditch acting as a ha-ha. The round pond or basin has lost its obelisk, gained an island reached by a wooden bridge and been transformed into an irregular shape. There is no sign however of the temple on the island which only appears in later impressions of the engraving, added in the top left hand side of the print. The approach avenue has been swept away but some of the east-west axial one remains in place. The main ride from the belvedere to the bowling green is still there but it has been extended to another cross axis on the fringe of the estate, which leads to the summit of the amphitheatre. A classical pavilion has been constructed at one side of the bowling green, a temple close to the house and a rustic cottage at the far of end of a smaller sheet of water. And there is a considerable multiplication of squiggly walks.

Most commentators have dated the pictures to around 1740. We know that Kent and the Duke fell out in 1747 or 1748 not long before the former's death. As has been suggested, this series might be a celebration of the completion of Kent's work, but the pictures accord far more closely with Rocque's 1750 plan than the 1738 one. The location of the viewpoint of five out of the six pictures can be pinpointed pretty exactly on the 1750 plan (297). The key evidence for this dating comes in the painting that includes the entrance drive from Farm Lodge, which goes past the re-sited obelisk and the Home Farm, with a little island in proximity to it (303). None of this complex was in place in 1738 but it was certainly all there in 1750. Nor is there any indication on the 1738 plan of the cascade that is firmly marked as number one on that of 1750. So in fact the date of the pictures could be as late as the 1750s.

It has to be assumed that Newcastle commissioned these pictures, but there is no provenance to prove it. Their utter freshness of vision surely gives us a remarkably truthful impression of a garden designed by Kent within years of its creation. One is a panorama of the house façade, now devoid of its approach avenues, and with Vanbrugh's belvedere soaring up behind it (299). There are two views of the lake, one with the amphitheatre to the right, with the lake's edge still stone lined and with Kentian seats arranged on the amphitheatre's mighty steps for viewing the prospect (293). The second picture looks towards the temple on the island and includes a modified version of the cascade as it was actually built (300). A fourth looks along a vista towards a picturesque thatched cottage at the end of a small sheet of water (301). To the right on a hillock is the temple recorded in the margin of the 1738 engraving. This was quite close to the house and the vista is to one side of it looking along almost to the boundary of the estate. The view of the Home Farm, has already been discussed leaving us with one conundrum, a grassy walk flanked by formal hedges clipped into bays and pilasters and with Kentian seats either side (302). Logic would suggest that we see something by Bridgeman softened by the hand of Kent in the scattered fir trees and clumps in the distance. But it would be difficult to guess which walk is recorded.

Even more than in Rysbrack's paintings of Chiswick we are given an acute feeling of what it must have been like to have experienced one of these innovatory gardens in its youth. A flower garden is recorded at the back of the house in the 1750 plan but it was evidently not thought appropriate for a picture. These green arcadian gardens called for a high degree of sophistication of perception, their tonality ranging through a wide repertory of foliage shades and demanding a masterly orchestration of groupings to frame or hide something or draw the eye onwards. Far more than in the Chiswick series are we made con-

301. Artist unknown, *Claremont. View to William Kent's temple on the island,* c. 1750, Private collection

302. Artist unknown, *Claremont. View of one of the topiary allées,* c. 1750, Private collection

303. Artist unknown, *Claremont. View of the stables and entrance lodge,* c. 1750, Private collection

scious of the role played by the cast shadows of trees and hedges. The absence of visitors or gardeners heightens the intense feeling of privacy, only the sheep indicate that the estate was actually worked as farmland.

Unlike so many of the other gardens essaying the new style Claremont emerges as a private elysium without an iconography. Any obvious allusion to the world of politics in which its owner was immersed for decades is eschewed. Perhaps Newcastle too saw the gardens of Claremont as the villa garden style of Rome translated to England. This in short was his Plinian villa. Nor should we forget that Newcastle's brother, Henry Pelham, lived next to Claremont. Esher Place was regarded by Horace Walpole as Kent's most accomplished creation and that too seems not to have had a schema. Both gardens probably reflect the decline in iconographic knowledge at the opening of the eighteenth century that paved the way for a style that was wholly visual.[81] Thomas Whately in his *Observations* (1770) describes Esher in these kind of terms, ones which could equally apply to neighbouring Claremont:

> The groups of trees are few and small; there was not room for larger or for more…the vacant spaces are therefore chiefly irregular openings spreading every way, and great differences between the trees are the principal variety…The trees sometimes overspread the flat below, sometimes leave an open space to the river; at other times crown the brow of a large knole, climb up a steep, or hang on a gentle declivity. These varieties more than compensate for the want of variety in the disposition of the trees.[82]

And it is this garden presented as a series of arcadian pictures or stage settings by Kent that we see caught so exactly in these canvases.

A PLINIAN VILLA: WESTCOMBE HOUSE

The ghost of Pliny and his villas haunts not only Hartwell and Claremont, but also the garden of Westcombe House, Blackheath, which was arguably more extraordinary than any of the other gardens which were to be the subject of a set of paintings. These are by the landscape artist, George Lambert, and one of them is usefully dated 1732 (304, 306).[83] Like Chiswick, Westcombe was a villa and, like Chiswick too, it was the direct expression of the personal taste of a single aristocrat, the 'Architect Earl', Henry Herbert, 9th Earl of Pembroke. Westcombe was built on rented land at Blackheath by the Earl when he was Lord Herbert before he succeeded his father in 1733. Unlike the taciturn Burlington, much is recorded about this remarkable man, all of it pointing to an original cast of mind and vision.[84] Here was an early vegetarian whose passion for his horses stretched to providing for them on his demise. Here too was a bold athlete, but yet endowed with all the attributes of the virtuoso. Herbert was also an architect, much respected at the time, exercising that role in a manner typical of the eighteenth century by using an amanuensis, in his case Roger Morris. Herbert had made the Grand Tour, meeting Kent in Rome, and, as a consequence, he became a passionate palladian and devotee of the architecture of both Palladio and Inigo Jones.

Herbert's speciality was the design of toy-like classical villas. Marble Hill, which he designed for George II's mistress, the Countess of Suffolk, is a monument to his exquisite if chaste classical taste. Westcombe, which we see in the pictures, was in the same vein, its exterior adorned with antique busts and its interior of a kind which the old Duchess of Marlborough lampooned as 'the

304. George Lambert with William Hogarth and Samuel Scott, *Westcombe House, Blackheath*, 1732. Collection of the Earl of Pembroke, and the Trustees of the Wilton House Trust

305. George Lambert, Site drawing for plate 304, British Library, Map Room, King's Collection, XLI/29/G.

306. George Lambert with William Hogarth and Samuel Scott, *Westcombe House, Blackheath*, 1732, collection of the Earl of Pembroke, and the Trustees of the Wilton House Trust

307. Detail of plate 309, Thomas Robins turns the ground of Painswick House into a rococo reverie of frolicking satyrs

most ridiculous thing that ever I saw in my life.'[85] The account of the interior, which she gives in her letter, makes it clear that it was extremely unusual. So was the garden.

The Duchess's visit was in 1732, when the house had just been finished. This information establishes that both it and the grounds were laid out in the immediate aftermath of Robert Castell's *The Villas of the Ancients Illustrated* (1728). This gave a groundplan of Pliny's Tuscan villa, with its irregular, winding walks that had influenced Lord Burlington's planting on the far bank of the Bollo Brook. Westcombe records a serious attempt to re-create an Ancient Roman villa garden. The hand of William Kent is nowhere in evidence.

George Lambert's paintings embody a radical departure from the usual house views, for the house hardly figures at all, being looked up to in two of the views and the other two looking into the surrounding grounds.[86] But, one might add, that way of looking at the house must have been dictated by the patron – surely the man in the red coat who appears in all four pictures. This indicates an interest not so much in recording the architecture of the house but the ambience of the whole *mise-en-scène*. The commission was made one year before Herbert succeeded to the title and to Wilton House.

George Lambert, like Rysbrack, was a theatrical scene-painter employed from about 1725 onwards by the Lincoln's Inn Theatre.[87] In 1732 he is recorded as painting scenery for Covent Garden. The theatrical link may be an important one for although virtually no stage design survives from this era the libretti of Handel's operas, for example, are full of garden scenes. One of these scenes on stage could well have triggered the notion of asking the same painter to paint an actual garden, in the same way as Burlington may have been inspired. But Lambert, like Rysbrack, could turn his hand to most things from copying old masters to Italianate landscapes. However, for the views of Westcombe Hogarth inserted the figures and Samuel Scott provided the river-

PANS LODGE

DBORN GROVE

Pan taykt in

LOS SHIRE

scape. In the case of the view from a pond looking to the house, Lambert's on-site drawing survives which corresponds in every detail with the finished painting, bar the foreground and the figures (305).

This garden takes the attempt to respond to the antique far beyond that at Chiswick. Here there is not even a trace of a lingering Bridgemanesque formality. Here are no Kentian temples, no statuary, no clipped hedges or articulated water. Instead we are confronted with an almost unnervingly natural, if arranged, terrain. Where there are hedges they remain fluffy, etching gentle winding walks through grass and trees that are arranged to afford vistas to the Thames and to the distant cityscape with its glimpse of the dome of St Paul's.

This juxtaposition is the key to their meaning, for this is a celebration of *otium* as against *negotium*, the civilised life of the villa in the country, as against that of public affairs in the city.[88] On the banks of the Thames we see a motif that looks back to one of the earliest of all the Medici villas, the Villa Medici at Fiesole, sited on its terraced gardens to afford vistas back to Florence. The presence in these pictures of rustics, farm workers, uniquely emphasises the role of the villa in the sense that Palladio designed it, for those along the Brenta were also working farms. Westcombe is never presented as a place of public parade by polite society.

Sixteen years later, in 1750, the Earl's son was to commission Richard Wilson to paint a parallel series of views, this time of the ancestral seat of the Herberts, Wilton (313, 314). In the case of Westcombe we have the earliest record of 'rural gardening' or the *ferme ornée* in which garden and working the land are welded into one. The vision remains resolutely English. There is no attempt to suffuse the domain with a false Claudean golden glamour. The Wilton pictures are of equal significance for in them we cross over from the age of the garden into that of the park.

The End of the Garden of Association: Thomas Robins the Elder

Garden painting was to take a very different direction by the close of the 1750s as ideal landscape under the aegis of 'Capability' Brown heralded the demise of the garden of association with its world of architectural fantasy and allusion. One artist, however, continued to record gardens in this vein and that was the provincial, naive painter, Thomas Robins the Elder, official 'limner' to the fashionable city of Bath.[89] To the modern eye these rococo visions offer total enchantment. Garlanded with flowers and at times peopled by nymphs and fauns, they conjure up a world about to vanish, one filled with Chinese kiosks and bridges, Gothic temples and pavilions, classical ruins and grottoes dotted asymmetrically either on summits or along serpentining walks edged with spindly trees. Robins's work oscillates between bird's-eye views, like those of Painswick House and its grounds (1748) (307–9), depicted in a manner which would not be altogether out of place in *Britannia Illustrata*, and those which are not so far distant from the work of Rysbrack at Chiswick or Nebot at Hartwell house. They belong firmly to the thought patterns of an earlier era.

Davenport House is in Shropshire and Robins painted views of its surroundings in 1753. On 15 July 1753 William Shenstone, creator of the famous *ferme ornée* of The Leasowes, wrote: 'Mr Davenport...is laying out his environs, and...has also a painter at this time taking views around his house.'[90] That

308. Thomas Robins the Elder, bird's-eye view of the gardens laid out between *c.* 1744 and 1748 by Benjamin Hyett at Painswick House, Gloucestershire. Private collection

309. Thomas Robins the Elder, Pan's Lodge in Coldbourne Grove, sited in a wood above the main gardens of Painswick House, Gloucestershire, 1748, Private collection

310. Thomas Robins the Elder, *Davenport House, Shropshire*, 1753, a view of the grounds laid out by Henry Davenport in the early 1750s, including a gothick temple, grotto, cascade and classical ruins. Private collection

311. Thomas Robins the Elder, *Davenport House, Shropshire*, 1753, another part of the grounds with a canal, gothick alcove seat and gothick *ferme ornée*. Private collection

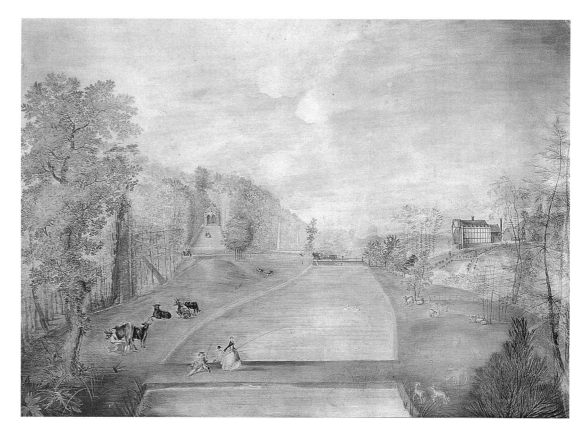

painter was Robins. In one view we look down on the house from a height and see serpentine plantings of young trees enfolding a Gothic pavilion on a mount. The pavilion is taken from a design by Batty Langley. Along a stream a cascade disgorges its waters into a stream below while, on an eminence in the foreground to the right there are ruins of two fragmentary classical arches. In the distance the middle ages are evoked with a baronial castellated tower (310). Here scattered across a single panorama are the features we know so well from great gardens like that at Stowe, monuments to bring to mind the heritage of the world of antiquity transported to England as well as England's own heroic past.

A second view looks up a long stretch of water. There is a fishing party in the foreground and there are vistas to a half-timbered farmhouse and also to a Gothic seat that should have been made of icing sugar (311). No other artist purveys quite that sense of the pure joy that such gardens must have brought to their privileged owners. They exude all the happiness and confidence in the world typical of the Enlightenment in its optimistic phase. But here, as in all his watercolours of gardens, one is also keenly aware that what we look at is transitory, a horticultural paradise of pasteboard, stage scenery dotted across the landscape, for the most part made of wood and *papier mâché*. And all of it too easily swept away, which indeed was what happened.

VI

GARDEN PICTURE
INTO LANDSCAPE PAINTING

THE TRIUMPH OF THE PARK

Up until the previous chapter we have searched for representations that might depict the reality of a garden. This has meant interpreting the horticultural evidence in emblems, studying the rare instances of pictures of gardens, or looking at prospects of country houses and their domain, whether in paint or in print. We have had little if any means of checking if what we see is accurate. The great series of garden pictures from the opening of the eighteenth century for the first time reverses that. Suddenly it seems that we can voyage through some of the most famous gardens of the age, savouring them in all their infinite variety. The scene would seem to be set for providing us henceforth with a plethora of visual material. But this was not to be, for, to a greater extent than in the previous centuries, the pictorial evidence after 1750 has left us a deeply flawed account of late Georgian gardens. Responsibility for this should be laid at the door of the patron, who no longer defined his status in terms of a garden, but of a park.

LANDSCAPE PARK AND LANDSCAPE PAINTER

In this new dialogue between patron and artist we will search in vain for garden views – we have entered the era of the park.[1] 'Capability' Brown's career took off in the 1750s and he and his contemporaries and followers, men like Richard Woods, shared his enthusiasm for parkland. A new generation discovered the beauties of the English landscape, resulting in an exaltation of the park, always a part of any substantial estate, and its expansion to embrace not only adjacent prospects, but also picturesque features such as crags, gorges and streams, previously looked upon as aberrations. Simultaneously the park encroached right up to the walls of the house and anything remotely recognisable as a garden vanished from the imagery.

The shift from the creation of gardens, works of high artifice, to 'improving' a pre-existing terrain, was a radical one; it demanded a succession of pictures. We are no longer confronted with pictures of gardens, but with idealised landscape paintings in the midst of which a house happens to be situated. Up until the 1750s gardens of association worked from the premise of a series of set pieces to be viewed as tableaux, whereas the new style was far freer and less constricted, offering multiple viewpoints, in particular those from the drive to the house and from the carriage pathway that encircled the estate. Both assumed movement less on foot than on horseback and in the new faster-moving, light carriages. Nature, of course, called for some rearranging, whether in

312. Richard Wilson at work, recording a view at Wilton House. Detail of plate 313

313. Richard Wilson, *Wilton House: view from the south-east with the house and bridge beyond the lake and basin, c.* 1758–9. Collection of the Earl of Pembroke and the Trustees of the Wilton House Trust

the era of Brown or in that of the Picturesque which succeeded it. Hills were made to undulate gently, irregular clumps of trees were planted, streams were turned into serpentine lakes, clearances were made and branches loped to afford vistas. The three decades after 1750 saw a landscape of Whig liberties, with few if any garden buildings. In the case of the Picturesque, the rearrangement of the existing domain allowed for a far greater tolerance of roughness, leaving peasants' huts and rickety bridges as they were, but it too was artifice and the aim was still to create a series of pictures.

Country-house owners now demanded of painters that their residence should be set in Utopia, a desire that fortuitously coincided with the coming of age of English landscape painting epitomised in the figure of Richard Wilson.[2] He was no hack topographer but a painter of high aspiration and determination, who, on his return from years of study in Italy, set out to elevate landscape painting, regarded as one of the minor genres, to the level of the Grand Style emulating the classical canvases of Poussin and Claude that had in part inspired the landscape garden.

Some time just before 1760 Wilson executed a set of five views of Wilton for

Henry Herbert, 10th Earl of Pembroke.[3] These show the park from various aspects with parts of the house visible in each. Pembroke had met Wilson on his Grand Tour. On his return he had commissioned Sir William Chambers to remodel the park which already included the famous palladian bridge designed by his father in association with Roger Morris in the 1730s.[4] Wilson's pictures form one of the first responses to the new format of the landscape park. Wiltshire is transmuted into the Roman Campagna and the house itself into an antique villa – all of it suffused by an unreal golden aura. The house, always glimpsed from afar, is depicted bathed in an evening sunset glow (313) or lit fitfully as the clouds momentarily part (314). In perhaps the most important of the series, the view from the south-east, Wilson emphasises the pictorial nature of his work by placing himself sketching in the foreground. Indeed this picture encapsulates what was to become a compositional cliché, reworked again and again by two generations of painters of country-house prospects. Always the foreground has a staffage of trees rising from a bank, which may or may not be peopled. Next came the artificial lake with its lyrical reflections and then beyond, generally elevated in the distance, the owner's house, framed by clumps of trees.

314. Richard Wilson, *Wilton House: view of part of the south front and the Palladian bridge to the east, c.* 1758–9. Collection of the Earl of Pembroke and the Trustees of the Wilton House Trust

315. Richard Wilson, *View of Tabley House,*
Cheshire, the grounds were laid out for Sir
Peter Leicester, *c.* 1765. Private collection

Wilson himself was to repeat the formula in his rendering, for instance, of Croome Court in 1758, a picture which celebrated 'Capability' Brown's transformation of an expanse of marshy land into spacious lawns through which a stream meandered.[5] The same treatment is accorded to Syon House, viewed from Richmond Gardens across the Thames,[6] and to Tabley House, Cheshire, across a lake (315).[7] In the case of Moor Park, Hertfordshire, a house set amid seemingly untramelled prospects, the scene lacks only the water. The painter purveys a never-ending verdant and watery emptiness evoking the order, tranquillity and harmony that the owning classes believed they embodied. The debt not only to painters of classical landscape in the previous century but also to Dutch panoramic views of the same period is patent.

Two of Richard Wilson's pictures, however, qualify as garden pictures in the old sense. At Kew Sir William Chambers continued the tradition of associational buildings, evocations of classical antiquity and foreign lands, like a mosque or the famous pagoda for the Princess Augusta, widow of Frederick, Prince of Wales. Wilson always aspired to royal patronage and he executed, about 1761–2, two views of the Dowager Princess of Wales's garden, one of the ruined arch and the other of the pagoda and the wooden bridge (316).[9] Both must have been painted in the hope of encouraging the young George III

316. Richard Wilson, *Kew Gardens: view towards the Pagoda and Bridge*, two features of the garden laid out by Sir William Chambers for Augusta, Princess of Wales, 1762. New Haven, Yale Center for British Art, Paul Mellon Collection

317. William Hannan, *View of the lake and cascade at West Wycombe Park, Buckinghamshire,* as laid out in the 1740s for Sir Francis Dashwood, 1752, West Wycombe Park

318. Artist unknown, *View of the lower lake at Studley Royal, Yorkshire,* part of the grounds laid out in the 1720s and 1730s for John Aislabie, probably 1750s, Vyner Trustees, Fountains Hall

to commission a complete series. From the early nineteenth century until 1949 the picture of the ruined arch laboured under the title of a view in the gardens of the Villa Borghese, indicating the origins of Wilson's treatment of the livestock and carriage entrance to the garden. Both pictures were shown to the king by Chambers himself. He was a friend of Wilson's leading patron, Benjamin Booth, who has left an account of the royal reaction: 'They were shewn Him, but a party for Zucharelli and Flemish artists getting the better of his Judgmt He did not express that Approbation of them as was wisht nor ever employed Him.'[10] And there it died.

This incident also probably reflects the slip from fashion of the sets of garden views typical of the first half of the century. Their finale might be said to be the eleven, once possibly fourteen, views of the surroundings of Studley Royal, Yorkshire (317).[11] At least one of these is said to be dated 1762 and signed by the painter of the Hartwell House set, Balthasar Nebot (281–8), although what we see bears little relation to his style. The costumes in some of the paintings seem to be earlier than the sixties and any serious study of this series, if indeed it is such, is precluded by their dispersal through the salerooms in the 1980s. But they do graphically record the great garden created by John Aislabie in the 1720s and 1730s, in which he made use of the waters of the river Skell which ran along a valley on the estate past the ruins of Fountains Abbey.[12] These were water gardens in the grand formal sense, ones of great splendour and elegance that incorporated a cascade flanked by finials and pavilions, the water falling into a semi-circular lake with a pyramid gushing water at its centre in the manner of Stowe. John's son, William, who inherited Studley in 1742 and who eventually purchased the ruins of Fountains in 1767, went on to add a Chinese landscape that is also recorded. But the Studley series is a remnant from an earlier decade. To it we can add two other groups to represent the tail end of a genre, the four murky views of Kew dated 1759 by Johann Jacob Schalch[13] and the two by William

319. John Constable, *View of Malvern Hall, Warwickshire*, 1809, the grounds were laid out by Henry Greswolde Lewis in the 1780s. Tate Gallery, London

Hannan of West Wycombe, Buckinghamshire, the Dashwood seat, dated 1752 (317).[14]

Sixty years after Wilson the young John Constable reworked exactly the same formula. In 1809 the artist was commissioned to paint a view of Malvern Hall, Warwick, the seat of Henry Greswold Lewis (319).[15] As in the case of Wilson's Wilton or Croome Court the composition is again a view from a bank across a stretch of artificial water to the house set amidst clumps of trees. Seven years on Constable was to paint a far more accomplished version of this type of view, this time of Wivenhoe Park, Essex (320), caught on a summer's day across the inevitable lake, in a picture which became a hugely extended panorama (he had to add strips of canvas to both sides) to include a deer house and a grotto: 'the great difficulty has been to get as much in as they wanted to make them acquainted with the scene.'[16] Pictures of this kind, and they are numerous and by a variety of hands, would almost suggest that the painting of gardens had become an extinct art.

That in fact was not so, but before exploring the trickle of works which will take us into the Victorian age we must turn to a far more significant development, the recording of English gardens in the mass visual media of the Georgian age, engraving.

Engraved Garden Views

Nothing could present clearer evidence that the status of gardens was changing than the emergence of a large market for engraved views of the most famous creations. Already by the 1740s garden visiting had become a popular pastime and that activity was only to escalate as the century drew to its close, particularly in the aftermath of the war with France in the 1790s, which eliminated travel abroad.

Until about 1750 the English had been on the receiving end of the international print trade based in Paris. By 1780 that situation had been reversed and

320. John Constable, *View of the grounds of Wivenhoe Park, Essex*, 1816, the seat of Major-General F. S. Rebow. National Gallery of Art, Washington, Widener Collection

Britain became instead Europe's major centre for the production of new prints, as Anglo-mania swept through the continent.[17] Foreign printmakers who had settled in London, men like John Rocque and Georges Chastelain, taught a new native generation better technique and draftsmanship. A system of subscription, built up through advertising and catalogues, ensured that the public was made aware of a continuous flow of new prints. This became dynamic after 1750 when that new generation of practitioners came to maturity. The print trade was aided also by the consumer boom, the ever expanding professional and middle classes having more disposable income to spend. That went hand in hand with a real sense of pride in the country's achievements in the arts. Add to that the desire for knowledge, which in an age before the camera could visually only be obtained by the means of the print.

Subject matter was never dictated other than by the marketplace. Gardens, as we have seen, already figured in the engraved tradition as part of the expansion in topographical publishing earlier in the century. But even then it was slow to take off. Knyff's *Britannia Illustrata*, first advertised in 1701, was still looking for subscribers in 1707 which it failed to find, although the project proceeded. We have already followed the sad saga of Rigaud's set of engravings of the gardens at Stowe in 1734 for which Bridgeman failed to find enough subscribers. It was not until the mid-1740s, and after they had been bought up by a consortium of printsellers, that these ravishing engravings were to see the light of day at what was half the original price. Even when that happened, in 1746, it was still a decade ahead of the explosion.

The boom in garden prints forms one aspect of the enormous demand for

321. J. B. Chatelain, *A perspective View of the Bowling Green...at Gubbins in Hertfordshire*, 1748, Bodleian Library, University of Oxford

views triggered by the discovery, about 1745, of the optical illusion of looking at prints through a concave glass.[18] In today's terms the experience would seem to be almost a naive one, but at the time looking at engraved views of the great gardens of the era must have had all the exhilaration of both discovery and experience. By means of a concave mirror and a reflector a print laid flat on a table could be viewed by looking through a lens placed at eye-level. This activity was first mentioned in a list of prints issued by Thomas and John Bowles which included a set of prints of Stowe as among those 'proper to be view'd in concave glasses.'[19]

To appreciate the escalation of the market it may be useful to tabulate the major print series:[20]

1743	George Bickham, *Deliciae Britannicae; or, the Curiosities of Kensington, Hampton Court and Windsor Castle Delineated*
1745	John Tinney and Anthony Highmore collaborate on eight views of Kensington and Hampton Court
1748	John Tinney publishes two views of Gubbins (321) Thomas Smith publishes views of Hagley and The Leasowes
1749	Thomas Smith publishes views including Hagley, Belton, Newstead and Exton Park
1750	George Bickham, *The Beauties of Stowe*
1754	Eight engravings by Paul Sandby after drawings by himself, his brother, Thomas, and others, published privately, of the Duke of Cumberland's improvements in Windsor Great Park
1757	John Tinney produces four views of West Wycombe and two of Whitton Park
1758	Robert Sayer publishes views of Studley Royal (322), Chatsworth and Castle Howard
1759	John Tinney combines with Thomas and John Bowles publishing six views by John Sullivan of Wilton, Oatlands, Ditchley, Cliveden, Esher and Woburn Farm (323)
1760	This consortium is joined by Robert Sayer and publishes views by

322. Anthony Walker, *View of Fountains Abbey and Tent Hill from the gardens of Studley Royal, Yorkshire*, 1758, Riddleston Hall, Yorkshire

William Woollett of Carlton House (324), Foots Cray, Combe Bank, Painshill and two of Hall Barn.

1763   Paul Sandby's etchings in Sir William Chambers, *Plans, Elevations, Sections and Perspective Views of the Gardens and Buildings at Kew in Surrey*.

1777   Francis Vivares's engravings after Coplestone Warre Bamfylde's watercolours of the lake at Stourhead.

These engraved views frequently record gardens planted decades earlier whose appearance will have changed considerably. Then, at the close of the 1770s, a new genre arrived, that leads on into the nineteenth century, the engraved view of the country seat. In 1779 publication began of William Watts's *The Seats of the Nobility and Gentry*. By 1786 some eighty-four copperplates had already been published after drawings by artists including Michael Rooker and Paul Sandby (325). This survey was continued from 1787 to 1800 in William Angus's *The Seats of the Nobility and Gentry in Great Britain and Wales, In a Collection of Select Views*. Like the paintings these uniformly present us with the isolated mansion house set in its swathes of parkland.

For the first time British engravers surpassed their continental rivals. Three in particular, William Woollett, Luke Sullivan and Paul Sandby, were outstanding. Woollett, the son of a flax-dresser, was a pupil of John Tinney, the most significant publisher of views of houses and gardens around London.[21] Indeed Woollett's earliest certain work, when he was twenty-two, was a set of views of the gardens of Sir Francis Dashwood's West Wycombe and another of the Duke of Argyll's garden at Whitton in 1757. These reveal a sophistication in the handling of the atmospherics of cloud formation and light as it fell onto trees, shrubs, grass and water that was admirably attuned to the new landscape style (327, 328). But Woollett's finest work lay elsewhere, starting with his engraving after Claude's *Temple of Apollo* in 1760.

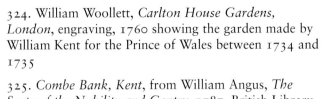

323. Luke Sullivan, *Woburn Farm, grounds south of the house*, 1759

324. William Woollett, *Carlton House Gardens, London*, engraving, 1760 showing the garden made by William Kent for the Prince of Wales between 1734 and 1735

325. *Combe Bank, Kent*, from William Angus, *The Seats of the Nobility and Gentry*, 1787, British Library

326. William Woollett, *Painshill Park,
Surrey. View of the lake to the west of the
grotto island*, 1760, part of the grounds laid
out by Charles Hamilton between 1738 and
1773

Luke Sullivan, an Irishman who owed his career to the patronage of the
Duke of Beaufort, responded to the new manner with a sharp eye for exquisite
detail and delicacy of observation, until drink and women led to an early
death.[22] He not only engraved but also drew the six views of the major gardens
published in 1759. These share a delight in placing in the foreground a large
tree in shadow always sited just off-centre leading the eye on to two contrary
perspectives to admire glimpses of the shimmering domain beyond and into the
far distance. He peoples his shadowed foregrounds with figures whose elegance
and animation can only be described as rococo.

The final outstanding contributor was Paul Sandby, whose series of etchings
after drawings by William Marlow, Thomas Sandby and John Joshua Kirby of
Kew gardens form a summit of achievement in late eighteenth-century garden
publishing. Sandby was of course a major artist, the watercolourist who raised
the art to the status previously only accorded to oil painting. His period of service with the Military Survey of Scotland early in his career ensured his abilities
as an accurate draftsman with an unerring eye for perspective. Like Luke
Sullivan he employed strong variations of light and shade to infuse his panoramas with life. Skies are often dramatic and although his treatment of trees tends
to be formulaic he invests his sparsely peopled scenes with a sense of mysterious rapture that captures the magic of the landscape garden at its finest.

Such engravings satisfied a home tourist market and exported the triumph of
English garden style across the globe. Many were retrospective records of gardens made earlier in the century which had attained status as points of reference. After 1770 the prints assume the monotony of the paintings, variations on
a theme, the ever present lake, undulating hills and clumps of trees either
smooth in the Brownian period or ragged in the Picturesque phase. One looks
in vain for anything which might remotely be described as a garden. But in fact
such things did exist.

THE SURVIVAL OF THE GARDEN PICTURE

Contrary to what the paintings and engravings suggest, the late eighteenth-century landscape park embraced the garden. Flower gardens and rosaries as part of 'the pleasure ground' were standard, indeed highly esteemed, features of any major country-house complex.[23] But they were hidden away behind screens of trees and shrubberies, so as not to disrupt the landscape composition framing the house. Thus representations of them are exceptionally rare and their existence is only generally signalled in groundplans, where time and again, even in the case of Brown himself, we find a formal arrangement of flowerbeds tucked away, but in proximity to the house.

Through the century the old wilderness, with its stiff hedges and radiating walks, evolved into the pleasure ground with its winding pathways and shrubberies. Within any landscape park there was always a pleasure ground in which the planting was far more ornamental, embracing the use of trees, flowering shrubs, flowers and bulbs arranged in a graduated planting and making use in particular of the new exotics which flooded in from America from the late 1730s onwards through the agency of Peter Collinson and John Bartram. Fleeting glimpses are all we can catch of this development in engravings like William Woollett's of the garden at Carlton House in 1760. It had been laid out by Kent in the thirties, and records an astonishing luxuriance of planting and flowers. On one side of the same artist's engraving of Grotto Island at Painshill (326) we can spot a cluster of exotics, including a spruce, a pine and a *Robinia pseudoacacia*[24] and in his depiction of the bowling green in the Duke of Argyll's garden at Whitton (327) we catch figures solemnly inspecting specimen cedars and pine trees.[25]

The actor David Garrick acquired Hampton House on the Thames in 1753. He employed Brown to lay out its modest terrain,[26] and Johann Zoffany painted a sparkling quartet of views of it. In one, *A View of Hampton House with Garrick reading*, specimens of the new exotics were literally just dotted

328. Johann Zoffany, *A view of the grounds of Hampton House*, 1762. The figure in the foreground is described as 'Garrick reading' in an early inventory; the grounds were laid out by 'Capability' Brown. Collection of Lord Egremont, Petworth House

into a shrubbery (328). In fact Zoffany's rendering of the horticultural content of the pictures is so general that it is little help in terms of information, excepting for its vivid record of a weeping willow – then a novelty. A group of them cascades behind the temple dedicated to Shakespeare while two others, clearly very recent plantings, are by the water's edge in proximity to Garrick's tea party (329).

As the century progressed the shrubbery gradually replaced the wilderness, but the term only came into general use after 1770. In the same way as the circuit of the park was made on horseback or by carriage, walks were taken through the pleasure ground, something that gradually developed into a circuit,

329. Johann Zoffany, *A view of the grounds of Hampton House with Mrs and Mrs Garrick taking tea*, 1762. Private collection

330. Thomas Robins, *The Chinese Kiosk, Woodside, Old Windsor, Berkshire*; the garden was laid out for Hugh Hamersley in the 1750s. Private collection

providing an opportunity for highly decorative planting. But it is a development which visually went unrecorded. Thomas Robins's view of the Chinese Kiosk (330) at Woodside, Old Windsor[27] from the late 1750s provides a rare record of one of these serpentine walks (331) which formed the essence of some of the great set pieces of the age like Philip Southcote's Woburn Farm or William Shenstone's The Leasowes.

332. Johan Heinrich Muntz, *Strawberry Hill, Twickenham, from the South*, with its floriferous shrub border, *c.* 1755–9. Lewis Walpole Library, Yale University

333. William Tomkins, *The Elysian Fields at Audley End, Suffolk, from the Tea House Bridge*, laid out in the 1780s as a hidden floral paradise, 1788, Audley End

Johan Heinrich Muntz's view of Strawberry Hill, *c.* 1755–9 (332), records a rarity, a mid-eighteenth-century theatrical shrubbery which fully lived up to the aim of its owner, Horace Walpole, in being '*riant*' and full of all 'the gaieties of nature'.[28] Only William Tomkins's paintings of the Elysian Fields at Audley End in 1788 as created by Sir John Griffin a few years earlier (333) conjures up the magic of floriferous walkways in which the visitor wandered along borders crammed with china roses, honeysuckle, pinks, lilies and clusters of African marigolds, candytuft and stocks. As Mark Laird has written: 'no other painting

331. A rare depiction of serpentine walks flanked by flowering trees and shrubs. Detail from plate 330

334. Paul Sandby, *The Flower Garden at Nuneham Courtney*, 1777; the garden was laid out by William Mason for the 1st Earl Harcourt in the 1770s. Private collection

335. William Pars, *The Flower Garden at Strawberry Hill, Middlesex*, 1772; it was created for Horace Walpole between 1769 and 1772. Victoria & Albert Museum, London

comes so close to capturing the essential qualities of an eighteenth-century pleasure ground.'[29]

Information about flower gardens is sparse, opening with William Marlow's record of that designed for Princess Augusta at Kew in the 1750s, its format still that of Lady Burlington's at Chiswick.[30] Flower gardens are in fact quite a mysterious feature – one strand formal, as at Kew, the other irregular, beds either circular or serpentine dotted into grass of the kind already seen in Dickie Bateman's garden at Old Windsor (213). This absence of pictorial sources forces probably overmuch attention onto the famous flower garden at Nuneham Courtney which was recorded in two views by Paul Sandby in 1777 (1, 334) that were engraved in the *Copperplate Magazine* by William Watts and issued in 1778. But of the unrivalled status of the garden there can be no doubt. It had been begun by the 1st Earl Harcourt under the influence of the poet William Mason and the philosopher, Jean-Jacques Rousseau.[31] It enshrined the familiar circuit walk through lawns studded with clumps of trees and shrubs in irregular beds planted thick with graduated flowers. The ensemble embraced both architectural and sculptural features: a conservatory, the Temple of Flora, a bower and a grotto besides statues and busts of philosophers and mythological figures. This flower garden was universally admired and also copied and the existence of these paintings is at least some compensation for their absence in the case of other great flower gardens of the era such as the Duchess of Portland's at Bulstrode or Queen Charlotte's at Frogmore.

One of the few other glimpses of a flower garden comes in William Pars's watercolour of Horace Walpole's one at Strawberry Hill in 1772 (335), painted shortly after its creation on land that he had acquired to the north of the villa three years before. The arrangement here is a formal geometric one, but by 1777 this no longer satisfied him and he was filled with a huge desire to emulate Nuneham Courtney: 'The Flora Nunehamica is the height of my ambition'.

336. William Henry Pyne, *Boy playing a drum in the garden of a Country House*, 1793; an attempt at a circular flowerbed filled with a graduated planting. New Haven, Yale Center for British Art, Paul Mellon Collection

337. John Constable, *The Kitchen Garden at East Bergholt House, Essex*, 1815. Ipswich Borough Council Museums and Galleries

A second watercolour from 1786 records this new passion, but the result hardly lived up to his horticultural aspirations.[32]

In these scattered pictures we look forward to the golden century of floral abundance to come. In them also we anticipate the re-emergence of the flower garden to public view instead of being hidden away behind a screen of trees and evergreen shrubs. In them even more we look forward to the spread of gardening to the middle classes that was to come in the work of John Claudius Loudon in the 1820s. That widening out from a narrow aristocratic circle is caught in William Henry Pyne's watercolour of a decayed old gentry house dated 1793 (336), whose garden already sports an imitation of the kind of graduated circular flowerbed seen in the grandest of gardens. Here the display is a valiant attempt rather than a spectacular reality.

In the same vein we might finally reach over into the new century with John Constable's unforgettable views of both the flower and kitchen gardens of his parents' house at East Bergholt, Essex (337, 338).[33] Together they form one dazzling panorama, the flower garden caught in a haunting late-summer evening light, the kitchen garden in the cool of a working morning. The flower garden was the creation of his mother the previous year, 1814, and she died in the following spring when Constable painted it. His father was still alive, an ailing man faced already with the legal wrangles which were to end in the break up of the family estate and the sale of the house. Both pictures have been recog-

338. John Constable, *The Flower Garden at East Bergholt House, Essex*, 1815; the garden created by the painter's mother shortly before her death. Ipswich Borough Council Museums and Galleries

nised as quite unlike anything else in nineteenth-century painting. Constable never sold these canvases, never exhibited them or even passed comment upon them. They remained with him until his death, perhaps an indication that they embodied some of his deepest emotional responses to grief. We look down from an upper room or the roof of the house onto his mother's flowerbed in its first summer, an image when set into context only periphery as evidence of the spread of the flower garden but far more as one of tragic intensity mourning the loss of a parent. In that picture we look forward to the kind of dialogue between painter and garden to come in Manet and Rueil and Monet and Giverny. And yet simultaneously we seem to have come back to where we started, the garden as emblem.

NOTES

INTRODUCTION

1. *Country Life*, 14 July 1994, p.52.
2. See for Italy Cristina Acidini Luchinat, 'Alle origini del "ritratto di giardini"', in *Giardini Regali. Fascino e Immagini del verde nelle grande dinastie: dai Medici agli Asburgo*, ed. Monica Amari, Milan 1998, pp. 159–64; for the Netherlands, Erick de Jong and Maureen Dominicus-van Soest, *Aardse Paradijzen. De Tuin in de Nederlandsche kunst 15de tot 18de eeuw*, Ghent 1996, pp. 202–4 (English summary).
3. Penelope Hobhouse and Christopher Wood, *Painted Gardens. English Watercolours 1850–1914*, London 1988; Eve Eckstein, *George Samuel Elgood. His Life and Work 1851–1943*, London 1995.

CHAPTER I: PRIDE OF POSSESSION

1. Oliver Millar, *Tudor, Stuart and Early Georgian Pictures in the Collection of H. M. The Queen*, London 1963, I, pp. 63–4 (43); Roy Strong, *Gloriana. The Portraits of Queen Elizabeth I*, London 1987, p. 49; Christopher Lloyd and Simon Thurley, *Images of a Tudor King*, London 1990, p. 116 (3).
2. Simon Thurley, *The Royal Palaces of Tudor England*, New Haven and London 1993, pp. 212-16; idem, *Whitehall Palace. An Architectural History, 1240–1690*, New Haven and London 1999, pp.52–62.
3. For which see Roy Strong, *The Renaissance Garden in England*, London 1979, pp.34–8; idem, 'Los jardines de los palacios de la Inglaterra Tudor', in *Jardin y Tanturaleza en el reindado de Felipe II*, ed. Carmen Anon and Jose Luis Sancho, Madrid 1998, pp. 113–18, which includes new material that has emerged since 1979.
4. On the compartment system see Claudia Lazzaro, *The Italian Renaissance Garden*, New Haven and London 1990, pp. 33 ff.; David Jacques, 'The *compartiment* system in England', *Garden History*, 27, 1999, pp. 32–53.
5. See John Harvey, *Medieval Gardens*, London 1981, p. 135; Jeanne Bourin, *La Rose et La Mandragore*, François Bourin 1990, pp. 66–70.
6. Robert G. Calkins, 'Piero de' Crescenzi and the Medieval Garden', in *Medieval Gardens*, ed. Elisabeth B. MacDougall, Dumbarton Oaks Colloquium on the History of Landscape Architec-

ture, IX, 1986, pp.155–73.
7. This passage is usefully translated in *ibid.*, pp. 172–3.
8. See A. D. Fraser, 'Cosimo de'Medici's Patronage of Architecture and the Theory of Magnificence', *Journal of the Warburg and Courtauld Institutes*, XXXIII, 1970, pp. 162–70.
9. See C. A. J. Armstrong, 'The Golden Age of Burgundy. Dukes that outdid kings', *The Courts of Europe. Politics, Patronage and Royalty 1400–1800*, ed. A. G. Dickens, London 1977, p. 74.
10. Anne Hagopian van Buren, 'Reality and Literary Romance in the Park of Hesdin', in *Medieval Gardens*, *op. cit.*, pp. 123–4.
11. Gordon Kipling, *Triumph of Honour. Burgundian Origins of the Elizabethan Renaissance*, Leiden 1977, p. 43 note 9.
12. Strong, *Gloriana*, *op. cit.*, pp. 113–14; *Dynasties. Painting in Tudor and Jacobean England 1530–1630*, exhibition catalogue, Tate Gallery, 1995, pp. 86–7 (41).
13. Strong, *Gloriana*, p.100.
14. See Kenneth Woodbridge, *Princely Gardens. The origins and development of the French formal style*, London 1986, p. 79; William Howard Adams, *The French Garden 1500–1800*, London 1979, pp. 34–5; Frances A. Yates, *The Valois Tapestries*, London 1959, pp.67–70.
15. Lauro Magnani, *Il Tempio di Venere. Giardino e Villa nella Cultura Genovese*, Sagep Editrice, 1987, pp. 125–50.
16. Ibid., p.148.
17. See Roy Strong, *Artists of the Tudor Court. The Portrait Miniature Rediscovered 1520–1620*, Victoria & Albert Museum exhibition catalogue, 1983, pp.159–61 (no.267) which lists all literature to that date, and subsequently *Dynasties*, *op. cit.*, 1995, pp. 128–9 (no.76); Lesley Lewis, *The Thomas More Family Group Portraits*, Leominster 1998, pp. 36–7; Roy Strong, 'Is this Thomas More's Garden?', *Country Life*, 9 March 2000, pp. 123–3.
18. George Vertue, *Notebooks*, v, Walpole Society, XXVI, 1937–8, pp. 10–11.
19. On this see *LCC Survey of London*, IV, *The Parish of Chelsea*, pt. 2, LCC, 1913, pp. 11, 20–7; *The Life of Sir Thomas More by his son-in-law, William Roper, Esq.*, ed. W. S. Singer, Chiswick, 1822, pp. 25–6; E. E. Reynolds, *Saint*

Thomas More, Burns Oates, 1953, pp. 184 ff.
20. Jacques, 'The *compartiment* system in England', *op. cit.*,
21. See P. W. Hasler, *The House of Commons 1558–1603*, London 1981, III, pp. 127–8; Gordon Nares, *Arbury Hall, Warwickshire*, Country Life, 1955.
22. Thomas Hyll (Didymus Mountain), *The Gardeners Labyrinth*, New York 1982, pp. 22–3.
23. *Ibid.*, p. 24.
24. (Francesco Colonna), *Hypnerotamachia. London 1592*, Theatrum Orbis Terrarum, 1969, pp. 42–4.
25. Woodbridge, *Princely Gardens*, p. 108, fig.106.
26. Mavis Batey, *Oxford's Gardens. The university's influence on garden history*, Avebury 1982, pp. 21–7. A goundplan of 1612 of the garden of Clothworkers' Hall records two knots, but not of the interweaving kind. See John Schofield, 'London Gardens 1500–1620', *Garden History*, XXVII, 1999, p.80, fig.5.
27. Gervase Markham, *The English Husbandman*, New York 1982, pp. 124–5.
28. Hasler, *House of Commons*, I, pp. 665–6.
29. For this period see Strong, *Renaissance Garden*, ch. 4 and 5.; John Dixon Hunt, *Garden and Grove. The Italian Renaissance garden in the English Imagination: 1600–1750*, London 1986, pp.119 ff.; Christopher Thacker, *The Genius of Gardening. The History of Gardens in Britain and Ireland*, London 1994, ch.6.
30. For previous literature see *Dynasties*, *op. cit.*, pp. 192–3 (no. 30).
31. George Scharf, *A Descriptive and Historical Catalogue of the Collection of Pictures at Woburn Abbey*, 1890, p.50 (no.70).
32. Alice Fairfax-Lucy, *Charlecote and the Lucys. The Chronicle of an English Family*, Oxford 1958, pp.126–7; information from Alastair Laing of the National Trust and Edward Morris of the Walker Art Gallery, Liverpool.
33. David Jacques and Arend van de Horst, *The Gardens of William and Mary*, London 1988, pp. 126–8; Jan Woudstra and James Hitchmough, 'The Enamelled Mead: history and practice of exotic perennials grown in grassy swards', *Landscape Research*, 25, no. 1, 2000, pp. 29–47.
34. André Mollet, *Le Jardin de Plaisir*, Editions du Moniteur, n.d., pp. 35–6.

35. For the portrait see Roy Strong, *Tudor and Jacobean Portraits*, London 1969, I, p.162 (no.4515). For Prince Henry's gardening projects see Strong, *Renaissance Garden*, pp. 97–103 and idem, *Henry, Prince of Wales and England's Lost Renaissance*, London 1986, pp.107–9; Sabine Eiche, 'Prince Henry's Richmond. The Project by Constantino de'Servi', *Apollo*, November 1998, pp. 10–13.

36. For previous bibliography and provenance see *Dynasties, op.cit.*, pp. 185–6 (no.126).

37. John Parkinson, *Paradisi in Sole, Paradisum Terrestris*, London 1629, p.610.

38. For a full bibliography of these see Roy Strong, 'The Renaissance Garden in England Reconsidered: A Survey of Two Decades of Research on the Period 1485–1642', *Garden History*, 27, no. 1, 1999, pp.6–7.

39. *The Glory of the Garden*, exhibition catalogue, Sotheby's, 1986, p. 39 (no. 24). The Byngs came from Kent. Sir George Byng, created Baron Byng of Southill , purchased Southill in the early eighteenth century. The portrait passed with the house to the Whitbreads in 1795. *Victoria County History, Bedfordshire*, ed. W. Daye, 1912, III, p. 258.

40. W.P. Hasler, *The House of Commons 1558–1603*, London 1981, I, p.662.

41. Richard W. Goulding and C. K. Adams, *Catalogue of the Pictures belonging to His Grace the Duke of Portland ... ,* Cambridge 1936, p. 208 (no. 520).

42. For previous discussions of the Arundel House garden see John Harris, Stephen Orgel and Roy Strong, *The King's Arcadia. Inigo Jones and the Stuart Court*, Arts Council exhibition, 1973, pp. 100–4 (nos 179–86); Strong, *Renaissance Garden*, pp. 69–74; Dixon Hunt, *Garden and Grove*, pp. 119–22; David Howarth, *Lord Arundel and his Circle*, New Haven and London 1985, pp. 57, 60, 63, 113, 120; John Schofield, 'London Gardens 1500–1620', *Garden History*, 27, no 1, 1999, pp. 74–6.

43. David Coffin, *Gardens and Gardening in Papal Rome*, Princeton 1991, pp.17–21; Elisabeth Blair Mac Dougall, '*Il Giardino all'Antico*: Roman Stuatuary and Italian Renaissance Gardens', in her *Fountains, Statues and Flowers. Studies in Italian Gardens of the Sixteenth and Seventeenth Centuries*, Dumbarton Oaks 1994, pp. 23–35; Lazzaro, *Italian Renaissance* garden, p. 80.

44. Mary S. Hervey, *Thomas Howard, Earl of Arundel*, Cambridge 1921, pp. 84, 94–5, 100 ff.; D. E. L. Haynes, *The Arundel Marbles*, Oxford 1975; Howarth, *Lord Arundel, op.cit.*, ch. IV.

45. Hervey, *Arundel*, p. 255.

46. *Dynasties,* pp. 208–11 (nos 140–1) including previous bibliography.

47. John Harris and Gordon Higgott, *Inigo Jones. Complete Architectural Drawings*, London 1989, pp.126–8 (no. 40), 308–9 (no. 116).

48. See Strong, *Renaissance Garden*, pp. 176 ff.

49. For earlier literature on this picture and discussions on the garden see Oliver Millar, *The Age of Charles I. Painting in England 1620–49*, exhibition catalogue, Tate Gallery 1972, p. 34 (no. 38); Harris, Orgel and Strong. *The King's Arcadia*, p. 200 (no. 388); Strong, *Reniassance Garden*, pp.

181–5; John Harris, *The Artist and the Country House*, London 1979, p. 22 (no. 12); Dixon Hunt, *Garden and Grove*, p. 132; Douglas D. C. Chambers, *The Planters of the English Landscape*, New Haven and London 1993, p. 37.

50. See G. E. C., *Complete Peerage*, s.v. Capell of Hadham; John Edwin Cussans, *History of Hertfordshire*, London 1870–3, I, pp. 189–94; *The Memoirs of Ann Lady Fanshawe...*, London 1907, pp. 348–51; *Hertfordshire Families*, ed., David Warrand, Victoria County History, London 1907, pp. 93–6.

51. Paul Everson, 'The Gardens of Campden House, Chipping Campden, Gloucesershire', *Garden History*, 17, no. 2, 1989, pp. 109–21.

52. See Margaret Whinney, *Sculpture in Britain 1530 to 1830*, London 1964, p. 29; W. L. Spiers, *The Note-Book and Account Book of Nicholas Stone*, Walpole Society, VII, 1919, pp. 60–3.

53. Spiers, *op. cit.*, p. 137.

54. Harris and Higgott, *Inigo Jones*, pp. 300–1.

55. William Lawson, *The Country Housewifes Garden*, New York 1982, p. 19.

56. *The Garden Book of Sir Thomas Hanmer Bart*, intro. Eleanour Sinclair Rohde, Gerald Howe, 1933, p. 13.

57. See Colin Simpson, 'Sir Robert Vyner and his Family by Michael Wright', *Leeds Arts Calendar*, 83, 1978, pp. 20–5; Sara Stevenson and Duncan Thomson, *John Michael Wright. The King's Painter*, exhibition catalogue, Scottish National Portrait Gallery, 1982, pp. 79–80 (no. 27).

58. Samuel Pepys, *Diary*, ed. Robert Latham and William Mathews, London 1972, VI, *1665*, pp. 214–15.

59. Oliver Hill and John Cornforth, *English Country Houses. Caroline 1625–85*, London 1966, p. 241.

60. Edward Croft-Murray, *Decorative Painting in England 1530–1837*, London 1962, p. 262.

61. David Jacques and Arend van der Horst, *The Gardens of William and Mary*, London 1988, pp. 111 ff.

62. Whinney, *Sculpture in Britain*, p. 64 and note 6; Rupert Gunnis, *Dictionary of British Sculptors 1600–1851*, London 1953, p. 234.

63. For example Stevenson and Thomson, *John Michael Wright*, pp. 29 (no. 82) and 84 (no.21).

64. Ellen D'Oench, *The Conversation Piece. Arthur Devis and His Contemporaries*, exhibiton catalogue, Yale Center for British Art, New Haven, 1980, p. 67 (no. 45).

65. For the portrait and previous literature see John Harris, *The Palladian Revival. Lord Burlington, His Villa and Garden at Chiswick*, New Haven and London 1994, p. 58 (no.8).

66. *Ibid.*, p. 57 (no. 7).

67. See Carole Fabricant, 'The aesthetics and Politics of Landscape in the Eighteenth Century,' *Studies in Eighteenth-Century British Art and Aesthetics*, ed. Ralph Cohen, Los Angeles 1985, pp. 49–81.

68. Edward Harwood, 'Personal Identity and the Eighteenth-Century English Landscape Garden', *Journal of Garden History*, 13, nos 1–2, 1993, pp. 36–48.

69. The importance and persistence of this phase is emphasised by Tom Williamson, *Polite Landscapes. Gardens and Society in Eighteenth-Cen-

tury England*, London 1995, ch, 2 and 3. On the emergence of the natural style in general see David Jacques, *Georgian Gardens. The Reign of Nature*, London 1983, ch. 1 and 2.

70. See Sacheverell Sitwell, *Conversation Pictures. A Survey of English Domestic Portraits and their Painters*, London 1969 edn; Mario Praz, *Conversation Pictures. A Survey of the Informal Group Portrait in Europe and America*, London 1971. For an up-to-date account see D'Oench, *The Conversation Piece, op.cit.*, and Marcia Pointon, *Hanging the Head. Portraiture and Social Formation in Eighteenth-Century England*, New Haven and London 1993, pp. 159 ff.

71. See Millar, *Tudor, Stuart and Early Georgian Pictures*, I, pp. 136–7 (no. 316); Harris, *The Artist and the Country House*, 1979, p. 51 (no.36); *The Treasure Houses of Britain*, ed. Gervase Jackson-Stops, exhibition catalogue, National Gallery of Art, Washington 1985, p. 162 (no.91); *The Glory of the Garden*, 1987 (no. 43); *The Anglo-Dutch Garden in the Age of William and Mary*, exhibition catalogue, *Journal of Garden History*, 8, nos. 2–3, 1988, pp. 241–2 (no. 97); George Royle, 'Family Links between George London and John Rose: new Light on the "Pineapple Paintings"', *Garden History*, 23, no. 2, 1995, pp. 246–9; John Harris, *The Artist and the Country House*, exhibition catalogue, Sotheby's, 1995 (no.8).

72. Robert Raines, 'Peter Tillemans, Life and Work, with a list of representative paintings', *Walpole Society*, XLVII, 1980, p. 58 (no. 79); *Manners and Morals. Hogarth and British Painting 1700–1760*, exhibition catalogue, Tate Gallery, 1987, p. 69 (no. 45); John Hayes, *The Portrait in British Art*, exhibition catalogue, National Portrait Gallery 1991, pp. 64–5 (no.16). See also Norman Scarfe, 'Little Hough Hall, Suffolk', *Country Life*, 5 June 1958, pp. 1238–41.

73. Millar, *Tudor, Stuart and Early Georgian Pictures*, I, p. 85 (no. 559); Ronald Paulson, *Hogarth: His Life, Art and Times*, New Haven and London 1971, I, pp. 313–18; Jenny Uglow, *Hogarth. A Life and a World*, London 1997, pp. 233–5.

74. *Manners and Morals*, p. 91 (no. 69).

75. See John Harris, 'The Fate of the Royal Buildings', *Country Life*, 28 May 1959, pp. 1182–4; Peter Willis, 'The Royal Gardens', in *Furor Hortensis. Essays on the history of the English Landscape Garden*, ed. Peter Willis, Ediburgh 1974, pp. 41–7; idem., *Charles Bridgeman and the English Landscape Garden*, London 1977, pp. 103–5; Kimerly Rorschach, *The Early Georgian Landscape Garden*, exhibition catalogue, Yale Center for British Art, New Haven, 1983, pp. 59–63; Peter Martin, *Pursuing Innocent Pleasures. The Gardening World of Alexander Pope*, Hamden, Conn. 1984, pp. 147–52.

76. Uglow, *Hogarth*, pp. 71–2, 99–101.

77. On whom see Sydney H. Paviere, *The Devis Family of Painters*, Leigh-on-Sea 1950, pp. 28–70; D'Oench, *Conversation Piece*, op.cit.; *Polite Society by Arthur Devis 1712–1787*, exhibition catalogue, National Portrait Gallery 1983–4.

78. It is easiest to cite as examples those illustrated in

D'Oench, *Conversation Piece*, pl. 1, 18, 7, 18, 25; *Polite Society*, pl. 22, 28, 40.

79. Formerly collection Paul Mellon, on loan to the National Gallery of Art, Washington; sold Sotheby's, 1981.

80. Paviere, *Devis*, p. 61; D'Oench, *Conversation Piece*, p. 89 (no. 179). In both she is listed as a member of the Lister family but for no apparent reason.

81. On the Orange Tree Garden see Harris, *Palladian Revival*, pp. 78–9.

82. *Ibid.*, pp. 188–9 (nos 77–8).

83. *Ibid.*, p. 243 (no. 105).

84. D'Oench, *Conversation Piece*, pp.57–7 (no. 155). There is a companion portrait of her husband.

85. *Polite Society*, p. 59 (no. 40).

86. G. E. C., *Complete Peerage*, s.v. Lincoln; John Ingamells, *A Dictionary of British and Irish Travellers in Italy 1701–1800*, New Haven and London 1997, s.v. Lincoln; Timothy Mowl, *Horace Walpole. The Great Outsider*, London 1996, passim.

87. Michael Symes, 'New Light on Oatlands Park in the Eighteenth Century', *Garden History*, 9, 1981, no. 2, pp. 136–53; Chambers, *The Planters of the English Landscape Garden*, pp. 92–4.

88. Jacques, *Georgian Gardens*, pp. 31, 54 f.

89. Quoted by Symes, *op. cit.*, p. 141.

90. On the gardens of Corby Castle see Gordon Nares, 'Corby Castle, Cumberland', *Country Life*, 7 January 1954, pp. 32–5; Barbara Jones, *Follies and Grottoes*, London 1974 ed., pp. 213–15; Jacques, *Georgian Gardens*, p. 100.

91. The picture was last recorded when sold at Christie's, 11 November 1999 (lot 2).

92. Quoted by Nares, *op.cit.*

93. All the information on Haytley is gathered in 'The Montagu Family at Sandleford Prior by Edward Haytley, 1744', in an *Exhibition of English Eighteenth Century Paintings*, Leger Galleries, London 1978.

94. *Polite Society*, pp. 66–7 (no. 54); Hayes, *The Portrait in British Art*, pp. 68–70 (no. 18); *Prospects of Town and Park*, Exhibition catalogue, Colnaghi, 1988, pp. 42–3 (no. 11).

95. John Steegman, 'An Eighteenth-Century Painting Identified', *Country Life*, 21 November 1963, pp. 1348–9; Harris, *The Artist and the Country House*, p. 219 (no. 236).

96. *Victoria County History, Lancashire*, IV, ed. W. Farrel and J. Brownhill, 1966, pp. 115–18.

97. Harris, *The Artist and the Country Houe*, pp. 220–21 (no. 237); *Manners and Morals*, p. 148 (nos 127–8); Emma Devapriam, 'Two Conversation Pieces by Edward Haytley', *Apollo*, August 1981, pp. 85–7; Ursual Hoff, *European Painting before 1800 in the National Gallery of Victoria*, Melbourne 1995, pp. 143–4. See also for the family Miss Burford Butcher, 'The Brockman Papers', *Archaeologia Cantiana*, XLIII, 1931, pp. 281–3.

98. The letter is quoted in full in Harris, *op.cit.*

99. Quoted Williamson, *Polite Landscapes*, p. 34.

100. Quoted David Coffin, *The English Garden. Meditation and Memorial*, Princeton 1994, p.6.

101. Desmond Shaw-Taylor, *The Georgians. Eighteenth-Century Portraiture and Society*, London 1990, pp. 130–2.

102. *The Glory of the Garden*, p. 100 (no. 151) with bibliography.

103. Shaw-Taylor, *The Georgians*, p. 194.

104. *Ibid.*, p. 195.

CHAPTER II: A PARADISE OF DAINTY DEVICES

1. John Harvey, *Medieval Gardens*, London 1981, p.98.

2. Howard M. Colvin, 'Royal Gardens in Medieval England', in *Medieval Gardens*, ed. Elisabeth MacDougall, Dumbarton Oaks Colloquium on the History of Landscape Architecture, IX, 1983, pp. 7–22; Harvey, *Medieval Gardens*, op.cit., pp.86–7.

3. For symbolic gardens in medieval art see Robert Hughes, *Heaven and Hell in Western Art*, London 1968, pp. 47–98; Terry Comito, *The Idea of the Garden in the Renaissance*, Harvester Press 1979, pp. 25–50; John Prest, *The Garden of Eden. The Botanic Garden and the Re-Creation of Paradise*, New Haven and London 1981, pp. 11–26; Marilyn Stokstad and Jerry Stannard, *Gardens of the Middle Ages*, exhibition catalogue, Spencer Museum of Art, University of Kansas, Lawrence, 1983, pp. 19–33; Marilyn Stokstad, 'The Garden in Art' in *Medieval Gardens*, op. cit., pp. 177–85; Jeanne Bourin, *Le Rose et La Mandragore. Plantes et jardins medievaux*, François Bourin 1990, pp. 105–28. The best gathering of images remains Sir Frank Crisp, *Medieval Gardens*, London 1924.

4. Stanley Stewart, *The Enclosed Garden. The Tradition and the Image in Seventeenth Century Poetry*, Wisconsin 1966, pp. 31–59; Brian E. Daley, 'The "Closed Garden" and the "Sealed Fountain": Song of Songs 4:2 in the Late Medieval Iconography of Mary', in *Medieval Gardens*, ed. MacDougall, pp. 255–78.

5. Comito, *The Idea of the Garden in the Renaissance*, pp. 89–147; John Y. Fleming, 'The Garden of the *Roman de la Rose*: Vision of Landscape or Landscape of Vision', in *Medieval Gardens*, ed. MacDougall, pp. 201–34.

6. For example see Harvey, *Medieval Gardens*, figs 23, 45, 47, 65; Stokstad and Stannard, *Gardens of the Middle Ages*, figs 21, 28, pl. IX, pp. 143 (25), 164–5 (35)

7. See Beatrijs Brenninkmeijer-de Rooij, *Roots of 17th Century Flower Painting. Miniatures, Plants, Books, Paintings*, Leiden 1996, pp. 14–20; Sam Segal, *Flowers and Nature. Netherlandish FlowerPainting of Four Centuries*, exhibition catalogue, Amsterdam 1990, pp. 19–23.

8. Robert G. Calkins, 'Piero de' Crescenzi and the Medieval Garden', in *Medieval Gardens*, ed. MacDougall, pp. 157–69.

9. Illuminations from it are reproduced in Harvey, *Medieval Gardens*, fig. 65 and Teresa McLean, *Medieval English Gardens*, London 1981, facing p.145.

10. I abridge here my own summary of the topic in Roy Strong, *Art and Power. Renaissance Festivals 1450–1650*, London 1984, pp. 22–8 and notes for bibliography; Mario Praz, *Studies in Seventeenth Century Imagery*, London 1939, remains fundamental.

11. The only general survey is Rosemary Freeman, *English Emblem Books*, London 1948.

12. Henry Peacham, *Minerva Britanna 1612*, English Emblem Books no.5, London 1975, p. 183.

13. For accession day *imprese* see Alan R. Young, *The English Tournament Imprese*, Arts Studies in the Emblem No. 3, Arts Inc., 1988, pp. 58 (93), 59 (100), 112 (175).

14. Michael Leslie, 'The dialogue between souls and bodies: Picture and Poesy in the English Renaissance', *Word and Image*, I, no. 1, 1985, pp. 16–30.

15. G. Scharf, *A Descriptive and Historical Catalogue of the Collection of Pictures at Woburn Abbey*, 1890, p. 23 (30); Roy Strong, *The English Icon. Elizabethan and Jacobean Portraiture*, London 1969, p. 31.

16. W. H. Matthews, *Mazes and Labyrinths. Their History and Development*, New York 1970 ed., pp. 110 ff.; Paolo Carpeggiani, 'Labyrinths in the Gardens of the Renaissance', in Monique Mosser and Georges Teyssot, *The History of Garden Design. The Western Tradition from the Renaissance to the Present Day*, London 1991, pp. 84–7.

17. Claude Paradin, *Devises Héroïques*, 1557, London 1971, p. 94.

18. *Dynasties. Painting in Tudor and Jacobean England 1530–1630*, ed. Karen Hearn, exhibition catalogue, Tate Gallery, 1996 (56); Sarah Bird, John Edmondson, Susan Nicholson, Katherine Stainer-Hutchins and Christopher Taylor, 'A Late Sixteenth-Century Garden: Fact or Fantasy. The Portrait of Sir George Delves in the Walker art Gallery, Liverpool', *Garden History*, 24, no. 2, 1996, pp. 167–83.

19. See P. W. Hasler, *The House of Commons 1558–1603*, The History of Parliament, London 1981, II, p. 29.

20. Anthony Wells-Cole, *Art and Decoration in Elizabethan England*, New Haven and London 1997, p. 209.

21. Vredeman de Vries, *Hortorum Viridiorumque elegantes… Antwerp, 1587*. Reprinted Amsterdam 1980; Ulbe Martin Mehrtens, 'Johann Vredeman de Vries and the *Hortorum Formae*', in Mosser and Teyssot, *The History of Garden Design*, pp. 103–5.

22. Roy Strong and V. J. Murrell, *Artists of the Tudor Court. The Portrait Miniature Rediscovered*, exhibition catalogue, Victoria & Albert Museum, 1983 (268).

23. Roy Strong, 'The Elizabethan Malady: Melancholy in Elizabethan and Jacobean Portraiture', *Apollo*, 79, 1964, pp. 254–9; reprinted in Roy Strong, *The Tudor and Stuart Monarchy. Pageantry. Painting. Iconography*, III, *Elizabethan*, Woodbridge 1996, pp. 295–302.

24. *The Complete Poems of Sir John Davies*, ed. A. B. Grosart, London 1976, II, p. 43.

25. Margery Corbett and R. W. Lightbown, *The Comely Frontispiece. The Emblematic Title-page in England 1550–1660*, London 1979, pp. 191–200.

26. On which see Roy Strong, 'Nicholas Hilliard's Miniature of the "Wizard Earl"', *Bulletin van het Rijksmuseum*, no. 31, 1983, pp. 54–62; reprinted in Strong, *Tudor and Stuart Monarchy*, III, *Elizabethan*, pp. 187–98; John Peacock, 'The "Wizard Earl" Portrayed by Hilliard and Van

Dyck', *Art History*, 8, no. 2, 1985, pp. 134–57.

27. David H. Horne, *The Life and Minor Works of George Peele*, New Haven 1952, p. 245.

28. See Arthur K. Wheelock, Jr., Susan J. Barnes and Julius Held, *Van Dyck Paintings*, exhibition catalogue, National Gallery of Art, Washington 1991, pp. 256–8 (65).

29. See *The Tate Gallery. Illustrated Catalogue of Acquisitions 1978–80*, London 1981, pp. 4–6; John Dixon-Hunt, 'The Portrait of William Style of Langley: Some Reflections', *John Donne Journal*, 5, 1986, pp. 291–310.

30. David Howarth, *Lord Arundel and his Circle*, New Haven and London 1985, colour plates 2 and 3.

31. *Henry VIII. A European Court in England*, ed. David Starkey, exhibition catalogue, National Maritime Museum, Greenwich 1981, p. 154 (XI. 22); Sydney Anglo, *Images of Tudor Kingship*, London 1992, p. 93.

32. Corpus Christi College, Cambridge MS 298 (no 8) quoted in Robert Withington, *English Pageantry*, Cambridge MA 1918, I, p. 177; Sydney Anglo, *Spectacle, Pageantry and Early Tudor Policy*, Oxford 1969, pp. 196–7. The French also had a tradition of the country as a garden as recorded in one of the pageants for Mary Tudor's entry into Paris in 1513 (Withington, *op.cit.*, p. 172): 'au bas dudict escharfault avoit ung beau iardin nomme la vergier de France seme de plusiers beaulx lys.'

33. Strong, *The Renaissance Garden in England*, pp. 45–49.

34. See Roy Strong, *Gloriana. The Portraits of Queen Elizabeth I*, London 1987, pp. 71–7 and for earlier bibliography.

35. Robert Dodoens, *A Nieuwe Herball*, trans. Henry Lyte, London 1578, sig. iii v.

36. For the text see *The Dramatic Works of Thomas Dekker*, ed. Fredson Bowers, Cambridge 1975, II, pp. 280–91; *Jacobean Civic Pageants*, ed. Richard Dutton, Keele 1995, pp. 19–25, 75–84. For studies see David M. Bergeron, *English Civic Pageantry 1558–1642*, London 1971, pp. 82–4; Graham Parry, *The Golden Age Restor'd. The Culture of the Stuart Court, 1603–42*, Manchester 1981, pp. 12–13.

37. *The English Garden. Literary Sources and Documents*, ed. Michael Charlesworth, Helm Information, 1993, I, p.141.

38. Margery Corbett and Michael Norton, *Engraving in England in the Sixteenth and Seventeenth Centuries*, III, *The Reign of Charles I*, Cambridge 1964, pp. 108–9 (23).

39. For a discussion of Henrietta Maria, her religion and court festivals, see Erica Veevers, *Images of Love and Religion. Queen Henrietta Maria's Court Entertainments*, Cambridge 1989.

40. Henry Hawkins, *Parthenia Sacra 1633*, intro. by Karl Holtgen, London 1993.

41. Quoted Stewart, *The Enclosed Garden*, p. 42.

42. Jane Ashelford, 'Female Masque Dress in Late Sixteenth-Century England', *Costume* 12, 1978, p. 45.

43. Frances A. Yates, *Astraea. The Imperial Theme in the Sixteenth Century*, London 1975, p. 215; Mario Praz, 'The Gonzaga Devices', in *Splendours of the Gonzagas*, ed. David Chambers and

Jane Martineau, exhbition catalogue, Victoria & Albert Museum, London 1981–2, pp. 64–80, fig. 79.

44. Young, *The English Tournament Imprese*, p. 71 (160).

45. John Nichols, *The Progresses of Queen Elizabeth*, London 1823, III, pp. 137–40.

46. Ellen Chirelstein, 'Lady Elizabeth Pope: The Heraldic Body', *Renaissance Bodies. The Human Figure in English Culture c.1540–1660*, ed. Lucy Gent and Nigel Llewellyn, London 1990, pp. 37–59. Oddly the author makes no attempt to interpret the significance of the laurel.

47. Orgel and Strong, *Theatre of the Stuart Court*, I, p. 116, ll. 26–8.

48. *Ibid.*, I, p. 119, ll. 402–3.

49. Hawkins, *Partheneia Sacra*, p. 152.

50. Orgel and Strong, *Theatre of the Stuart Court*, I, p. 407, ll. 196–200.

51. Excellently developed in chapter II of David R. Coffin, *The English Garden. Meditation and Memorial*, Princeton 1996, pp. 57–80.

52. See Freeman, *English Emblem Books*, pp. 114–32; Stewart, *The Enclosed Garden*, pp. 88–90, 103–4.

53. Freeman, *English Emblem Books*, pp. 140–7; George Wither, *A Collection of Emblemes 1635*, English Emblem Books no. 12, London 1968.

54. Freeman, *English Emblem Books*, pp. 198–203.

55. Coffin, *The English Garden*, pp. 58 ff.; also see Paul Taylor, *Dutch Flower Painting 1600– 1720*, New Haven and London 1995, pp. 36 ff. and for the wider Catholic context Marcello Fagiolo and Adriana Giusti, 'Giardini come esercizi spirituali', in *Lo Specchio del Paradiso. Il giardino e il sacro dell'Antico all'Ottocento*, Milan 1998, pp. 115–61.

56. Quoted Stewart, *The Enclosed Garden*, p. 115.

57. Qoted *ibid.*, p. 116.

58. Quoted *ibid.*, p. 127.

59. *The English Garden*, ed. Charlesworth, I, pp. 165 ff.; David Leatherbarrow, 'L'Uso spirituale di un frutteto', *Rassegna*, 8 (*La Natura dei giardini*), 1981, pp. 81–7.

60. *Ibid.*, I, pp. 183–5

61. All of which are reproduced in Stephen Orgel and Roy Strong, *The Theatre of the Stuart Court*, London and Los Angeles 1973.

62. Orgel and Strong, *Theatre of the Stuart Court*, I, p. 139 l.9

63. On developments in garden design 1603–42 see Roy Strong, *The Renaissance Garden in England*, London 1979, pp. 73 ff.

64. Orgel and Strong, *Theatre of the Stuart Court*, I, p. 194 ll. 170–232.

65. *Ibid.*, I, p. 196 ll. 351–2, 355.

66. *The Masque of Flowers* is reprinted in H. A. Evans, *English Masques*, London 1909, pp.100–13.

67. Gervase Markham, *The English Husbandman* (1613), Garland Publishing, 1982, pp. 112-13.

68. Orgel and Strong, *Theatre of the Stuart Court*, I, p. 273 ll. 155–9.

69. I am much indebted here to John Peacock, *The Stage Designs of Inigo Jones. The European Context*, Cambridge 1991.

70. For which see A. N. Nagler, *Theater Festivals of the Medici 1539–1637*, New Haven 1964, pp.

80–1; *Feste e Apparati Medicei da Cosimo I a Cosimo II*, exhibition catalogue, Florence 1969, pp. 80–1 (39); *Il Luogo Teatrale a Firenze*, exhibition catalogue, Florence 1975 p. 113 (8. 12).

71. Orgel and Strong, *Theatre of the Stuart Court*, I, p. 407 l. 163.

72. *Ibid.*, II, p.421 ll. 163-65.

73. Ibid., II, pp. 483–85 (216); For the Parigi garden see Nagler, *Theater Festivals of the Medici*, pp. 106–7; *Feste e Apparati Medicei*, pp. 114–15 (61); *Il Luogo Teatrale*, p. 120 (8. 32).

74. Orgel and Strong, *Theatre of the Stuart Court*, II, p. 480 ll. 51–66.

75. *Ibid.*, pp. 514–15 (259).

76. Pointed out by Peacock, *Stage Designs of Inigo Jones*, pp. 198–99.

77. Orgel and Strong, *Theatre of the Stuart Court*, II, pp. 552 ll. 624–30; 562 (271).

78. *Ibid.*, II, pp. 518–19 (252).

79. Strong, *Renaissance Garden in England*, p. 188.

80. Orgel and Strong, *Theatre of the Stuart Court*, II, p. 579 ll. 1114–1021.

81. *Ibid.*, II, pp. 586–8 (281).

82. For whom see Lucia Tongiorgi Tomasi, *An Oak Spring Flora*, Upperville 1997, pp. 69–73; Margaret McGowan, *The Court Ballet of Louis XIII. A collection of working designs for costumes 1615–33*, Victoria & Albert Museum, n.d.

83. Orgel and Strong, *The Theatre of the Stuart Court*, II, pp. 633 ll. 137–42; 654 (330).

84. *Ibid.*, II, pp. 706 ll. 30–3; 708 ll. 240–3.

85. Nagler, *Theater Festivals of the Medici*, pp. 168–9; *Il Luogo Teatrale*, pp. 141–2 (9. 40).

CHAPTER III: PORTRAIT OF A PLACE

1. John Harris, *The Artist and the Country House. A history of country house and garden view painting 1540-1870*, London and New York 1979; idem, *The Artist and the Country House from the Fifteenth Century to the Present Day*, exhibition catalogue, Sotheby's 1995.

2. Claudia Lazzaro, *The Italian Renaissance Garden*, New Haven and London 1990, ch.9, pl. 20, 206.

3. *Ibid.*, ch. 10, pls. 24, 227.

4. *Ibid.*, pl.21, 45.

5. Daniela Mignani, *Le Ville Medicee di Giusto Utens*, Arnaud 1980.

6. Lazzaro, *The Italian Renaissance Garden*, pp. 219–20.

7. For a valuable survey of the multiplication of garden prints see Virginia Tuttle Clayton, *Gardens on Paper. Paintings and Drawings 1200-1900*, Philadelphia 1990, ch. II and III. See also Maurizio Gargano, 'Villas, Gardens and Fountains of Rome: The Etchings of Giovanni Battista Falda', *The History of Garden Design*, ed. Monique Mosser and Georges Teyssot, London 1991, pp. 166–8.

8. See Roy Strong, *The Renaissance Garden in England*, London 1979, pp.220–1; Harris, *The Artist and the Country House*, p. 36 (29).

9. *Ibid.*, p.54 (41).

10. Mark Girouard, *Robert Smythson and the Elizabethan Country House*, New Haven and London 1983, *passim*.

11. J.-A. du Cerceau, *Les Plus Excellents Bastiments de France*, ed. David Thomas, Paris 1988, pp. 14 ff.; Françoise Boudon, 'Illustrations of Gardens

in the Sixteenth Century: "The Most Excellent Buildings in France"', *The History of Garden Design, op. cit.*, pp. 100–2.

12. Clayton, *Gardens on Paper*, pp.83–92.

13. *Ibid.*, pp.92–8.

14. Erik de Jong and Marleen Dominicus-van Soest, *Aardse Paradijzen*, I, *De tuin in de Nederlandse kunst 15de tot 10de eeuw*, Ghent 1996, p. 27 (16).

15. *The Anglo-Dutch Garden in the Age of William and Mary*, ed. John Dixon Hunt and Erik de Jong, *Jorunal of Garden History*, 8, nos 2–3, 1988, pp. 200–1.

16. *The Anglo-Dutch Garden*, p. 108 (2); *Aardse Paradijzen*, p. 36 (23).

17. A. M. Hind, *Engraving in England in the Sixteenth and Seventeenth Centuries*, I, *The Tudor Period*, Cambridge 1955, pls. 34, 114, 115.

18. Antony Griffiths, *The Print in Stuart Britain 1603–1689*, British Museum Press, 1998, pp. 97–8 (131).

19. John Harris, '"A grand design of an ichnographical survey": A Tour of London's gardens with John Rocque', in *London's Pride. The Glorious History of the Capital's Gardens*. London 1990, pp. 103–21.

20. Hind, *op.cit.*, I, pl. 86, 87.

21. A. M. Hind, *Engraving in England in the Sixteenth and Seventeenth Centuries*, II, *James I*, Cambridge 1955, pl. 40; see Strong, *The Renaissance Garden in England*, pp. 63–9.

22. Roy Strong, 'The Renaissance Garden in England Reconsidered. A Survey of two decades of research on the period 1485–1642', *Garden History*, 27, no.1 ,1999, p. 5 ; James Boutwood, 'A Vanished Elizabethan Mansion', *Country Life*, 23 March 1961, pp. 638–9.

23. For the latest account of Wyngaerde see *The Panorama of London circa 1544*, ed. Howard Colvin and Susan Foister, London Topographical Society in association with The Ashmolean Museum, Publication no. 151, 1996, pp. 1–4; David Blayney Brown, *Ashmolean Museum, Oxford. Catalogue of the Collection of Drawings*, IV, *The Earlier British Drawings...*, Oxford 1982, pp. 6–13 (nos 10–14).

24. For Hampton Court see Strong, *The Renaissance Garden in England*, pp. 25–34; David Jacques, 'The history of the Privy Garden', *The King's Privy Garden 1689–1995*, London 1995, pp. 23–5; Roy Strong, 'Los jardines de los palacios de la Inglaterra Tudor', *Jardin y Naturalieza en el reinado de Felipe II*, ed. Carmen Anon and Jose Luis Sancho, Madrid 1998, pp. 106–11.

25. Griffiths, *The Print in Stuart England*, p. 113 (67); Harris, *The Artist and the Country House*, p. 23 (13). Mention should also be made of the garden view in a second set of Hollar *Seasons*, rep. Griffiths, p. 115 (68a).

26. *Ibid.*, pp. 124–5 (75).

27. Timothy Mowl, 'New science, old order: the gardens of the Great Rebellion', *Journal of Garden History*, 13, nos 1–2, p. 17.

28. Strong, *The Renaissance Garden in England*, pp. 186 ff.

29. On Loggan see Griffiths, *The Print in Stuart Britain*, pp. 198–200.

30. See Harris, *The Artist and the Country House*, pp. 93–5.

31. *Ibid.*, p. 61 (54); Harris, 1995 exhibition catalogue, p. 40 (11); Strong, *The Renaissance Garden in England*, p. 186.

32. Harris, *The Artist and the Country House*, pp. 91–2.

33. *Ibid.*, p. 44.

34. T. H. Fokker, *Jan Siberecht*, Paris and Brussels 1931; Harris, *The Artist and the Country House*, pp. 46–8.

35. *Ibid.*, p. 122 (121).

36. William T. Stearn, 'The origin and development of garden plants', *Journal of the Royal Horticultural Society*, XC, 1965, p. 326. For a useful introduction see Penelope Hobhouse, *Plants in Garden History*, London 1992, ch. IV and more especially Lucia Tongiorgi Tomasi, *An Oak Spring Flora*, Upperville 1997, pp. 109–13.

37. See Georgina Masson, 'Italian Flower Collectors' Gardens in Seventeenth Century Italy', in *The Italian Garden*, First Dumbarton Oaks Colloquium on the History of Landscape Architecture, ed. David Coffin, 1972, pp. 63–80; David Coffin, *Gardens and Gardening in Papal Rome*, Princeton 1991, pp. 207–10.

38. Elisabeth Blair MacDougall, A Cardinal's Bulb Garden: A Giardino Segreto at the Barberini Palace in Rome', *Fountains, Statues, and Flowers. Studies in Italian Gardens of the Sixteenth and Seventeenth Centuries*, Washington 1993, pp. 219 ff.

39. See those reproduced, for example, in *Fleurs et Jardins dans l'Art Flamand*, exhibition catalogue, Musée des Beaux-Arts, Ghent, 1960; *Aardse Paradijzen, passim*.

40. For the development of the flower garden in France see Kenneth Woodbridge, *Princely Gardens. The origins and development of the French formal style*, London 1986, pp. 97–107.

41. Quoted *ibid.*, p. 37.

42. *Ibid.*, pp. 139–41.

43. Irène Frain, *La Guirlande de Julie*, Paris 1991, pp. 69 ff.

44. *Ibid.*, ch. 10.

45. *Ibid.*, pp. 228–30; Eleanor P. DeLorme, *Garden Pavilions and the 18th Century French Court*, Woodbridge 1996, pp. 66–9.

46. Harris, *The Artist and the Country House*, p. 33 (138); 1995 exhibition catalogue, pp. 50–1 (20–1).

47. On whom see G. E. C., *Complete Peerage*, s.v. Fauconberg; P. Hasler, *The House of Commons 1558–1603*, London 1981, s.v. Henry and Thomas Bellasis; Hugh Aveling, *Northern Catholics. The Recusants in the North Riding of Yorkshire 1558–1790*, Geoffrey Chapman, 1966, pp. 184–5, 272–3.

48. John Cornforth, 'Newburgh Priory, Yorkshire – I', *Country Life*, 28 February 1974, pp. 426–9.

49. Girouard, *Robert Smythson*, pp. 81–3 for Wollaton.

50. *Ibid.*, pp. 179–80.

51. *A New Orchard and Garden*, New York 1982, sig A 2 – sig A 2 v.

52. See Masson, 'Italian Flower Collectors' Gardens', *op. cit.*

53. John Parkinson, *Paradisi in Sole...*, London 1629, p. 5.

54. *Ibid.*, p. 6.

55. *Ibid., loc. cit.*

56. R. T. Gunter, 'The Garden of the Rev. Walter Stonehouse at Darfield Rectory, in Yorkshire, 1640', *The Gardener's Chronicle*, 15 May 1920, pp. 240–1; Mea Allen, *The Tradescants. Their Plants, Gardens and Museum 1570–1662*, London 1964, pp. 190–1; David Sturdy, 'The Tradescants at Lambeth', *Journal of Garden History*, II, i, 1982, pp. 1–16; Prudence Leith-Ross, *The John Tradescants. Gardeners to the Rose and Lily Queen*, London 1984, pp. 121–2.

57. Laure Beaumont-Maillet, *Le Florilège de Nassau-Idstein par Johann Walter 1604–1676*, Anthese, Arcueil 1993; *So Many Sweet Flowers. A Seventeenth Century Florilegium. Paintings by Johann Walter 1654*, ed. Jenny de Gex, London 1997.

58. Parkinson, *op. cit.*, p. 3.

59. *The Garden Book of Sir Thomas Hanmer, Bt.*, introduction by Eleanour Sinclair Rohde, London 1933. See Ruth Duthie, 'The Planting Plans of Some Seventeenth-Century Flower Gardens', *Garden History*, 18, no. 2, 1990, pp.83–7; Jenny Robinson, 'New Light on Sir Thomas Hanmer', *ibid.*, 16, no.1, 1988, pp. 1–7.

60. *Ibid.*, pp.xvii–xix; for an accurate transcript see Duthie, *op.cit.*, pp. 83–4.

61. Prudence Leith-Ross, 'The Garden of John Evelyn at Deptford', *Garden History*, 25, no. 2, pp. 138–52.

62. Harris, *The Artist and the Country House*, pp. 70–1 (67).

63. Vertue, *Notebooks*, II, Walpole Society, XX, 1932, p. 86.

64. *Ibid.*, p. 24.

65. Walpole, *Notebooks*, I, Walpole Society, XVIII, p. 131.

66. On which see Blanche Henrey, *British Botanical and Horticultural Literature before 1800*, Oxford 1975, I, pp. 195–8; Peter Goodchild, 'John Rea's Garden of Delight: Introduction and the Construction of the Flower Garden', *Garden History*, 9, no. 2, 1981, pp. 99–109; Tomasi, *An Oak Spring Flora*, pp. 125–30. For more on flower gardens Ruth Duthie, *op.cit.*

67. Goodchild, *art. cit, Garden History*.

68. Harris, *The Artist and the Country House*, pp. 86–7 (86); see also Alastair Rowan, 'Yester House, East Lothian – I', *Country Life*, 9 August 1973, pp. 358–61 which records the purchase in 1686 of four pedestals for lead garden statues.

69. E. H. M. Cox, *A History of Gardening in Scotland*, London 1935, pp. 55–6.

70. Mark Laird and John Harvey, '"Cloth of Tissue of Divers Colours": The English Flower Border, 1660–1735', *Garden History*, 21, no 2, 1993, pp. 158–205.

71. Mark Laird, *The Flowering of the Landscape Garden. English Pleasure Grounds 1720–1800*, Philadelphia 1999, ch.i.

72. Henrey, *op.cit.*, p. 198.

73. Samuel Gilbert, *The florists vade-mecum*, London 1682, p.7.

74. Harris, *The Artist and the Country House*, pp. 104–5 (92).

75. *The Journeys of Celia Fiennes*, ed. Christopher Morris, London 1947, pp. 57–8.

76. Duthie, *op. cit.*, pp.88–97. See also Gloria Cottesloe and Doris Hunt, *The Duchess of Beaufort's Flowers*, Exeter 1983.

77. Laird, *The Flowering of the Landscape Garden*, pp.198–9; John Harris, *The Palladian Revival. Lord Burlington, His Villa and Garden at Chiswick*, New Haven and London 1994, p. 243.

78. John Harris, 'Some Imperfect Ideas on the Genesis of the Loudonesque Flower Garden', in *John Claudius Loudon and the Early Nineteenth Century in Great Britain*, Dumbarton Oaks 1980, pp. 55–7; John Harris, *Gardens of Delight. The English Rococo Landscape of Thomas Robins the Elder*, London 1978, pp. 11–12; Laird, *The Flowering of the English Landscape Garden*, pp. 184–7.

79. *London's Pride. The Glorious History of the Capital's Gardens*, ed. Mireille Galinou, London 1990, pp. 44–5; John Schofield, 'City of London Gardens, 1500–c.1620', *Garden History*, 27, no. 1, 1999, pp.73–88.

80. Harris, *The Artist and the Country House*, p. 62 (57); *The Anglo-Dutch Garden*, p. 248 (100)

81. Harris, *The Artist and the Country House*, p. 114 (108).

82. Dan Cruikshank and Neil Burton, *Life in the Georgian City*, London 1990, ch. 4.

83. See P. Borsay, *The English Urban Renaissance: Culture and Society in the Provincial Town 1660–1770*, Oxford 1989.

84. *The Journeys of Celia Fiennes*, p. 72.

85. J. H. Plumb, *The Pursuit of Happiness. A View of Life in Georgian England*, exhibition catalogue, Yale Center for British Art, New Haven, 1977 (137); Harris, *The Artist and the Country House*, p. 114 (109); *The Anglo-Dutch Garden*, pp. 240–1 (96).

86. For the Pierreponts see *The House of Commons 16601690*, ed. Basil Duke Henning, London 1983, II, pp. 242 ff.; Duncan Gray, *Nottingham through 500 Years*, City of Nottingham, 1960, pp. 79–82, 124–5.

87. For the Nottingham background see Adrian Henstock, 'The Changing Fabric of the town, 1550–1750', in *A Centenary History of Nottingham* ed. John Beckett, Manchester 1997, pp. 107–31.

88. George London and Henry Wise, *The Retir'd Gard'ner (1706)*, New York 1982, pp. 237–8.

89. For Marshal Tallard's garden see London and Wise, *op.cit.*, appendix to vol. II; David Green, *Gardener to Queen Anne. Henry Wise (1653–1738) and the Formal Garden*, Oxford 1956, pp. 125–7.

90. Daniel Defoe, *A Tour through England and Wales*, Everyman ed., 1928, II, p. 144.

91. Paul Stamper, *Historic Parks and Gardens of Shropshire*, Shrewsbury 1996, pp. 32–7.

92. *The Journeys of Celia Fiennes*, p.227.

93. Defore, *Tour*, II, p. 75.

94. Information from the present occupant, Mr Gordon Manser. For Dogpole and its residents see H. E. Forrest, *The Old Houses of Shrewsbury. Their history and Associations*, Shrewsbury 1920, pp. 75–7.

95. *The Journeys of Celia Fiennes*, p. 227.

96. John Davis, *Antique Garden Ornament. 300 Years of creativity: Artists, manufacuers & materials*, Woodbridge 1991, ch. 1.

97. John Harris, *Gardens of Delight*, pp. 14–15.

98. John Harris, '"Gardenesque": the Case of Charles Grevile's Garden at Gloucester', *Journal of Garden History*, I, no 2, 1980, pp. 167–78; 'knick-knackery' is Harris's phrase.

99. Laird, *The Flowering of the Landscape Garden*, pp. 178–9.

CHAPTER IV: EVERY PROSPECT PLEASES

1. The exception to this is a Ph. D. dissertation by Linda Marie Cabe, 'Sets of Painted Views of Gardens, c.1728–140, and the Relationship between Garden Design and Painting in England in the first half of the eighteenth century', Yale 1988.

2. The account of the Wilton garden given here is based on Roy Strong, *The Renaissance Garden in England*, London 1979, pp. 147–64; John Dixon Hunt, *Garden and Grove. The Italian Renaissance Garden in the English Imagination: 1660–1750*, London1986, pp. 139–42 (but who ignores the francophile and Netherlandish elements in the garden) and John Bold, *Wilton House and English Palladianism*, London 1988.

3. This has since been the subject of a reprint: Isaac de Caus, *Wilton Garden*, New York 1982; see also Antony Griffiths, *The Print in Stuart England 1603–1688*, London 1998, pp. 124–5 (no.75).

4. *The Diary of John Evelyn*, ed. E. S. de Beer, Oxford 1955, s.v. 20 July 1654.

5. For Stent see Alexander Globe, *Peter Stent, London Printseller c.1642–1665*, Vancouver 1985, pp. 158–60.

6. Salomon de Caus, *Le Jardin Palatin. Hortus Palatinus*, ed. Michel Conan, Paris 1981.

7. See Richard Patterson, 'The "Hortus Palatinus" at Heidelberg and the reformation of the World', *Journal of Garden History*, I, 1981, no. 1, pp. 67–104; no. 2, pp. 179–202.

8. See Griffiths, *The Print in Stuart England, op. cit.*

9. Strong, *The Renaissance Garden in England*, pp. 164-65.

10. See J. Harris and A. A. Tait, *Drawings by Inigo Jones...at Worcester College*, Oxford 1979, p. 47.

11. See Michel Conan in his edition of André Mollet, *Le Jardin de Plaisir*, Paris 1981, pp. 106–7.

12. Griffiths, *The Print in Stuart Britain*, ch. 3 passim.

13. John Harris, *The Artist and the Country House*, London and New York 1979, p. 128 (no. 129).

14. Cabe, 'Sets of Painted Views of Gardens', ch. 1, covers the French origins of the English garden panorama but is unaware of the Netherlandish aspect.

15. Virginia Tuttle Clayton, *Gardens on Paper. Prints and Drawings 1200-1900*, National Gallery of Art, Washington 1990, pp. 66–7.

16. *Ibid.*, pp. 83–92.

17. On the London print market, see Griffiths, *The Print in Stuart Britain*, pp. 23–31.

18. See Tuttle Clayton, *op. cit.*, pp. 92–8.

19. 'The Anglo-Dutch Garden in the Age of William and Mary', ed. John Dixon Hunt and Erik de Jong, *Journal of Garden History*, 8, nos. 2–3, pp. 112–13; Erik de Jong, 'For Pleasure and Profit: The Function and Meaning of Dutch Garden Art in the Period of William and Mary, 1650–1702', in *The Dutch Garden in the Seventeenth Century*, ed. John Dixon Hunt, Washington 1990, pp. 13–48.

20. Willemien B. de Vries, 'The Country Estate Immortalised: Constantine Huygens's Hofwyck', in *The Dutch Garden in the Seventeenth Century*, pp. 81–97.

21. *The Anglo-Dutch Garden*, pp. 109–112 (no.3); Erik de Jong and Marleen Dominicus-van Soest, *Ardse Paradijzen, I, De tuin in de Nederlandse Kunst 15 de tot 18de eeuw*, Snoeck-Ducaju & Zoon 1996, pp. 42–3 (no. 27 a–c).

22. *The Anglo-Dutch Garden*, pp. 122–4 (no. 11). A series by Romeyn de Hooghe of the garden at Cleve has been dated *c.* 1680 by Wilhelm Didenhofen but the costume, above all the female headdresses, precludes any date before the nineties. See his '"Belvedere", or the Principle of Seeing and Looking in the Gardens of Johan Maurits van Nassau-Siegen', in *The Anglo-Dutch Garden in the Seventeenth Century*, pp. 49–80.

23. Many of these are reproduced in *The Anglo-Dutch Garden*, pp. 139–42 (Dieren), 144–55 (Het Loo), 163–79 (Zorgvliet), 179–84 (Clingendael), 188–91 (Roosendael), 193–8 (Heemstede). On the role of these prints and propaganda see pp. 200–1.

24. *The Anglo-Dutch Garden*, fig. 32; de Jong and Domincus-van Soest, *Aardse Paradijzen*, I, p. 53 (no. 35).

25. This is reprinted in *De Lusthof Het Loo van de Koning-Stadholder Willem III en zijn gemalin Mary II Stuart*, The Hague 1984.

26. This is fully covered in V. Cazzato, M. Fagiolo and M. A. Giusti, *Teatri di Verzura. La Scena del Giardino dal Barocco al Novecento*, Florence 1993.

27. Joseph Spence, *Observations, Anecdotes of Books and Men*, ed. J. M. Osborne, Oxford 1966, I, p. 252 (no.606).

28. Horace Walpole, *The History of the Modern Taste in Gardening*, Introduction by John Dixon Hunt, New York 1995, p. 56.

29. The best account of Kent with a catalogue and plates of all his designs is in John Dixon Hunt, *William Kent. Landscape Designer*, London 1987.

30. For John Rocque see Hugh Phillips, 'John Rocque's Career', *London Topographical Record*, XX, 1952, pp. 9–25; Jean O'Neill, 'John Rocque as a Guide to Gardens', *Garden History*, 16, 1988, no. i, pp. 8–16; Harris, *The Artist and the Country House*, p.159.

31. Harris, *The Artist and the Country House*, pp. 172–3 (nos 1178 a–d); 180 (no. 186); Robin Fausset, 'The Creation of the Gardens at Castle Hill, South Molton, Devon', *Garden History*, 13, 1985, ii, pp. 103–5. Mention perhaps should be made of the multiple glimpses we have of the garden at Euston Hall, Suffolk, in the watercolours by the antiquary, Edward Prideaux, 'The Prideaux Collection of Topographical Drawings', *Architectural History*, 7, 1966, pp. 26–7 (nos 28–32)

32. There is a substantial literature on this garden but the most important publication is the most recent by John Harris, *The Palladian Revival. Lord Burlington, His Villa and Garden at Chiswick*, New Haven and London 1994, esp. ch.5. Items which I have found of particular importance in respect of the garden are Peter

Willis, *Charles Bridgeman and the English Landscape Garden*, London 1977, pp. 64–6; Cinzia Maria Sicca, 'Lord Burlington at Chiswick: Architecture and Landscape', *Garden History*, 10, 1982, i, pp. 36–69; Richard Hewlings, *Chiswick House and Gardens*, London 1989, pp.18–32; R. T. Spence, 'Chiswick House and its gardens, 1726–1732', *Burlington Magazine*, 1993, pp. 525–31.

33. This recent reassessment of Burlington is to be found in *Belov'd of Ev'ry Muse: Richard Boyle, 3rd Earl of Burlington and 4th Earl of Cork (1694–1753)*, Georgian Group, 1994 and *Lord Burlington: Architecture, Art and Life,* ed. Toby Barnard and Jane Clark, London 1995.

34. Dixon Hunt, *William Kent*, p. 127 (no.31).

35. John Macky, *A Journey Through England*, 4th ed., London 1724, pp. 86–7.

36. For the Rysbrack views see Harris, *The Artist and the Country House*, pp. 182–3 (no.187); Harris, *The Palladian Revival*, pp. 44 (pl.43), 75 (pl.57); nos 6, 27, 29, 81, 82, 90; Cabe, 'Sets of Painted Views of Gardens', pp. 65–94.

37. Cabe, 'Sets of Painted Views', p.67.

38. Vertue, *Notebooks*, III, Walpole Society, XXII, 1934, p. 42.

39. Harris, *The Palladian Revival*, p. 57.

40. For the Rigaud drawings see Harris, *The Palladian Revival*, nos 28, 30, 75, 79, 83, 95, 100; Jacques Carré, 'Through French Eyes: Rigaud's Drawings of Chiswick', *Journal of Garden History*, 2, no. 2, 1982, pp. 133–42.

41. Vertue, *Notebooks*, IV, Walpole Society, XXIV, 1936, p. 64; also *ibid.*, III, Walpole Society, XXII, 1934, p. 73.

42. Harris, *The Palladian Revival*, nos 112, 113.

43. *Ibid.*, nos 117–22; Michael Symes, 'John Donowell's Views of Chiswick and other Gardens', *Garden History*, 7, 1987, i, pp. 43–57.

44. Quoted Walpole, *The History of the Modern Taste in Gardening*, p. 7.

45. *Ibid.*, p. 8.

46. Thierry Mariage, *The World of André Le Nôtre*, Philadelphia 1999, pp. 87–9.

47. Linda Cabe Halpern, 'The Duke of Kent's Garden at Wrest Park', *Journal of Garden History*, 15, 1995, no.3, p. 161. For Tillemans see Robert Raines, 'Peter Tillemans – Life and Work with a List of Representative Paintings', *Walpole Society*, XLVII, 1980, pp. 21–59; Harris, *The Artist and the Country House*, pp. 224–5.

48. Harris, *The Artist and the Country House*, pp. 140–1; *The Anglo-Dutch Garden*, p. 228 (87). Neither of these accept Tillemans's authorship but Raines unequivocally does, 'Peter Tillemans', *op.cit.*, p. 51 (42).

49. For these references see Halpern, 'The Duke of Kent's garden at Wrest Park', p. 152.

50. I am much indebted for this discussion of the Wrest paintings to the work of Halpern, 'The Duke of Kent's garden at Wrest Park'. Also for her earlier discussion in Cabe, *Sets of Painted Views of Gardens*, pp. 125–62.

51. Halpern, 'The Duke of Kent's garden at Wrest Park', p. 151.

52. Vertue, *Notebooks*, Walpole Society, XXX, 1955, p. 194.

53. *Ibid.*, III, Walpole Society, XXII, 1934, p. 69.

54. *Ibid.*, VI, *op. cit.*, p. 194.

55. See George B. Clarke, *Stowe Gardens in Buckinghamshire, Laid out by Mr Bridgeman...*, BW Publications 1987. This is a facsimile edition of the engravings with an account of their history.

56. Vertue, *Notebooks*, III, *op.cit.*, p. 69.

57. For an up-to-date bibliography on Stowe see 'The Political Temples of Stowe', ed. Patrick Eyres, *New Arcadian Journal*, nos 43/44, 1997, pp. 109–21. For this account I have drawn on George Clarke, 'The Gardens of Stowe', *Apollo*, 97, January 1973, pp. 558–65; idem, 'Grecian Taste and Gothic Virtue: Lord Cobham's gardening programme and its iconography', *ibid.*, pp. 566–71; Willis, *Charles Bridgeman*, pp. 106–27; John Martin Robinson, *Temples of Delight. Stowe Landscape Garden*, London 1990.

58. Peter Willis, 'Jacques Rigaud's Drawings of Stowe in the Metropolitan Museum of Art', *Eighteenth Century Studies*, VI, 1972, pp. 85–98. Richard Quaintance, 'Who's making the scene? Real people in eighteeth-century topographical prints', in *The Country and the City Revisited. England and the Politics of Culture 1550–1850*, ed. Gerald MacLean, Donna Landry and Joseph P. Ward, Cambridge 1999, pp. 134–59.

59. Quoted, Willis, *Charles Bridgeman*, p. 118.

60. For the Bickham and Chatelain views see Willis, *Bridgeman*, pp. 124–5; Clayton, *The English Print*, p. 161.

61. For the Hartwell paintings see John Harris, 'Views of an 18th-Century Garden. Hartwell, Buckinghamshire', *Country Life*, 15 March 1979, pp. 707–9; Harris, *The Artist and the Country House*, pp. 188–89 (no. 194); Terry Friedman, *James Gibbs*, New Haven and London 1984, pp. 182–9; *The Glory of the Garden*, exhibition catalogue, Sotheby's, 1986 (nos. 76 a-h); *The Anglo-Dutch Garden*, pp. 229–30 (no.88); Cabe, 'Sets of Painted Views of Gardens', pp. 180–203; *Manners and Morals*, pp. 106–7 (87–90); Roy Strong, 'Pictures paint a Royal Mystery', *Country Life*, 23 March 2000, pp. 118–20. I am particularly grateful to Eric Throssell for allowing me to make use of his as-yet unpublished research on Hartwell House and garden.

62. For Nebot see C. H. Collins Baker, 'Nebot and Boitard: Notes on two early Topographical Painters', *Connoisseur*, LXXV, 1926, pp. 3–6; Harris, *The Artist and the Country House*, pp. 160–1.

63. For the Lees see the *DNB* under Sir William and Sir George; J. Burke, *The Extinct and Dormant Baronetcies...* London 1844, pp. 304–5; *Complete Baronetage*, ed., G. E. C., Alan Sutton, 1983, III, pp. 111–12; Basil Duke Henning, *The House of Commons 16601690*, London 1983, II, pp. 718–23; Romney Sedgewick, *The House of Commons 1715–1754*, London 1970, II, pp. 205–6.

64. Cabe, 'Sets of Painted Views of Gardens', p. 183 note 7.

65. Compare for example, the profile in John Wotton's *Shooting Party,* see Oliver Millar, *Tudor, Stuart and Early Georgian Pictures in the Royal Collection*, London 1963, pl. 195. For

66. Frederick's visit to Stowe, Robinson, *Temples of Delight*, p. 95.

66. What little documentation there is is given in Friedman, *James Gibbs*, pp. 291–2.

67. Suggested by Harris in the article cited and followed by both Friedman, *James Gibbs*, p. 184 and John Dixon Hunt in *The Anglo-Dutch Garden*, p.230.

68. W. H. Smyth, *Aedes Hartwellianae*, 1851, p. 39.

69. Cabe, 'Sets of Painted Views of Gardens', p. 187, note 14.

70. On the squiggly walk phenomenon see John Harris, 'The Antinatural Style', in *The Rococo in England. A Symposium*, ed. Charles Hinde, Victoria & Albert Museum, 1984, pp. 8–20.

71. The essential idiosyncratic elements of Bridgeman's style are well summed up in Willis, *Charles Bridgeman*, pp. 130–3.

72. Cabe, 'Sets of Painted Views of Gardens', pp. 201–3.

73. See Friedman, *James Gibbs*, p. 186 and pl. 211.

74. Dorothy Stroud, Capability Brown, London 1975 ed., p. 228; Cabe, 'Sets of Painted Views of Gardens', p. 196 note 21; Fiona Cowell, ' Richard Woods (1716–93): A Preliminary Account', *Garden History*, 14, no. 2, 1986, p. 89.

75. On the paintings see Harris, *The Artist and the Country House*, pp. 186–7 (nos 192–93), Harris, *The Artist and the Country House*, Exhibition catalogue, p. 78 (nos 49–54); Cabe, 'Sets of Painted Views of Gardens', pp. 204–47.

76. On which see Dorothy Stroud, 'The Gardens at Claremont', *National Trust Yearbook, 1975–76*, pp. 32–7; Willis, Charles Bridgeman, pp. 48–50;Kimerly Rorschach, *The Early Georgian Landscape Garden,* Yale Center for British Art, New Haven, 1983, pp. 53–5; John Harris, 'The Beginnings of Claremont. Sir John Vanbrugh's garden at Chargate in Surrey', *Apollo*, CXXXVVII, 1993, pp. 223–6; C. H. Beharrell, *Claremont Landscape Garden*, London 1995.

77. Quoted G. E. C., *Complete Peerage*, IX, p. 530 note b.

78. Harris, 'The Beginnings of Claremont', *op. cit.*

79. Historic Manuscripts Commission, *Carlisle*, pp. 143–4.

80. Dixon Hunt, *William Kent*, p. 141 (nos 60–1), 147 (69).

81. See John Dixon Hunt, '"Ut Pictura Poesis": The Garden and the Picturesque in England (1700–1750)', in *The History of Garden Design. The Western Tradition from the Renaissance to the Present Day*, ed. Monique Mosser and Georges Teyssot, London 1991, pp. 231–41.

82. Thomas Whately, *Observations on Modern Gardening*, London 1770, pp. 146–51.

83. For which see Sidney, 16th Earl of Pembroke, *A Catalogue of the Paintings and Drawings in the Collection at Wilton House, Salisbury, Wiltshire*, London 1968, p. 23 (nos 34–7); Elizabeth Einberg, *George Lambert*, exhibition Catalogue, Kenwood House, Greater London Council, 1970, p.8;Harris, *The Artist and the Country House*, p. 258 (no. 273); *Manners and Morals*, pp. 104–5 (nos 85–6); Cabe, 'Sets of Painted Views of Gardens', pp. 163–79.

84. For whom see James Lees-Milne, *Earls of Cre-*

ation. Five Great Patrons of Eighteenth Century Art, London 1962, pp. 60–100; John Ingamells, *A Dictionary of British and Irish Travellers in Italy 1701–1800*, New Haven and London 1997, s.v. Herbert, Henry Herbert, Lord.

85. Quoted *ibid.*, p. 95.
86. *George Lambert, op. cit.*, p. 8.
87. For Lambert see *ibid.*, and Harris, *The Artist and the Country House*, pp. 246–7.
88. See Cabe, *op. cit.*
89. The definitive work is John Harris, *Gardens of Delight. The Rococo English Landscape of Thomas Robins the Elder*, London 1978.
90. *Ibid.*, p. 22.

CHAPTER V: GARDEN PICTURE
INTO LANDSCAPE PAINTING

1. This is particularly brought out in Tom Williamson, *Polite Landscapes. Gardens and Society in Eighteenth Century England*, London and Baltimore 1995, ch. 4.
2. For a discussion of Wilson's country house views see David H. Solkin, *Richard Wilson. The Landscape of Reaction*, Tate Gallery, exhibition catalogue, 1982, pp. 113–34.
3. W. G. Constable, *Richard Wilson*, London 1953, pp. 188–9 (58–60); John Harris, *The Artist and the Country House*, London and New York, 1979, pp. 249–50, 276–7 (198a–e); Solkin, *Richard Wilson*, pp. 195–6 (81a–b).
4. Kimerly Rorschach, *The Early Georgian Landscape Garden*, Yale Center for British Art, exhibition catalogue 1983, pp. 47–51.
5. Constable, *Richard Wilson*, p. 173 (33a–b); Harris, *The Artist and the Country House*, p. 271 (293); Solkin, *Richard Wilson*, p. 196 (82); *Manners and Morals. Hogarth and British Painting 1700–1760*, Tate Gallery, exhibition catalogue, 1988, pp. 228–9 (213).
6. Constable, *Richard Wilson*, pp. 184–6 (54a–b); Harris, *The Artist and the Country House*, p. 272 (294).
7. Constable, *Richard Wilson*, pp. 186–7 (56a);

Harris, *The Artist and the Country House*, p. 274 (296); Solkin, *Richard Wilson*, p. 231 (124).
8. Constable, *Richard Wilson*, pp. 178–80 (41a–b); Leslie Parris, *Landscape in Britain c.1750–1850*, Tate Gallery, exhibition catalogue, 1973, pp. 30–31 (35); Harris, *The Artist and the Country House*, p. 277 (299); Solkin, *Richard Wilson*, pp. 209–12 (97–99).
9. Quoted Solkin, *Richard Wilson*, p. 19.
10. Harris, *The Artist and the Country House*, pp. 194–5 (197a–d).
11. Christopher Hussey, *English Gardens and Landscapes 1700–1750*, London 1967, pp. 132–9; Douglas D. C. Chambers, *The Planters of the English Landscape Garden. Botany, Trees and the Georgics*, New Haven and London 1993, pp. 149–55.
13. Oliver Millar, *The Later Georgian Pictures in the Collection of H. M. The Queen*, London, 1969, p. 113 wrongly identified as Frogmore; Harris, *The Artist and the Country House*, p. 199 (204).
14. Harris, *The Artist and the Country House*, p. 200 (205a–b).
15. Parris, *Landscape in Britain*, pp. 96–7 (223); Harris, *The Artist and Country House*, p. 355 (404); Malcom Cormack, *Constable*, Oxford 1986, p. 56; Graham Reynolds, *The Early Paintings and Drawings of John Constable*, New Haven and London 1996, I, pp. 131–2 (09.17).
16. Cormack, *Constable*, pp. 98–9; Graham Reynolds, *The Late Paintings and Drawings of John Constable*, New Haven and London 1984 (14.32).
17. For all of this see Timothy Clayton, *The English Print 1688–1802*, New Haven and London 1997.
18. *Ibid.*, pp. 140–41.
19. *Ibid., loc.cit.*
20. Based on *ibid.*, ch. 5. But see also Harris, *The Artist and the Country House*, p. 162; David Jacques, *Georgian Gardens. The Reign of Nature*, London 1983, pp. 95–6; Virginia Tuttle Clayton, *Gardens on Paper 1200–1900*,

National Gallery of Art, Washington, 1990, pp. 115–22.
21. Clayton, *The English Print*, 1997, p. 163.
22. Michael Symes, 'The Landscape Park Engravings of Luke Sullivan,' *Journal of Garden History*, IV, 1984, no. 2, pp. 179–89.
23. See Mark Laird, *The Flowering of the Landscape Garden. English Pleasure Grounds 1720–1800*, Philadelphia 1999. Also Williamson, *Polite Landscapes*, pp. 87–92.
24. Laird, *Flowering*, p. 67.
25. See Michael Symes and John H. Harvey, 'The Plantings at Whitton', *Garden History*, 14, no. 2, 1986, pp. 138–72; Chambers, *The Planters of the English Landscape Garden*, pp. 85–9; Laird, *Flowering*, pp. 84–8.
26. Mary Webster, *Johann Zoffany 1733–1810*, National Portrait Gallery, exhibition catalogue, 1976, pp. 26–8 (11–13); Harris, *The Artist and the Country House*, p. 280 (303a–b); Laird, *Flowering*, pp. 158–63.
27. John Harris, *Gardens of Delight*, London 1978, II, pl. 9.
28. Laird, *Flowering*, pp. 163–72.
29. *Ibid.*, pp. 341–50; Michael Sutherill, *The Gardens of Audley End*, London 1995, pp. 32–3.
30. Laird, *Flowering*, p. 201.
31. Mark Laird, '"Our Equally Favourite Hobby Horse": The Flower Gardens of Lady Elizabeth Lee at Hartwell and the 2nd Earl Courtney at Nuneham Courtney', *Garden History*, 18, 1990, no. 2, pp. 103–54. This article also deals with discrepancies and alterations in relation to the pictures and the plans. See also p. 138 note 1 for earlier bibliography; Laird, *Flowering*, pp. 350–60.
32. Laird, *Flowering*, pp. 176–8.
33. Cormack, *Constable*, p. 92; Reynolds, *The Early Paintings*, I, p. 208 (15.22); M. Rosenthal, 'Golding Constable's Gardens', *Connoisseur*, 187, 1974, pp. 88–91; Stephen Daniels, 'Love and Death across and English Garden,' *Huntington Library Quarterly*, LV, 1992, pp. 433–53.

INDEX

Page numbers in *italic* indicate illustrations

PHOTOGRAPHIC ACKNOWLEDGEMENTS

Howard Allen (Allen Studio), Middleburg, Virginia 223; Art Resource, NY 97; The Bridgeman Art Library 330, 331; © Christie's Images Ltd 76; The Country Life Picture Library 174; Conway Library, Courtauld Institute of Art 65, 80, 151, 155, 228, 238, 239, 252; Photographic Survey, Courtauld Institute of Art 36, 136, 137, 138, 140, 248; © English Heritage 83, 333; Paul Gurner 1, 20, 21, 45, 79, 307, 308, 309, 315, 317, 328, 334; John Hammond 222; Photo RMN 242; Glen Segal 145, 173, 329; Sotheby's Picture Library 75, 77, 123, 225, 293, 299, 300, 301, 302, 303; Stowe School Photographic Archives 279.